TEACHERS AND POWER

The Story of the
American Federation of
Teachers
by **Robert J. Braun**

SIMON AND SCHUSTER   NEW YORK

First printing

SBN 671-21167-6
Library of Congress Catalog Card Number: 73-189743
Designed by Jack Jaget
Manufactured in the United States of America

To my mother,
Mrs. Frances Petrena,
for her confidence
and that Western Union typewriter
so long ago . . .

Acknowledgments

A particular word of thanks to those who opened a variety of doors—George Flynn; Herb Jaffe, Mort Pye and Jerry Izenberg, of *The Star-Ledger;* Lewis Kaden, James Mundy, Joseph Cascella, Paul Giblin and Carole Graves. Considerable help was provided by the staff of the Rutgers University Library, especially the students. Danny Moses of Simon and Schuster deserves credit for his understanding of both the writer and the written word. A special kind of thanks to Bernie, who stood watch with me on many long nights. But enough gratitude can never be expressed to my wife, Lyn, who patiently sacrificed so much to prod, to counsel, to criticize and, most importantly, *to believe,* for so many months.

Contents

Foreword

"THE AMERICAN FEDERATION of Teachers is determined to control the public schools of the United States. And someday it will. Just as the American Medical Association controls American medicine and as the American Bar Association controls the legal profession." The young man who expressed those sentiments, one of the A.F.T.'s dozen or so national organizers (the number changes almost yearly), might have been talking out of an inflated sense of self-importance.

Yet there was good reason to heed the young man's words. Not a month before, he and a small cadre of teachers, all fiercely loyal to the A.F.T., managed to end all instruction in a city of 400,000 population. Not the mayor, not the courts, not the governor, not the Chief Justice of the State Supreme Court could reopen those schools as long as he and his A.F.T. colleagues wanted them closed. And when he decided that enough had been granted to resume instruction, the schools reopened. While admittedly negative and temporary, that is control.

He continued. "And why not? Better an organization of teachers should control the schools than some hack politicians.

Or the local bankers." He was growling now. All A.F.T. organizers growl. I am personally convinced it is a part of their training. Talk to one organizer on the phone, and you have talked to all of them. Their voices are almost indistinguishable. But here too there was some considerable truth in what the man was saying. Only fools and those in control of the schools are willing to say the free public system is in reality both free and public. It is variously and in combination controlled by federal bureaucrats, state bureaucrats, local bureaucrats, a multitude of "professional" educational associations, national corporate interests, local corporate interests, angered community groups, concerned citizens' committees of all political hues, hack politicians and local bankers. The people of a local community are, of course, allowed to pay for the schools. And, very often, to suffer in silence when the young and creative minds that belong to their children are reduced to inefficient magnetic recording tapes. This country's institutions, the public ones, always have been the almost willing victims of vested interests. The schools are no exception.

It is useless to argue with this man about the ultimate desirability of a public-school system which is genuinely public, open to participation by a broad cross section of the local populace. He is a warrior in a cause and he believes the cause to be just. Philosophy and theory are the responsibility of others, people in the national A.F.T. office in Washington. His job is to organize a local, win a collective-bargaining election, prepare timid teachers for a strike, force angry teachers back to work, negotiate a contract. If he or his colleagues on the national staff are heavy drinkers, it is probably because many a contract has been gained by winning a heavy drinking bout with the paid negotiator for the local school board. David Selden, the A.F.T.'s national president, is fully aware of the power of creative inebriation. At a reception to celebrate his release from prison for supporting the 1970 Newark, New Jersey, teachers' strike, he told his knowing supporters, "We're going to have a lot of fun in this fight for the freedom of teachers. There'll be a lot of booze. . . ." If an A.F.T. organizer swears heavily, it is probably because many a school board has been intimidated into hard bargaining through the use of carefully chosen, adequately punctuated four-letter words. A.F.T. organizers are not teachers, not theorists, not advocates of social betterment. They are soldiers.

They are soldiers, and it is wartime in the public schools. The past masters are, for a variety of reasons, leaving the field open. School matters have, in hundreds of communities, become too controversial, too complex; and the local political machine is more likely to be hurt than be helped by control of them. The solid "professional" front, made up of thousands of associations affiliated with the once monolithic National Education Association, is breaking up, atomizing. It is not good corporate relations for local industry to have a top executive on a school board which votes on an issue likely to offend one group or the other.

The withdrawal from the fray is more spiritual than physical. The same people, or at least the same kinds of people, may occupy the seats every month at the board meeting. They are there, not so much to control, but to formalize, with varying degrees of willingness, the slow dissolution of their control of the schools. Where they have withdrawn, there is a battlefield. The students demand control over dress and disciplinary codes, a say in the selection of teachers and administrators, the right to bring speakers of their choice into the public schools, the right to have draft counselors and birth-control information. Those of the political left, allied with minority groups, demand community control over personnel policies, access to the schools, an expansion of the school function to include a whole range of social-welfare services. Those of the political right, allied with the bewildered, frustrated, fearful and sometimes racist middle class, demand the unconstitutional return of prayers, lower taxes, an end to sex-education courses, neighborhood schools, the removal of "leftist" educators and "outside agitators," a return to the old days, when respected teachers taught respect for God, duty, honor, country, flag, police, law, order, free enterprise, patriotism, veterans organizations, the sanctity of the American Way and the human body. Much more quietly, of course, come the seemingly endless lists of guidelines from the state and federal governments, the new regulations, the thinly veiled warnings that this year no more mistakes will be tolerated on the application for federal funds, funds for the handicapped, funds for busing parochial-school children, funds for the preschoolers, the culturally, educationally, economically and socially deprived, funds for the adult-education program, the hot lunches and the hot or cold breakfasts—no more mistakes, you understand, or else, no more funds.

And then, in an ever-increasing number of school districts throughout the country, there are the soldiers from the A.F.T. and its local affiliates. They are demanding more control, too, over salaries and benefits, of course, but over many board-of-education prerogatives—assignment, promotion, transfer, curriculum development, class size, textbook selection, supplies, teacher aides and substitutes, school hours, principals, superintendents, district lines, extracurricular activities, lighting and plumbing. The union teachers join the fray with a vengeance. They are organized, disciplined, financed, loyal (to the union, not the board) and willing to face harassment, court, fines and jail to clear the field of competing interests and establish firm control. The New York City teachers took on all comers in the fall of 1968; they won. Tall, glib Albert Shanker may spend time in jail, he may not possess a seat on the school board, but little of importance is done in the schools of New York without his, or his union's, assent.

The warriors of the A.F.T. are well trained and think of themselves not as educators, but as professional organizers and negotiators. Since there are so few of them—the entire A.F.T. staff numbers only about thirty men and women—the union's field representatives lead the lives of missionaries. They are away from their families more than they are home. Like good soldiers, they are always on duty. They have no hours. And their pay is, for the work they perform, relatively low—less than $17,000 a year in 1971, plus expenses, which are carefully scrutinized by a miserly A.F.T. national headquarters. They are genuine fanatics, driven by the smell of battle, and often by a paranoid hatred of mayors, school-board members, injunction-granting judges, superintendents, representatives of community groups and especially the National Education Association. "I joined the union," one field organizer explained, "because there are about sixty school boards in this country I would really like to f--k. I was a state representative for the National Education Association, and those bastards wouldn't let me f--k the boards. Now I won't quit until I can f--k the N.E.A. too."

Beyond their shared hatreds, the A.F.T. organizers care little for ideology or educational philosophy. During the crisis at San Francisco State College, the organizers aligned themselves with radical students, hippies, Crazies, Panthers, and a Gay Activist brigade. Anyone who would hate Reagan and Hayakawa was a friend to the A.F.T. In New York City, Albert Shanker's United Federation of Teachers found support in some of the most conservative elements of the Legislature, including John Marchi, the Conservative-Republican who defeated Mayor John Lindsay in the 1969 Republican mayoralty primary. A.F.T. teachers in Newark carefully cultivated a "relationship" with Anthony Imperiale, the vigilante leader whose cadre of young, antiblack toughs wore black steel helmets and Army fatigues while out on "jungle patrol" in the city's wretched Central Ward. It matters little to the A.F.T. warriors that the teachers' union had a proud history of leadership in civil rights, an uncomfortably close (for them) tie with American Socialists and Communists. What matters is the battle. In some cases, even the victory has secondary importance.

The A.F.T. warriors, thus motivated, tend to write the rules of war as they go along. If it means, as it did in New York

City in 1968, keeping teachers out so long that the school children suffer measurable damage in terms of reading skills, then that is war. If it means, as it did in New Orleans in 1969, giving silent consent to, or at least not stopping, the operations of an "anarchy committee," the teacher-members of which may slash school-bus tires, distribute cherry bombs to all-too-willing high-school students and, in an act of desperation, firebomb a school building, then that, too, is war. If it means wrecking a man's career, deliberately frightening an entire city with rumors of racial upheaval, then so be it. "It is," said the young man from the A.F.T., "a real war between power groups. We don't cry when our people are fired or sent to jail. We try to get out of it. But we don't cry. School boards shouldn't cry, either." Not every A.F.T. action requires such drastic measures, of course. Much more is accomplished through the studied control of the minds of teachers, through skillful manipulation of the media and through collective bargaining. But when the outlook is not too bright, some A.F.T. strikes include vandalism, violence and harassment. The resort to total war is never ruled out.

The instrument of peace is almost always the contract settlement. A contract will be the articles of occupation when, or if, the A.F.T. as a strong national teachers' union takes over the public-school system. Now, of course, the contract settlement is just a temporary list of concessions, a phased withdrawal by the school board from the field of battle. In the course of the last fifty years, the teachers have added more and more to their contracts. In some less developed areas, an A.F.T. local may have control over only the setting of salaries and financial benefits. In the strongest A.F.T. areas, such as New York, the A.F.T. local is more than an equal partner with the board in the operation of the city schools. Control by contract requires, now at least, no promise of accountability, no real worries about the public's role in the operation of the schools.

Present union-board contracts do not actually put the school system in the hands of the union. But the A.F.T. has a program ready for that day. It is called the More Effective Schools project (M.E.S.). Much to the credit of the A.F.T., and particularly to A.F.T. staffer Simon Beagle who put the M.E.S. package together, the project includes, in simple, ready-to-apply form, many desirable educational reforms—smaller classes, team teaching, vastly expanded psychiatric and social services, special attention for poor and for gifted students, expanded use of technical materials, community participation, and so on. But the school boards that agree to sign a contract which guarantees the creation of an M.E.S. school have practically signed away their right to control anything about the school except the way it will be financed. The M.E.S. program gives the A.F.T. affiliate veto power over any change, any expansion, any deviation from the M.E.S. formula. If all schools in a district were M.E.S. schools, the A.F.T. local in that district would have almost complete control. In New York City, the A.F.T. has more than a score of M.E.S. schools.

If throughout this consideration of the American Federation of Teachers, there is a distinct and perhaps unsettling lack of union concern for the values of education, the principles of popular participation in the operation of social institutions or the lofty reliance we like to place in the schools as the transmitters of knowledge and all that is best in American culture, that is because to the A.F.T. warriors these concerns are better left to others. As my conversation with the young organizer drew to a close, he dismissed all such considerations as, simply, "bullshit." They were, to him, diversionary tactics of the present masters of the schools. Only after the schools were firmly in the control of their rightful masters—that is, unionized teachers—would such discussions have any meaning. Until then, only the battles were important. And the tactics devised to win them.

To those who have an interest in the future of the public-school system, but do not have the interest to join in the fray, this book, hopefully, will serve as a useful guide. To those who believe that education is much too important to be left to educators, who believe that the battles should be, not for control over the schools, but to rid them finally of any form of control by special interests, who believe that popular control, while often illusory, is yet desirable, this book may remind you that "the wise learn many things from their enemies."

 If We Are Good Teachers . . .

DOUBTLESS there are many in the United States who suspect that life in this country would have been much simpler without Chicago. I know that many school-board members do. Chicago was where the American Federation of Teachers began. A good many more uncomfortable events have had their origins in the city with "restless, violent hands and casual tongue." But Chicago is, after all, America, a scene of great social upheaval because it grew too large, too quickly, and with too little concern for what that growth meant.

Chicago began as a hamlet of twelve families and a military garrison during the War of 1812. The military garrison was charged with the grand and glorious conquest of Canada. But somehow, in Chicago, things never turn out as expected. The garrison surrendered with hardly a shot when the soldiers began to think of what the British might tell the Indians to do if the Americans didn't surrender. Twenty years later, Chicago had four thousand residents. During the Civil War, the city's population grew to 100,000. Even Mrs. O'Leary's cow failed to stunt Chicago's phenomenal growth. By the turn of the century, it was a sprawling urban center, with sprawling urban problems and a population of more than a million.

When a city experiences such rapid growth, there are bound to be problems. Problems such as how all the people can be provided with jobs that pay enough to keep them in food, shelter and clothing; how social services can be provided to keep pace; and how the school system can be adequately expanded and kept up to date. Fortunately, however, those few whose responsibility it was to bear the burdens of governing Chicago found solace in yet another certainty of fast-growing-city life—graft. A growing population meant a growing construction business, especially in schools. With a friend on the school board or in city hall, one could discover opportunities for great wealth, as long as moral scruples provided no barrier. Even in this fertile field, however, Chicago had problems delivering. While most states were developing tax-supported public-school systems in the 1830's and the 1840's, it took Chicago-dominated Illinois until the Civil War to decide to have free schools.

Graft and corruption were not the only possibilities in a city grown too quickly. There were many in the city who harbored a distinct dislike for the capitalists and the way they did business. The city became a magnet for labor agitators and others who preached the equality of the worker. Many were immigrants. Shortly after the Civil War, German anarchists grouped in defense and educational societies. A national conference of "social revolutionaries" was held in 1881. Obviously, the few who made money on the poor wages of others would think such sentiments totally un-American. They did all in their power to quash the rising labor movement. As a result, Chicago, possibly more than any other American city, witnessed constant and invariably bloody labor-management clashes. After the railroads announced a 10 percent wage cut in 1877, police, National Guardsmen and even federal troops were required to put down the almost continuous fighting and sabotage.

The strife reached a frightening zenith in 1886, when the newborn American Federation of Labor called for a nation-wide labor push for the eight-hour day. The campaign began May 1. Massive strikes gripped the nation's major cities, including, of course, Chicago, where, as might be expected, events took a tempestuous turn. Many of the frustrated workers had come under the strong influence of anarchist groups— one of which called for a huge protest rally at Haymarket Square for May 4.

Few more than three thousand people showed up to protest the use of strikebreakers at the McCormick Harvesting plant, one of the city's largest employers. Many of these drifted away as speaker after speaker denounced capitalism and local working conditions. Just as the meeting was about to break up, someone in the ranks of the police watching the rally drew a sword, marched up to the speaker's platform and, in words which didn't work for the British in Lexington almost exactly a century earlier, ordered the workers to go home: "I command you in the name of the people to immediately and peaceably disperse." Who threw it was never proved, but suddenly an 1886 version of the Molotov cocktail exploded in the crowd. The resulting riot left scores of police and demonstrators injured. Four anarchist leaders were eventually hanged for their part in the incident, which gave to the international labor movement the May 1 labor holiday. Only in America, where it originated, May 1 is Law Day; throughout the rest of the Western world it commemorates the struggle of the worker for a better life. The disaster also gave the American people the impression that the nascent labor movement was, in the words of one antilabor writer, a "bomb-throwing, foreign-accented, beer-sodden fanaticism." And that certainly didn't help the attitudes toward unionized teachers.

Social unrest continued in Chicago. It became the proving ground for groups concerned with child welfare, consumer protection, unwed mothers, derelict men. In 1893 and 1894, the Illinois National Guard was called out more often to put down civil disturbances than ever before. A few years later, the notorious and ill-fated International Workers of the World, the "Wobblies," was founded in the city. To make matters worse, a red-haired young elementary-school teacher began to ask embarrassing questions about the use of land ceded to the city for use by the public-school system, land which ended up beneath the buildings of some of the city's largest corporations, including the powerful Chicago *Tribune*. Her name was Margaret Haley, a woman now considered the spiritual mother of teacher-unionism in the United States.

Miss Haley didn't have much luck with her questions about the use of school land. But her early experiences caught the attention of a number of local reformers and state legislators, particularly among the powerful Irish bloc. Her incessant criticism of the failure of the big corporations to pay taxes on the school lands won her a reputation as "the lady assistant mayor," that "nasty, unladylike woman," and more. To make matters worse, Miss Haley was a feminist and a suffragette. It took time to overcome the chronic timidity of female teachers, but in 1897 the hard-driving Miss Haley finally convinced them to form the Chicago Federation of Teachers. The cause around which the group formed was the state pension bill that had cleared the Illinois legislature in 1895. Controlled by some less-than-trustworthy politicians, the pension fund always seemed to lack enough money to provide even a meager living to retired teachers—teachers who, while working, could not make more than $825 a year.

The Chicago Federation of Teachers was not the nation's first teacher organization. Less than twenty years after the Revolution, New York teachers formed the Society of Associated Teachers. In 1799, Connecticut pedagogues formed discussion clubs. The National Teachers Association, established in 1857, merged a year later with a number of other groups to become the National Education Association. But these groups either didn't last very long or, as in the case of the National Education Association, spoke more for the principals and superintendents, the "natural aristocracy," than they did for the classroom teachers. The teachers in these groups held firm to the popular idea that "sacrifice is the essence" of the teaching profession and that any talk of salaries, security, or even pension, was strictly nonprofessional. Not for Miss Haley's ladies, however. At their first meeting in that cold March of 1897, they issued a statement declaring they would strive "for the rights to which they were entitled." They were revolutionary just in believing that teachers possessed rights. The new Federation wanted a teacher-controlled pension board, a higher salary—$825 had been the ceiling since 1877—and relief from the overcrowded classrooms, which, at the time, contained seventy children or more.

It would not be easy for the fledgling group. The twenty-one member Chicago school board, when not declaring itself completely free and independent from any interest save that of its members, usually was controlled by the mayor. More often than not, the mayor was controlled by the city's large corporations. State law empowered the board to supervise every function of the school system without delegating any authority to an administration. The teachers often received personal visits from the board members, who took the opportunity to remind them of how much trouble they could get into by joining "radical teacher unions." The superintendent, the theoretical "top of the professional staff," was little more than a clerk.

But Haley's raiders were a stout group. From that initial meeting, the women spread out to the mayor's office, the City Council chambers and the legislature, asking, demanding, requesting, cajoling for reforms in the educational system. "The school system," lamented a member of the board just months after the founding of the Federation, "is in the grip of Margaret Haley." An estimated five thousand teachers joined the Federation ranks. The group gained momentum. Within a year, the pension law was reworked and teachers gained representation on the controlling board. The maximum salary was increased to $900 a year. Miss Haley left her teaching job and, to show spiritual if not actual ties with the local labor movement, became the Federation's business manager.

A year later, the school board gave the Federation its first real challenge. Four months into the school year, just before the Christmas break, the board announced it had simply run out of money. Therefore, would the teachers mind taking a salary cut back to the 1897 level of $825—just to save the schools from bankruptcy, you understand? The move infuriated the teachers and, with legal and financial assistance from the local labor council, Miss Haley began the "Christmas Crusade" for more funds for the system. She traveled to the offices of the Cook County clerk and dug up some information which should have made the board very happy. It seemed that a score of corporations, all no doubt with friends at City Hall, held franchise properties worth two hundred million dollars on which they paid no taxes. If the schools, as they were legally entitled, received the revenue from that property, there certainly would be no need to cut salaries. With all the information in hand, Haley appeared before the city tax assessor. He said thank you. And nothing happened. The Federation then went to a local judge and obtained an order putting the properties on the tax list. On to Springfield went Haley's raiders, to the state tax board. The board also said thank you. Again nothing happened. The Federation then went back into the courts, the Illinois Supreme Court, and obtained an order directing the state tax board to make an assessment.

The corporate interests, however, were not inactive. Their attorneys appeared before the state tax board and won a nominal assessment for the newly listed properties. The teachers apparently were ready; they went back into court, charging the board with fraud. Again the courts decided in favor of the teachers. The nominal assessment was voided. A levy of $2,300,000 yearly was slapped on the huge corporations, among them McCormick Harvesting Machine, the Chicago

Tribune, and a number of banks. The corporate interests were down but not out; they appealed and eventually won a modification of the lower court's ruling. Finally, an annual tax bill of $600,000 was given to the corporations. But it still was a phenomenal success for the Federation. While it won them the undying hatred of some of the most powerful people in Chicago, the court actions drew nationwide attention and gained the praise of labor groups and reform organizations—including Jane Addams' Hull House—throughout the city.

The school board apparently was not happy with the unexpected windfall. Although the 1901–02 salary scale was raised back to the $900 maximum, it was again reduced by $50 in midyear, apparently as a retaliatory move urged by the corporate interests. The shock of having fought so hard, only to be slapped down again, crystallized the suspicion among teachers that they were probably worse off than common laborers—despite all the lip service given to the profession. They managed to have the salary cuts reversed by court action. More important, however, the Chicago Federation of Teachers declared its solidarity with the labor movement and, in the fall of 1902, formally affiliated with the American Federation of Labor's Chicago Central Labor Council. It would now be the Chicago Federation of Teachers, A.F.L.

While the city's female elementary-school teachers were the first such group to adopt a union's-eye view of their relationship with the school board, and while it was the first such group to seek openly the support of the A.F.L., it was not the first teacher group to formally affiliate with the growing labor movement. Even educational revolutionaries had problems doing things right in Chicago. Two months before Haley's raiders accepted a charter from the Chicago Central Labor Council, a group of teachers in San Antonio, Texas, became Local 10303 of the American Federation of Labor. The date: September 23, 1902.

The San Antonio union local represented nearly half of the city's instructional staff. In February of 1903, it became the first teacher group to develop and present before a local school board a package of salary and benefit demands with a request for negotiation. But the school board would have nothing to do with collective bargaining. Furthermore, it was explained that the board had nothing to do with spending for education; that was, more or less, the state's problem. Thus ended the first collective-bargaining campaign of unionized teachers in the United States. From trying to get virtually powerless board members to negotiate on a package, the infant teacher union turned toward a public-relations campaign aimed at getting the local gentry to vote for the passage of referendums which would bring more power to the local board. And more money, too. The union succeeded in 1903 and 1907. But the union in San Antonio never really accepted the long-held labor tradition of equal pay for equal work. The high-school teachers who dominated Local 10303's leadership made more money than the elementary-school teachers and were content to allow the arrangement to continue. The dissension caused by this attitude set teacher against teacher, instead of teachers against the board. By 1910, only a handful of teachers showed up for union meetings. A year later, Local 10303 surrendered its A.F.L. charter. San Antonio soon became a stronghold of the rival National Education Association.

Meanwhile, the union marched on in Chicago. In 1909, Miss Haley managed to place a personal friend and strong union supporter, Mrs. Ella Flagg Young, in the schools' superintendency. She became a recognized force in Illinois politics, carrying a lot of weight with the Irish legislators. Two other Chicago teacher groups, the Chicago Federation of Men Teachers and the Chicago Federation of Women High School Teachers followed the lead of Haley's group and formally affiliated with the labor council. Nearly every teacher in the city was a union member. Miss Haley managed to pack the state pension board with prounion teachers and prounion school-board members—there were some—by arranging an organizational meeting of the panel while no one was looking. At the state level, the Chicago teachers increased the public's contribution to the pension fund and killed a pet project of the board, the so-called "Cooley Bill." This legislation would have created a dual-track educational system, assuring that the children of blue-collar workers would themselves be blue-collar workers and offering college preparatory courses only to the "natural aristocracy." For this action, Miss Haley and the Chicago teachers' union won the deep gratitude of Samuel Gompers, then A.F.L. president. "It shows what *organized* women can do," he said.

The organizing action spread. Two New York City teachers, Henry Linville and Abraham Lefkowitz, founded the Teachers' League, a group which adopted the Haley line almost entirely. The League put out a modest journal, *The American Teacher,* which soon became the official voice of unionized teachers. The slogan of the journal, "Democracy in Education; Education for Democracy," became the motto of all unionized teachers. Working through "teachers' councils," advisory groups permitted by the city school board, the League developed surprisingly thorough wage and benefit packages, which included provisions for salary increments, tenure, sabbatical leaves, the elimination of clerical work by teachers, placing teachers in committees developing curriculum and selecting textbooks. (They also devised a simplified orthography, spelling such words as *thought, thot,* and *thorough, thoro.* It absolutely infuriated nonunion teachers.)

The New York City teachers who favored a union found a strong ally in famed educational philosopher John Dewey, who actively urged all instructors to take common cause with the laborer. "We have not had sufficient intelligence to be courageous," he told an organizational rally in New York City. "We have lacked a sense of loyalty to our calling and to one another and on that account have not accepted to the

full our responsibilities as citizens of the community. . . . The
great reason for forming organizations of this kind, and organizations which are affiliated with other working organizations that have power and attempt to exercise that power
like the American Federation of Labor [is] the reflex effect
upon the body of the teachers themselves in strengthening
their courage, their faith in their calling, their faith in one
another, and the recognition that they are servants of the
community, and not people hired to do a certain job at their
beck and call." Roughly translated, if Dr. Dewey will for-
give, he meant "Power to the Teachers." (Many undergradu-
ate education majors will tell you they have read Dewey
several times and somehow never understood exactly what
the philosopher was saying. Which is probably why traditionalists blame him for almost everything from the A.F.T. to
progressive education.) Dr. Dewey and others provided a
philosophical argument for teacher unionism, a factor almost
completely lacking in the rough-riding political tactics of the
Chicago teachers. Other educational opinion leaders—most
of them not classroom teachers—joined in the call for a
fearless nationwide union of teachers to liberate the schools
from the unenlightened forces of capitalism and political interference.

The New York group followed the line, making the most
of every opportunity to charge the school board with serving
the corporate interests. *The American Teacher* printed article
after article about the struggles of teachers for economic and
academic freedom throughout the United States. When teachers in Herefordshire, England, struck, the League's leadership
was overjoyed, and no doubt they frightened many in the
city with this editorial analysis of the action: "We must recognize that the strike is a legitimate weapon." In March of
1916, the League changed its title to Teachers Union of New
York City and set out on a recruiting campaign that doubled
its membership.

Elsewhere in the nation, teacher-union locals and quasi-union teacher organizations were proliferating. In Montana, Idaho, Illinois, California, Michigan, Texas, the District of Columbia, Indiana and Missouri, tidy teacher discussion clubs suddenly emerged as angry union locals, applying for A.F.L. charters. Gompers was pleased and always willing to send out his organizers to assist in arranging affiliation and, of course, the payment of per capita dues to the A.F.L. He consistently urged the development of a nationwide teacher union which could develop its own method of providing skilled-labor personnel for crisis situations. But the unionized teachers were quite content to worry only about their local problems without committing themselves to a nationwide movement. Then in Cleveland, Ohio, something happened to change all that. That something, while a superficial victory for the cause of unionized teachers, signaled the beginning of the end for the infant teacher-labor movement.

Late in 1913, the Cleveland Grade Teachers Club became a magnet for Cleveland teachers who were dissatisfied with low salaries and the strict supervision of teacher performance. The group presented to the school board a list of demands which included higher pay and abolition of the supervisory arrangement. The school board replied, as school boards have been wont to reply ever since, that it had no extra money for higher salaries. As for supervision, that was simply not something teachers were supposed to talk about. But the teachers were ready to show the board what happened to a school board that refused to negotiate. The local leadership announced the formation of a teacher union; it invited Gompers to speak to an organizational rally. "Grit your teeth and organize!" Gompers urged. And organize the teachers did. Within days, some eight hundred teachers, nearly 70 percent of the instructional staff, voted to affiliate with the Cleveland Federation of Labor. The central labor body set loose negotiators, legal assistance and researchers.

The school board was ready. Now it would show what happened to teachers who joined unions. It announced that no member of the instructional staff who was a member of a labor union would be rehired the following fall. With the backing of Gompers and local A.F.L. officials, the Cleveland teachers went into court and obtained an order against the board decision. But in June, the school board published a list of rehired teachers, a list which, not coincidentally, failed to carry the names of the union leaders. Now it was the court's turn to show what happened to school administrations that refused to obey court orders. When the school superintendent refused to put the fired teachers back on the payroll in September, he was fined five hundred dollars and sentenced to ten days in jail for contempt of court. The teachers were rehired and, ostensibly, the union movement won a substantial victory. But school-board members across the country were watching Cleveland, and the idea of firing union teachers sounded much too attractive to allow court orders to stand in the way. Besides, teachers were then, as a few are today, timid folk. The idea of being fired, despite eventual remedies, was frightening.

The school-board members in Chicago apparently thought their Cleveland counterparts had something going there. The sentencing of a superintendent to jail was really not too high a price to pay to rid themselves of the wretched unions. After all, Haley's raiders had embarrassed the city with revelations of corruption, had humiliated the local political machine by defeating pet projects in the legislature, and had more control over the superintendent than the board had. Now, in 1915, all the teacher federations were backing a bill that would give women teachers equal pay and benefits. Jacob Loeb, the brother of one of the city's most powerful corporate captains, was now the president of the school board. He was an experienced in-fighter who had survived several attempts to remove him from his position and even managed to survive an attempt to overhaul the school system and remove the board from him. He felt himself a match for Miss Haley.

On August 23, 1915, the Loeb-dominated rules committee

of the school board adopted a resolution which forbade Chicago teachers to belong to any organization affiliated with the A.F.L. or to any organization which employed a full-time business agent. Not coincidentally, of course, Margaret Haley served as the full-time business agent to the Chicago Federation of Teachers. When the full board met a week later, the meeting almost broke out in a brawl. Mrs. Young threatened to resign. (Nothing, however, would have made Loeb happier.) Finally, the school board voted 11 to 9 to adopt the plan which later became known as Loeb I.

But Miss Haley was still a strong force in Chicago. She mobilized the city's labor unions in support of the teachers and organized a rally of more than five thousand supporters. Mrs. Young appeared and denounced her employers. Gompers appeared and pledged the full cooperation of the national labor movement. The board's action, an enraged Miss Haley shouted, was an attack on the right of teachers and working people everywhere to organize. Back into court went the teachers and they obtained a temporary injunction against the Loeb resolution. The school board lost an appeal to the State Supreme Court. The Chicago teachers resumed their work, their union cards intact. But the board hadn't quit. It cut the teachers' salaries nearly 10 percent. That measure too was rescinded by the courts. The apparent decision of the Chicago school board to wreck the union movement was, however, having an effect. More and more teachers expressed uneasiness about their affiliation with organized labor. The court battles were beginning to put a drain on the union purse. Very quietly, the Chicago teachers sought support from other teacher groups. A letter was sent out proposing the formation of a national teacher union which would "bring associations of teachers into relations of mutual assistance and cooperation" and "obtain for teachers all the rights to which they were entitled." The new union also would "raise the standards of the teaching profession by securing the conditions essential to the best professional service."

The reaction was not exactly thunderous. Thirteen teachers representing four teacher organizations—the three in Chicago and one in Gary, Indiana—met at the home of Charles Stillman, president of the men teachers' federation in Wilmette, Illinois. They left after forming the American Federation of Teachers. The date: April 15, 1916. Four more teacher groups—from New York City, Oklahoma, Scranton, and Washington, sent letters asking to be chartered as locals. The eight groups claimed a total membership of two thousand dues-paying members. Stillman became the A.F.T.'s first president and operated the union out of his frame-house home until 1924. Fittingly, Margaret Haley became the first national organizer, the first "A.F.T. warrior," and her federation was chartered Local 1. New York City's Linville gave the A.F.T. *The American Teacher* and was elected a vicepresident. (Practically everybody was a vice-president.) On May 9, 1916, Gompers personally delivered an A.F.L. charter to the newborn group, predicting it would "bring light and hope to the lives of American educators and give and receive mutual sympathy and support which can be properly exerted for the betterment for all who toil and give service —aye, for all humanity."

Unfortunately school-board members didn't see it that way. Bad enough that local teacher unions provided local irritation; but now a national organization, an international union with close ties to the bothersome A.F.L.—this was too much. Particularly in Chicago. Mailed fists began to fall. Less than two months after the A.F.T. was founded, Jacob Loeb decided it was time for another test of strength.

In early June, the school board passed a resolution dissolving the right of tenure for Chicago teachers. That was Loeb II. On June 27, the board published the list of teachers who would not be rehired—a total of sixty-eight. Of these, forty were members of Local 1, A.F.T. Of these forty, twenty-one had been formally rated "excellent" by Superintendent John Shoop (Mrs. Young had followed up on her threat to resign

and was now making speaking tours in behalf of the A.F.T.),
five "superior," eleven "good," and three received no ratings
at all. Nearly all of the remaining twenty-eight teachers on
the list had been marked inefficient. None of the union teachers had been so graded. It was most obviously an attack on
the core of the Federation. Every one of the union teachers
had been recommended for reinstatement by his principal,
his district superintendent and the city superintendent. But
Jacob Loeb was not fooling around.

Once more the Federation went into the courts. This time,
however, its string of successive legal victories was broken.
In the summer of 1917, the Illinois Supreme Court upheld
Loeb II, and the Chicago Federation of Teachers, for twenty
years the symbol of the potential power of organized teachers and the backbone of the American Federation of Teachers,
faced disaster. The decision of the state's highest court read:

> The board has the absolute right to decline to employ or to
> employ any applicant for any reason whatever or for no
> reason at all. The board is responsible for its action only to
> the people of the city from whom, through the mayor, the
> members have received their appointments. It is no infringe-
> ment upon the constitutional rights of anyone for the board to
> decline to employ him as a teacher in the schools, and it is
> immaterial whether the reason for the refusal to employ him
> is because the applicant is of fair complexion or dark, is or
> is not a member of a trades-union, or whether no reason is
> given for such a refusal. The board is not bound to give any
> reason for its action. It is free to contract with whomsoever it
> chooses.

The ruling, of course, applied only to Local 1 and the Chicago board. But its implications were national. It set a precedent and provided disgruntled school-board members across
the country with a clean method of disposing of teacher
unions. A.F.T. Local 1 withdrew from the national union.
They justified their action on the grounds that, after all,

maybe an international union was not the best solution to strictly local problems. To this day, a vestige of that original Chicago Federation of Teachers remains. And a few of Haley's raiders are still alive. But they refuse to acknowledge their connection with the formation of the A.F.T. (and one aging veteran refused to receive a present A.F.T. officer who was seeking information about Miss Haley—simply because he was an A.F.T. officer).

The A.F.T. national leadership took the stinging defeat philosophically. An editorial in the November, 1917, *American Teacher* recorded the loss of Local 1, but quickly added that four new charters had been issued—to teacher groups in the District of Columbia, Pennsylvania and Tennessee. The strong action of the Chicago board served to strengthen the position of the more radical members of the new union —most of whom taught in New York. The teacher-union members increasingly identified with the more wretched of the earth and sought parallels for their condition in other countries. "But the setbacks," that same editorial reassured the union members, "or even apparent failures of revolutionists never seem to discourage them permanently." So the teacher-union members were "revolutionists" now. It was a bad time to talk about revolution. Many were frightened, that November of 1917, by what was going on in Russia, where a moderate constitutional government had just been overthrown by the Bolsheviks. The union teachers too were aware of what was going on there. But they were encouraged, not frightened. They were soon to promote the idea of a distinct connection between the A.F.T. and the rise of the Soviets. It would be a connection which would return to haunt them not many years later.

For the moment, at least, the A.F.T. was making gains, even without Local 1. The 1917–18 school year ended with twenty-three A.F.T. locals, the union presence stretching from New York City to Vallejo, California, from St. Paul, Minnesota, to the Canal Zone in Panama. Two more charter locals,

Oklahoma and Scranton, were forced out of existence by Chicago-like action. In March, 1919, the A.F.T. claimed forty-five locals, including two on university campuses. Teachers were showing, said one A.F.T. officer then, "a phenomenal interest in unionism." By the end of 1919, there were more than one hundred locals and a total membership of nearly ten thousand teachers. The membership, however, was extremely unstable. Not all the locals were active and dues-paying. Many locals were still suffering the pains of birth when local school boards pounced on them, scaring many teachers away and forcing the surrendering of charters.

Still, the growth of the new union could not be denied. The A.F.T. was becoming an educational organization which school-board members and traditionalists simply could not wish away. Much of the early growth of the union was credited to L. V. Lampson, a young Washington, D.C., teacher who replaced Margaret Haley as chief warrior after the Chicago Federation withdrew in 1917. Lampson traveled throughout the country by train, his suitcases filled with union literature and blank copies of A.F.T. charters. He scanned the nation's newspapers for hints of cities or towns with dissatisfied teachers. When a local crisis arose, Lampson was sure to appear in a matter of days. During 1919, the young organizer spent nearly two thousand dollars on train fares and union literature. According to the A.F.T.'s audit report for that year, Lampson "has prepared and distributed a vast amount of literature and circular letters. He has written hundreds of personal letters and has reached by letter and in person, tens of thousands of teachers." Within a span of a few months, he had traveled to Missouri, Oklahoma, Texas, Mississippi, Georgia, Pennsylvania, Virginia, Maryland, New Jersey, Rhode Island and Maine. The A.F.T. gave him credit for personally chartering more than fifty locals.

In his speeches and informal sessions with teachers, Lampson stressed the poor economic condition of the teachers and the anxiety many of them felt about strict supervision by administrators and school-board members. "We are, in fact, subject to a form of economic oppression and intellectual repression." He calmed many timid teachers who had fears about the union's ideological position and the consequences of affiliation with the labor movement. "We are neither Socialist nor Bolshevik. We believe in cooperation with our employers." But won't unionized teachers strike? No, replied Lampson. The A.F.T. did not have to honor any other union's picket lines. What's more, the A.F.T. had ruled out the use of the strike as a weapon in negotiation. "The American Federation of Teachers does not endorse the strike as a means of getting results, but depends upon publicity, organization and political action. There have been no strikes among union teachers." Lampson was convincing. As World War I waned, as costs soared and salaries, particularly for public employees, stagnated or were cut, more teachers declared for the union than for the National Education Association.

But Lampson's efforts were being undermined both by fellow A.F.T. officials and by events which the teachers' union could not possibly control. While the organizer assured conservative teachers that the A.F.T. was "neither Socialist nor Bolshevik," *The American Teacher,* sent to all union members, was having a public love affair with the Soviet Union. It carried editorials admiring the concept, inherent in the Soviets, of workers determining the exercise of their particular trade or profession. While many Americans were being frightened by general anti-Soviet propaganda, *The American Teacher* was saying:

"Democracy is knocking at the gates. Whether we like it or not, the revolution is upon us. We shall have to assume responsibilities. We shall have to take counsel together. We shall have to make decisions. We shall have to become experts. The world has looked to America for lessons in democracy. If we are good teachers, we should be prepared to learn from Russia."

More and more, the A.F.T., or at least its official organ,

adopted a pro-Soviet, antiwar line. A number of teacher locals refused to participate in Liberty Bond drives. *The American Teacher* consistently opposed World War I and, in language familiar today, called for a reordering of the nation's priorities from war to education and other domestic concerns. The A.F.T. drew close parallels between the nation's leaders and the former masters of Russia, reducing those parallels to the conditions of teachers, comparing school-board members to dictators. When a number of New York City school-board members condemned the union for its leftist views, *The American Teacher* answered: "Let the teachers be wise and note that the hands of the dictator-destroyers are trembling. They are doing foolish things, for they fear the end is near."

In fine, the A.F.T. did little to convince the general public that it was not Socialist, not Bolshevik. And the public was not convinced that teachers' unions would not strike, despite the disavowal by most public-employee unions. The events in Boston in the fall of 1919 did not lead to an easing of the fear of public strikes. The Boston police commissioner flatly refused to allow his men to affiliate with the A.F.L. To put teeth in his order, he fired a number of prounion officers. In retaliation, the police struck, leaving one of the nation's largest cities to the mercy of looters and self-appointed vigilantes. The news spread across the nation. The specter of Soviet-style disruption and anarchy struck home. Although the walkout did not last long, many in the nation found comfort in the actions of Massachusetts Governor Calvin Coolidge, who sent in the militia to end the strike. The taciturn governor said simply there was "no right to strike against the public safety by anybody, anywhere, anytime." The words and the actions made the obscure New England governor a national hero; they also made him Vice-President and, ultimately, President of the United States.

The A.F.T. was fast losing its control over its theretofore most powerful weapon—public opinion. The final blow came in March, 1920, when the National Education Association took two far-reaching steps. It developed a delegate assembly, which gave classroom teachers some voice in the organization, thereby neutralizing the union's contention that the rank-and-file teacher could not be represented by the N.E.A. And the Association's department of superintendence, still the most powerful group within the organization, began a strong anti-union publicity campaign. Up to that point, many A.F.T. officers, as many do now, had hoped that the two organizations might someday merge, with the A.F.T. working for teacher-welfare programs while the N.E.A. developed professional-improvement strategy. Not only was that dream destroyed, but also the A.F.T. itself was practically destroyed by the torrent of antiunion rhetoric provided by N.E.A. members and supporters:

The union teachers are Communists. They are nonprofessional. They are partisans in a great class conflict and will poison the minds of the young. They are the dupes of clever labor organizers. They can do nothing, nor can they refuse to do anything, without the consent of the American Federation of Labor. They pay exorbitant dues to the A.F.L. They support disruptive and illegal public strikes. They are more concerned with money than with education. They will "be losers in freedom of spirit." They will drag the profession down to the level of the common laborer. "If democracy is to be safe," wrote one critic, "the teachers of our future citizens must be able to remain free from class prejudices as professional public servants, must see the justice of the claims peculiar to any class, and must labor to dispel the ignorance and cultivate the unselfishness which make class disputes impossible."

The rhetoric was willingly picked up by school-board members and administrators. In city after city, school boards refused to hire union teachers, and their decisions were upheld by the courts. Board members declared that "these teachers will be asking for rubles soon." And the school superintendent of Fresno, California, received nationwide notoriety for his remark that the only way to deal with A.F.T. members was with "baseball bats and Gatling guns." The almost hysterical dread of the A.F.T. worked rapidly to halt the group's growth. After 1920 until the Depression, not one local was organized. Membership dropped to fewer than three thousand. Even as early as December, 1920, only twenty-two locals cared enough to send delegates to the national convention— although the A.F.T. claimed 160 locals.

As the country danced and speculated its way into the late 1920's, the A.F.T. was dead, although it refused to lie down. Any vital signs of life registered only in a few big-city locals —Chicago (where a number of pro-A.F.T. men teachers had refused to follow Margaret Haley out of the national organization), New York and Washington. As a national organization, however, it ceased to function. Its first president, Charles Stillman, resigned, and although he was replaced, the event marked an end to the first phase of A.F.T. life. The A.F.T. would grow again, but not until the country was in the midst of a depression.

2

Let Them Fire All of Us!

I T HAS BEEN generally conceded by reasonable analysts that the economic depression which began in 1929 was an unfortunate turn of events for the country and its people. History does record, however, the words of men of such stature as Andrew Mellon, Herbert Hoover's treasury secretary, who, after surveying the poverty-stricken human wreckage, offered this comment: "People will work harder, live a moral life." Most have pointed out that Mellon's remark, aside from its questionable taste, was generally inaccurate. It was difficult to work hard when there were no jobs. Twelve million were unemployed; fifty million found themselves working for nearly nonexistent wages. Three billion dollars in family savings evaporated in the simple act of closing a bank door and locking it—more than 4,300 bank doors.

The American landscape was decorated with shanty towns. Millions lined up for bread and coal. A third of a nation, Franklin Delano Roosevelt was to say later, was ill-clothed, ill-housed and ill-fed. Local, state and national governments responded to the social and economic plight of the people in a not atypical fashion: they cut social, welfare and educational services. The country's hundred largest cities ceased making welfare payments completely; scores of smaller towns just stopped making welfare payments to black families. The move would, no doubt, under Mellon's paradigm, make people work even harder at jobs they did not have.

The nation's public schools were singled out for particular attention by expense-cutting local governments. No fewer than 13,000 cities and towns throughout the country closed their school doors temporarily or drastically reduced educational offerings. Large numbers of teachers were "laid off"—the Depression phrase for "fired"—in a third of the country's school systems. In more than two thirds, their salaries were reduced—and even completely eliminated.

By 1933, perhaps the blackest year of the Depression, instructional positions were awarded to the lowest bidder—with some bids recorded as low as forty-five dollars a year. Some teachers took jobs for room and board, often in a teacherage —a kind of secular convent found primarily in sparsely populated states of the Pacific Northwest, but also in such states as New Jersey and Pennsylvania—where drinking, smoking, dancing and courting were expressly forbidden and regular church attendance was a standing house rule. A few teacherages, however, allowed one night a week for courting purposes, and perhaps even two, if churchgoing was particularly regular.

In that same year, two thousand schools in twenty-four states simply failed to open. In those districts fortunate enough to maintain schools, such nonessential services as kindergarten, vocational training, physical education and medical and nursing services were discontinued.

Through it all, the American Federation of Teachers, which somehow managed to survive into another decade, performed like a pathetic cheerleading squad, trying to persuade its underpaid constituents that the Depression was actually doing a little good for their union. "Rejoice!" cried out one editorial in *The American Teacher*. And the reason for rejoicing?

Things had become so bad for teachers in Arkansas that twenty-five new A.F.T. locals were chartered in one day!

The entire American labor movement had some reason to rejoice over the Depression. As millions looked to collective organization for protection from the apparently flawed laissez-faire capitalist system, the American Federation of Labor began an unprecedented membership drive. Strengthened by Section 7A of the 1933 National Industrial Recovery Act, which forbade employer interference in the organization of unions, the A.F.L.—prompted by John L. Lewis as chief of an organizing committee—began chartering thousands of new locals. Union membership climbed from three million in 1933 to nine million in 1939.

The economic catastrophe that was the Depression opened new opportunities for the economically—and politically—oriented A.F.T. Its membership in the 1920's was, on paper at least, somewhere between 5,000 and 10,000—depending on the year and whether one chose to count only dues-paying members. By the end of the 1930's, however, the A.F.T., with its hard line against economic retrenchment and its espousal of radical causes, included more than 30,000 dues-paying members.

But the teachers' union could hardly be considered a unified entity. It was split into two camps—the action-oriented Midwest locals, led by the several Chicago unions and the leftist-leaning amateur politicians and rhetoricians of the New York City Teachers Union. It would be a division to haunt the A.F.T. to the present day; but in the 1930's and early 1940's, it led to a union which was hardly more than a noisy, unproductive debating society.

More than anyone else, John M. Fewkes personified the restless, angry mood of teachers in the Chicago school system of the Depression. A high-school and college athlete, the compact and muscular gym teacher and swimming coach was revered by fellow union members as the "teachers' John L. Lewis." His oratory was defiant, though free of the polarizing radical slogans which had become a trademark of professional unionists in the East. "Let them fire all of us," he once told a rally of unpaid teachers, his raised fist clenched, his great shock of black hair falling on his broad and receding brow, "and I hope they heard that loud and clear."

But more important, Fewkes had rare organizational skill. He was popular among the sports-minded students in the city high schools; to uneasy parents, he represented perhaps the only public figure interested in ridding the school system of a corrupt City Hall machine. Not since Margaret Haley had taken on the tax-evading corporations and the entire school board in the new century's opening years did the Chicago teachers have such a popular and dynamic hero.

And they needed one. In the years immediately following the 1929 crash, Chicago teachers were alternately paid with cash (in reduced amounts), tax warrants, and a worthless scrip at which merchants sneered. The scrip—theoretically—could be redeemed for cash as, and if, the city's largest corporations paid their municipal taxes. But fewer and fewer corporations were willing to pay their taxes until finally, in April of 1932, the school board went over completely to payment by scrip; there simply was no more cash.

The business community, organized as the Chicago Citizens' Committee under industrialist Frederick Sargent, justified their actions by charging the city had done too little to lower its expenditures. What was worse, the committee added, the school board had ignored Sargent's demand for a massive layoff of teachers and a doubling of class sizes in order to cut spending. No cuts; no taxes.

By the winter of 1932–33, the strain of virtually payless paydays had become unbearable for many of the city's teachers. According to the union's accounts—which might not have been literally true but did, nonetheless, form a big part of the belief system of a typical Chicago teacher—more than four hundred instructors had had physical or mental breakdowns, and some were locked up in sanatoriums; four had gone absolutely mad in the midst of spelling or arithmetic or whatever; one teacher had slowly starved to death and another, a female physical-education teacher, simply dropped dead while putting her class through push-ups. It was a combination of nervous strain, malnutrition and sheer physical exhaustion.

Whether true or not, the horror stories aided Fewkes as he guided his teachers—and students—toward what was to become the teachers' days of rage the following spring. The school board scoffed at Fewkes's warnings of disruption and just to show the city he was not to be laughed at, he unleashed fifteen thousand students in the Loop on April 5, 1933. The students, who knew Fewkes at least by sight because of his regular attendance at high-school football games (where, the legend goes, he bought as many of them ice cream as he could afford), made a lot of noise, broke a few windows and demanded full pay for their instructors.

Ten days later, Fewkes demonstrated his popularity among the city's parents, leading a march of twenty thousand parents and children around the Loop and to the offices of Mayor Edward Kelly. It is not recorded whether the mayor was impressed by the large showing of voters—he was known to have his greatest popularity among the graveyard bloc—but he did explain to Fewkes that the city simply had no money for teachers' salaries, for police salaries, or for anyone else's salary. The large corporations simply were not paying their taxes; and the city's largest banks were simply holding on to any other income the city could muster.

While Fewkes's New York colleagues in the A.F.T. were denouncing banks as "capitalist oppressors," the Chicago union leader was planning actions against the bankers, actions more in line with those of other Midwest dissidents, the farmers, who postponed foreclosure with shotguns. April 24, 1933, was a school holiday, part of the annual Easter recess. It was typically chilly and overcast, but the five thousand teachers Fewkes and his lieutenants in the union assembled in the

Loop offered little complaint. This was to be a silent march, a solemn protest against the slow starvation of teachers.

The teachers themselves were not aware of exactly what they were supposed to do. Marching orders in sealed envelopes were given to group leaders, orders which were not to be read until the march began. The policemen who lined the streets were not unsympathetic; they, too, were being paid in worthless scrip.

At noon, the great body of teachers began to stir, to march slowly and resolutely, apparently to the office of the mayor. Suddenly the crowd split into five distinct units, marching, at a faster pace now, each in a different direction. The police stared quizzically; small groups of children began to run after each group. Soon it all became clear. The *banks*—the teachers were marching to the banks. The uniformed guards, caught in their curiosity at the teachers' actions, rushed to lock the doors. The unpaid police laughed in wonderment at the sheer gall of the notoriously timid teachers—and somehow didn't hear the frantic calls for help from the bank guards. Within minutes, five of the city's largest banks—the First National, the Harris Trust and Savings, the City National, the Northern Trust, and the Continental-Illinois—were swarming with teachers shouting, "Pay us! Pay us! Pay us!"

Inkwells were torn from the desks and splashed against marble walls; teachers jammed their bodies into the tellers' windows and grinned stupidly at confounded tellers; the contents of wastepaper baskets floated down over counters and desks; desks were overturned; overwhelmed guards and intimidated senior tellers were lectured in basic economics by schoolmarms and angry gym teachers; top executives locked their doors and called frantically for police protection.

At City National, Fewkes and his thousand demanded the presence of General Charles G. Dawes, chairman of the board of directors. Finally, the livid financier and former U.S. Vice-President came down from his office and confronted the teachers. "Hey, Charley, give us our money," one teacher

shouted; and the group chimed in, "Pay us! Pay us!" Dawes
stamped his foot angrily, demanding attention, his white hair
contrasting with the high-blood-pressure scarlet of his face.
Someone shouted, "Let him speak!" and the din quieted.

Dawes glared about him, at the teachers and the ransacked
bank. "I have only one thing to say to people like you," the
former diplomat snorted. "To hell with troublemakers."

The roar was deafening, but Dawes ignored it, turned and
went back to his office as the teachers tore down draperies
and generally completed the havoc they had begun. When
their passions were spent, most returned home. Fewkes led a
small delegation to City Hall, where once more Mayor Kelly
said there was no money.

Two days later, the teachers returned to the Loop, a smaller
crowd but apparently an angrier one. Unlike the first groups
two days earlier, the majority of the three thousand teachers
were men—many of them carrying schoolbooks. Again, there
was no prior announcement of the planned route of march.
Just an unnerving silence. This time the streets were filled with
mounted policemen, many of them superior officers who, the
rumor was, would lose their ill-paying jobs if they allowed a
repetition of the early rampage. Foot patrolmen stood three
deep at the doors of the five banks the teachers had visited
two days previous. Behind the doors, reinforced teams of bank
guards were prepared, armed with clubs.

But the teachers, with an unsmiling Fewkes leading them,
marched past the five banks, followed closely by the mounted
police. The popular coach seemed to be leading them to City
Hall, but without warning, all three thousand teachers began
running toward the Chicago Title and Trust Company, a bank
ignored in the earlier demonstrations. The mounted police
charged into the crowd, attempting to split them up, to isolate
"controllable" groups. But the teachers demonstrated a novel
use for their hard-cover textbooks. They hurled the books at
the mounted police and their horses. The animals shied and
bucked, delaying the police action long enough for a sizable

group of teachers to smash their way into the bank. Scores more crashed through the building's plate-glass windows and ran into the staid, tall lobby of Chicago Title and Trust. Within minutes, the foot patrolmen were on the scene, pushing back the crowd, unpaid cops clubbing unpaid teachers. Women screamed and fainted, tying up the entrance. They were dragged unceremoniously from the doorway and left lying on the sidewalk. One woman had to be pulled away from a bank guard she had attacked. With the doorway cleared, the police rushed in, to find nearly every office in the building ransacked, tellers cowering in corners as hysterical teachers smashed windows, mirrors, office partitions. In less than a half hour, the rage was ended. Several teachers and policemen were injured. Nearly every window was smashed. The policemen led several bank executives to safety, including Holman Pettibone, who walked dazedly over the broken glass and the schoolbooks. He was saying, "But we pay our taxes—*we do.*"

At the now unprotected City National Bank, a small group of teachers made their way into the lobby and chanted a poem, no doubt to remind all who could hear that they still were, in fact, teachers:

> *We called on cursing Charley Dawes*
> *To ask about our money.*
> *You ought to see him show his claws—*
> *Perhaps he thinks he's funny!*
>
> *Cursing Charley, guard your tongue!*
> *Your record's not so pretty.*
> *We may be coming round again—*
> *Oh, that would be a pity!*

Something must be said for the flexibility of an educational system which produces teachers who, after ransacking six bank buildings and terrorizing their employees, still could feel offended by being told to go to hell.

In any event, Fewkes ended his second day of rage with a

meeting with Mayor Kelly and Governor Henry Horner, who
had come from Springfield to investigate the "unbelievable"
episodes of the first day's violence. Union accounts of the story
insist that President Roosevelt himself demanded an end to the
spectacle of half-starved teachers chucking books at policemen
and smashing bank windows. But, from wherever the pressure had been applied, it apparently worked. When the
schools resumed the following week, the Chicago teachers
were paid—not all of their back pay, but some. And it was in
cash.

The chaos in Chicago made Fewkes a national hero to
teachers and gave the A.F.T. an image as a tough and disciplined group, perhaps the only teachers' organization that
could salvage the economic rights of a badly depressed teaching corps. Just weeks after the demonstrations, the president
of the National Education Association had urged teachers to
return part of their salaries to help bail out bankrupt school
systems; but she was not a teacher. But the new image of the
A.F.T. was not to persist unscathed. Five days after John
Fewkes led his assault against the financial princes of the Midwest, the scholarly John Dewey was reading a report to an
unruly group of New York teachers, a report denouncing most
of the fellow union members for their insistence on tearing
apart the union for the benefit of outside political parties.
Dr. Dewey, who at his death carried A.F.T. card number I,
was booed off the podium before he finished his report. Dewey
had been the A.F.T.'s—and New York Local 5's—intellectual guru, the union's most prestigious claim to legitimacy
(with the possible exception of Albert Einstein, who, it is
rumored, was often delinquent with his dues). Dewey had
once said that he cherished his union card second only to his
teaching certificate; but now, along with Henry Linville and
Abraham Lefkowitz, two other elder statesmen of the adolescent union, Dewey was prepared to provoke the split which
would set union teacher against union teacher, make the
A.F.T. a pawn in the power game between the A.F.L.'s Wil-

liam Green and the C.I.O.'s John L. Lewis and retard the growth of the teachers' union for more than twenty years.

The split began with the birth of teacher-unionism in New York. Linville and Lefkowitz, organizers of A.F.T.'s New York Local 5, always had been enamored of what Linville called "some form of collectivism." When the Bolsheviks seized power in Russia, Linville used the pages of *The American Teacher,* the A.F.T.'s official journal, to urge teachers to prepare for a Soviet-like revolution. All of which did very little to help the Midwest bloc, which was trying to woo teachers into the union, assuring them that the A.F.T. was in no way "Socialist."

But as the Bolshevik revolution ran into problems at home and throughout the world, the pro-Soviet American intellectuals found themselves divided into a number of opposing camps. Since Linville felt no constraint about using *The American Teacher* for political discussion, leaders of the various leftist factions felt justified in using meetings of the teachers' union to denounce one another's revisionism.

While most of the New York teachers claimed to be individualists and spent hours making generally boring speeches at union meetings to prove it, loyalties were divided among four opposing camps. There was the Fosterite faction, for one, followers of William Z. Foster, who, like Stalin, believed that the Bolshevik revolution would have to be transferred whole to the United States. They were opposed, and particularly hated, by the Lovestoneites, disciples of Jay Lovestone, who argued that America's Communist revolution would have to be home-grown, a kind of working within the system for a violent overthrow of the government. Attempting to keep these two groups from turning rhetoric into fisticuffs was the Administration group, or the Organized Union Majority, the Silent Majority of its field and day, which believed that a teacher union should have something to do with teachers and education. Still another group, the Socialists, believed all three groups were wrong; they, however, felt that arguing with the others demeaned their true Marxist pedigree, so at least they didn't add to the pandemonium of the union meetings.

Since the positions of all factions changed with considerable frequency, the members often found themselves arguing their opponent's position. It was all very bothersome and untidy, and it finally drove Linville, who always wanted to be known as a civil libertarian, to the House Un-American Activities Committee (HUAC) to vent his spleen against his fellow union members.

Linville also turned to A.F.T. President Raymond Lowry in June of 1935 and asked him to "do something" about the raucous condition of his union, even if it meant revoking Local 5's charter. After a few days in New York, Lowry admitted it was a pretty noisy bunch, but did Henry really want him to throw out a third of the union? Linville said yes, and the A.F.T. president agreed to take it up with the national union's executive council. The council agreed to suspend the offending local; but its precedent-setting decision was roundly overturned at the 1935 convention. When the national conference repudiated Lowry, Linville and the union's governing board, the local's administration group walked out of the A.F.T. and took nearly seven hundred members with them. Linville, Dewey, Lefkowitz and a number of other charter members of the New York local formed the nonunion Teachers' League—a move roughly equivalent to Benjamin Franklin setting up his own republic somewhere else. These men were the founding fathers of teacher-unionism in the city and the nation. But, ironically, their absence from the New York local did not hurt a membership drive, and by 1939 the city's teacher union had multiplied its 1933 membership by ten.

In the current A.F.T. mythology, Linville and Dewey and the others who withdrew from the union are major heroes because they led the drive to expel Communists from their ranks. That is not precisely true. By the mid-30's, the A.F.T. was becoming a rather large organization; its per capita dues and its contribution to the parent A.F.L. were sizable. As a result, it was losing its innocence—the drive to expel Communists was not half so important to the union's national leadership as the drive to keep the A.F.L. leadership happy. By 1935, the A.F.L. was very unhappy—primarily because of a man named John L. Lewis and the Committee for Industrial Organization.

The American Federation of Labor under William Green was indistinguishable from Samuel Gompers' American Federation of Labor. It was a conglomeration of craft unions, an exclusive organization that shied away from the ethnic and racial minorities, repudiating any attempt to organize on an industry-wide basis to bring in the less skilled and the unskilled. Lewis didn't see it that way; he wanted to open up the union to the less prestigious industrial jobs. The feud degenerated into intense personal animosity, until finally, in 1935, Lewis called Green a "sonuvvabitch" and punctuated his remarks by starting a brawl on the floor of the A.F.L. convention. Several Green supporters were badly injured. And Lewis walked out with his C.I.O. In his rage, Green wanted the entire five-million-member Federation to join him in a campaign to quash the fledgling C.I.O. Like Linville in the A.F.T., Green went to HUAC with charges of Communism against Lewis. He even used the union's considerable lobbying power to help continue appropriations to the HUAC staff. To Green, it was purely a matter of survival; the nation was not big enough to hold two rival union organizations and two rival union bosses. The Midwest bloc of the A.F.T. opted for Green; the New York local favored Lewis. Green wanted New York out; using Linville's charges of Communist influence in the local, he revoked Local 5's membership in New York's Central Labor Council on August 28, 1935, one day before the A.F.T. opened its national convention.

Green kept up the pressure through 1936; but the bulk of the A.F.T. members, always mindful of the charges by other teacher organizations that the teachers' union was a mere puppet in the A.F.L.'s hands, resisted. At the 1936 A.F.T. convention, the membership's delegates elected as president Yale professor Jerome Davis, a wiry, soft-spoken faculty member at the university's Divinity School. Davis was an outspoken supporter of the C.I.O. but fancied himself too much of a diplomat to lead his entire organization out of the Federation.

Davis also felt that he could heal the New York division through the sheer weight of his reputation as a fighter for academic freedom—an important quality to city teachers. Shortly after his election to the A.F.T. presidency, Davis was suspended from his Yale post, primarily because of the scathing criticism of the economic system in his book *Capitalism and Its Culture.* He began a long correspondence with fellow philosopher Dewey, determined to unite the independent New York Teachers League with the A.F.T.-affiliated union, a group which, save for its pro-C.I.O. stance, had been behaving.

To the angry Midwest bloc, Davis made appeals for tolerance: "As teachers, we must insist that the highest patriotism, the greatest democracy demands freedom of speech, of press and of association. Within our own great federation, locals should have the right to differ in policies, programs and attitudes."

But Green was in no mood for tolerance. Lewis' C.I.O., with its no-nonsense, hard-line approach to organization (which included fighting it out with the Pinkertons and seizing plants), was effectively raiding the A.F.L.'s membership. Now the A.F.T. would have to bend. The showdown was to be the 1937 convention in Madison, Wisconsin, where teachers from New York, Philadelphia and California were planning to put the A.F.T. in Lewis' camp.

When the convention opened, the pro-Green, Midwest bloc was organized under Henry Ohl, Jr., who had been president of the Wisconsin Federation of Labor for twenty years. In small caucuses, he argued that C.I.O. affiliation would lump

the teachers together with janitors, cooks, boiler-room workers, and everyone else who worked around the school. Drop-
ping remarks about what a "deep shade of red" the A.F.T.
was becoming, Ohl urged the Midwestern teachers to rid the
A.F.T. of the pro-C.I.O. locals immediately, without further
discussion. "One cannot ride two horses simultaneously, unless of course, he is a trick rider, and teachers are not trick
riders," Ohl said.

Davis found himself in a difficult position. The pro-A.F.L.
teachers were stronger—and angrier—than he had imagined.
He sought to avoid, at any cost, a head-on confrontation between the C.I.O. and the A.F.L. factions. "We must not," he
pleaded in the convention's opening address, "we cannot be-
tray the organized workers of America by fighting the C.I.O.
It is the historic mission of the A.F.T. to support every progressive and successful labor movement. How can we possibly
ignore the C.I.O. and be true to our heritage?" Davis was
shouted down, jeered, despite his attempts to keep the C.I.O.
partisans happy while trying not to force the A.F.T. out of
the A.F.L. "You represent the C.P.," shouted an angry Chicago teacher, "but we don't know whether that stands for
college professors or Communist Party."

When Ohl took the floor later in the convention, he would
not hear of reconciliation. "Their [the C.I.O.'s] every activity
shouted treason to the world. . . . The full drama of betrayal,
as evidenced by recent events, exposes a treachery never before perpetrated in the annals of labor anywhere." But Davis'
quiet diplomacy prevailed over Ohl's shouting. By the time
the convention ended, he had put the question of A.F.L. or
C.I.O. off until the results of a membership referendum were
known—a vote never taken—and had engineered resolutions
condemning Green's suspension of all C.I.O. unions and praising Lewis' "great organizational success." He also managed to
be reelected by a comfortable margin over Charles B. Stillman, the Federation's first president and the titular leader of
the pro-A.F.L. bloc. He had brought the A.F.T. out, still to-

gether, still uncommitted to either major labor organization; but the battle had been exhausting, and an enraged A.F.L. leadership kept up the pressure by immediately revoking the A.F.L. membership of all pro-C.I.O. locals.

Davis embarked on one last campaign to bring his union together. He pleaded with A.F.L. unionists not to go running to Washington to rat on the A.F.T. membership, and he attempted to produce guidelines for an immediate unification of the New York teachers. "Over and over again, we receive demands that either all Communists or all Fascists be expelled from the union. Just who is a Fascist or a Communist is not always easy to ascertain. But in any case it is a fundamental principle of our Federation not to discriminate against any member because of race, religious faith or political belief. Republicans, Democrats, Socialists, Communists, even those who sympathize with the programs of Hitler and Mussolini, have the right to belong to the American Federation of Teachers."

But his efforts failed. The A.F.L.-C.I.O. split was too wide; teachers had accused their colleagues of being un-American in testimony before red-baiting politicians, thereby wrecking careers and lives. To make matters worse for the Eastern leadership of the A.F.T., Chicago's John Fewkes had managed to unite all the various factions in Chicago into a new A.F.T. Local 1 and now was determined to bring unity to the national—under Chicago's leadership. Davis went into the 1938 convention resigned to compromise.

And compromise he did. He squelched the Eastern locals' drive to go C.I.O.; he threw his support behind a number of resolutions backed by the Midwest bloc. Davis even supported the election of two Chicago teachers to the union's executive council. He bowed to Green's demand to set aside a percentage of per capita dues as an anti-C.I.O. war chest but convinced the A.F.L. president to allow the A.F.T. to use it for organizational purposes. Neither faction was deliriously happy, but Davis managed to win reelection as president over Chicago's

Lillian Herstein by sixty-two delegate votes out of more than six hundred cast.

The uneasy peace lasted only a few months. Green, backed by a number of well-known professors in New York, demanded that the A.F.T. throw out every pro-Communist (read pro-C.I.O.) member and local. Again, the labor leader went to Washington and reported to HUAC that the American Federation of Teachers itself was "dominated by Communists." He vowed he would cut off all financial and organizational assistance—at that point vital to the continued existence of the A.F.T.—unless Davis and the New York, California and Philadelphia locals were thrown out. Davis futilely denied the Communist charge and pleaded in vain for the various factions to concentrate on education, not vilification. But even his former supporters in New York, angered by what they believed was a sellout to Green at the 1938 convention, refused to support Davis.

On February 13, 1939, Green gave the A.F.T. three months to clean house "or face reorganization" by the American Federation of Labor. Davis announced he would not stand for reelection; the purge was about to begin.

The actual "reform" was to fall to Dr. George S. Counts, a Columbia University philosopher who came to the 1939 convention vowing to rid the A.F.T. of "divisive" elements. Most likely, his candidacy would have provoked a serious split in the union, but he received a big boost from an unlikely quarter; the convention opened the day the Molotov-Ribbentrop nonaggression treaty was signed, completely demoralizing the more leftist New York delegates and uniting the conservative Midwest bloc in anger. Counts, who with noted theologian Reinhold Niebuhr (yes, he too was a union member, as was Mike Mansfield, Paul Douglas and Hubert Humphrey) had tried unsuccessfully to take over New York Local 5, easily won election to the presidency and immediately pledged to clean house. But his executive council, still containing a pro-Davis majority, rebuffed him. Green re-

taliated by cutting off all financial and organizational assistance. Counts finally got his majority on the executive council
at the 1940 convention. Three months later, the bespectacled
philosopher and former editor of *Socialist Frontier* brought
Local 5 and other C.I.O.-oriented unions up on charges—
charges of dual unionism, of causing disharmony, of "creating
hysteria," of losing members (actually the local was growing)
and of being generally "inimical to democracy." A month
later, the executive council voted to recommend that the
A.F.T. membership expel the local. *The American Teacher*
carried article after article bewailing the threat of Communism, and when the votes were counted in May, 11,256
teachers voted for revocation of charter, 8,250 against. In
just a few months, the A.F.T. managed to confirm suspicions
of A.F.L. domination, engage in what smacked of very unin-
tellectual red-baiting and throw out easily a third of its
membership without offering them the chance to answer the
charges. The A.F.T. carved out for itself a second-class position; it stayed there for twenty years.

Green applauded the move, curiously reminding the teachers that what the A.F.T. should be looking for was "quality,
not quantity." He restored financial assistance to the crippled
union and even provided enough money for the A.F.T. to hire
its first two full-time organizers. Whether or not the two A.F.T.
warriors would have made a difference will never be known;
the entry of the United States into World War II ground all
membership drives to a halt.

The A.F.T. of the war years bore little resemblance to the
scrappy, outspoken teachers' union it had been for the first
twenty-five, admittedly precarious years of existence. It became a part, probably a very insignificant part, of the great
war machine. Fewkes finally took over the presidency in
August of 1942 and pledged a five-point "victory" program
which included the statement that "the schools of America
must teach America to think America!" No doubt every labor
union was dedicated to defeat of the fascist dictatorships, but

the A.F.T. acted as if it were trying too hard to overcome its previous pacifist-intellectual image. The convention which elected Fewkes, for example, offered as its guest speaker Colonel Frederick Swanson, who was, of all things, Director of Internal Security for the State of Illinois. There is no record of anyone cringing when the officer told the teachers:

"During the present crisis, every effort should be made to keep the schools running on a sane basis. Teachers should concentrate on the idea that their only mission in life is to do a good job teaching students the subjects they are assigned and not be influenced by every incident that is prone to distract attention from the job at hand. I should like to urge each of you and your students to be good soldiers. Set a definite objective for each lesson and make it difficult to attain. Then do not stop short of the objective but try to go beyond it. In this manner those of you in civil life can best supplement the efforts of those in uniform and lay the foundation for a better future which we all hope is not too far away."

Ten years earlier, he would have been hit with a book in Chicago, or slowly talked to death in New York. But this was an A.F.T. exhausted from controversy, gun-shy, trying desperately to be respectable.

Joseph Landis of Cleveland, another Midwest president (Fewkes quit in 1943 to take a job with the Roosevelt Administration), told his fellow union members in 1944: "Our phenomenal output of planes, ships, tanks, guns, munitions and supplies attests to the fundamental soundness of a training which has emphasized adaptation and utility as concomitants of mental development." Ten years earlier, Landis would have been hit with a book—in New York.

The A.F.T. tried in vain to hold on to the institutional respectability it thought it had, even after the war was over. It commissioned Dr. Counts to write a book on America's future relations with the Soviet Union; it sent its members to early meetings of UNESCO and promoted a pro-United Nations campaign. The teachers' union became a proponent of international education. By 1946, it was probably sponsoring more studies, conducting more seminars, participating in more workshops than the National Education Association, an organization that the A.F.T., at one time in its now unusable past, accused of doing little but sponsoring studies, conducting seminars and participating in workshops. But the A.F.T. had a past, unusable as it seemed then, and the postwar inflation was about to catch up with it.

America was a child emerging from a nightmare when the war ended. It wanted no reminders of the horror that had once seemed interminable. And that included wartime economic restraints. Price controls were allowed to expire; federal agencies charged with monitoring inflationary trends were dissolved. Prices soared while wages stagnated; the working people were angered, and in the immediate postwar months there were more serious labor disputes than in the entire ten-year period before that. That made a Congress dominated by Ohio Senator Robert A. Taft angry, and they almost legislated industry-wide labor unions out of existence—which made labor even angrier. America's teachers were particularly restless. Unlike workers in the private sector, they had no right to strike; and the postwar inflation drove costs so high that many school boards felt they had to postpone salary increases demanded by teachers. Although the A.F.T. did little, if anything, to support its teachers, the rank-and-file members were preparing for a war of their own. On September 20, 1946, teachers in Minneapolis and St. Paul presented to their school boards a package of demands. They wanted raises totaling nearly two million dollars, including a fifty-dollar-a-month cost-of-living bonus, and a salary range from $2,400 to $5,000 a year. After two months of aimless discussions, 1,160 members of the St. Paul Federation of Teachers walked off their jobs, closing 77 schools to 30,000 children. It was the biggest strike by teachers in the nation's history, and the first by a major local of the A.F.T. Two weeks later, Minneapolis teachers reached agreement with the school board without a strike—perhaps because of the presence of Mayor Hubert H. Humphrey, a member of A.F.T. Local 444, in the negotiation.

For six weeks, the St. Paul teachers walked the picket line in the cold Minnesota winter. And they walked virtually alone. The A.F.T. all but ignored the walkout; *The American Teacher* never mentioned it. When the strike ended, as all strikes must (that, incidentally, is a favorite phrase of A.F.T. organizers), the teachers really had less than they had before the strike. Weeks later, teachers in Buffalo, New York, walked out of their classrooms in a short but effective strike; but this time it was an affiliate of the National Education Association that provoked the strike, and the A.F.T. was looking more and more like a tissue-paper tiger. The A.F.T.'s executive council answered with a reaffirmation of their no-strike policy. Again and again, in New York, Pennsylvania, Vermont, Georgia, Rhode Island, teachers struck, demanding salaries which would bear a slight relation to the current economy. In May, 1951, teachers in Pawtucket, Rhode Island, walked out with a demand for a $410 cost-of-living bonus and a maximum salary of $5,000; they won their demands and despite whatever the A.F.T. headquarters was saying, union teachers had no no-strike policy.

The A.F.T. was stagnating in other ways. In 1952, the convention voted not to defend the rights of any teacher found to be a Communist. Two years later, they voted to recommend that any teacher proven to be a Communist be blacklisted from teaching anywhere in America. The union's long history of defense of academic freedom became an unfunny joke as union leaders cringed before Senator Joseph R. McCarthy.

The vegetative state of what had once promised to be the most militant of all educational organizations drove many of their best leaders out; but a sandy-haired, cowlicked young teacher felt that he could, if given the chance, revive the somnolent giant. His name was David Selden.

Selden was a Midwesterner, an admirer of Fewkes's resort

to action and a disciple of Walter Reuther. The Michigan classroom where he first taught had a view of the underpass at the River Rouge plant of the Ford Motor Company where Reuther had been beaten by Pinkerton guards. He felt he could live with both the A.F.L. and the C.I.O.; in 1940, he joined the American Federation of Teachers. His success as a local union leader ultimately won him a job as a full-time organizer with the A.F.T., his salary and some of his orders coming from the A.F.L. From 1949 to 1953, he traveled the country, his bags bulging with A.F.T. literature, leaving a local behind whenever he left a town. In four years, Selden personally chartered more than a hundred locals, none of which lasted more than a few months. They were simply not big enough, and they were not getting the national help they needed to survive. After complaining about his lot to Carl Megel, another Chicago teacher, who was elected to the A.F.T. presidency, Selden was sent to New York with orders to build a strong local, an order unaccompanied by any promise of financial support. That might have been the beginning of the bad relations between Selden and his boss; New York was a nightmarish collection of tiny empires, each representing no more than a fraction of the city's 40,000 teachers. The A.F.T.'s affiliate was the old Teachers' League, which had been given Local 5's charter after the 1941 purge. Selden's comment on the building of a united federation was simply, "Impossible."

But something was stirring in the American labor movement, and his name was Walter Reuther. He realized that both the A.F.L. and the C.I.O. were losing membership—combined losses were nearly a half million from the late 1940's to the early 1950's—and he felt that the future of the movement rested on its ability to organize the white-collar worker and the professional. In his own U.A.W., 68,000 jobs had been lost to automation. The merger of the A.F.L. with the C.I.O. in 1955 was, at least in part, due to this uneasiness over the disappearing membership. And the merger gave Reuther a new and bigger base from which to begin his drive to organize the professionals. Nicholas Zonarich, ex-miner, ex-farmworker, joined him in the development of the Industrial Union Department (I.U.D.). Reuther was to be president; Zonarich, chief organizer.

"We know," Zonarich told an early A.F.L.–C.I.O. convention, "that in the past twelve to fifteen years, American labor unions have not kept pace with the growth of the labor force. We have been successful in organizing the basic industries, the durable-goods industries. Now we have to go after the white-collar and service industries if the American labor movement is to survive."

The new approach reflected Selden's thinking. From his outpost in New York, he could see the A.F.T. going nowhere; in 1956 the union again threw out a large segment of its membership—7,000 teachers—when it revoked the charters of all racially segregated locals in the South. The membership figures in the mid-1950's were not very different from those of the late 1930's. But Selden felt he was unable to convince Megel of the importance of a big push in New York; apparently, the Midwestern mistrust of anything New York continued. Finally, Selden went directly to Reuther. New York was a liberal town, a labor town; if professional unionism wouldn't work here, if teacher-unionism wouldn't work here, neither movement had a chance anywhere in the country. But money was needed, and that's where Reuther came in. Walter and his brother Victor, and Zonarich and organizers from the Auto Workers, the Communications Workers and other unions came to the big town to help lay the foundation for a membership drive for the A.F.T. local. The first breakthrough came in March, 1960, when the Teachers' League merged with a small group of high-school teachers to become the United Federation of Teachers. Membership represented little over 10 percent of the teaching force.

But the U.F.T. was now in the hands of professional organizers, and negligible membership means little when there is a war to be won. Standard A.F.T. organizing tactic number 1 was probably first developed in New York—*even if you don't represent anybody, act as if you represented everybody,* including the children and the parents. Standard A.F.T. tactic Number 2 also was put into effect in 1960—select a president who will not object to the organizational procedures of the staff workers. Charles Cogen, a high-school teacher with impressive academic credentials and a long record of involvement with Liberal party politics, was just the man. So what if he was only five feet tall? He'll be known as fighting little, scrappy little, fiery little Charlie Cogen. And that's precisely what the A.F.T. and U.F.T. staffers called him, despite his mild-mannered approach to nearly everything.

Days after the formation of the U.F.T., Cogen demanded a bargaining election to determine the official representative at the negotiating table for the city's 40,000 teachers. Superintendent of Schools John Theobald replied, "I will not bargain with members of my own family." And the U.F.T. was on its way. They called for a strike to begin on May 17, a day which just happened to be Teacher Recognition Day in New York City. It was a gamble, and Selden knew it; the U.F.T. could not possibly muster enough strength to make even a laughable showing in a walkout. But the school board gave the U.F.T. something it could call a victory—an agreement to hold a bargaining election if 30 percent of the teaching staff wanted one. The strike was called off. By June, Selden had the signatures of more than 30 percent of the teachers petitioning for a bargaining election and the U.F.T. had a growing reputation as the only one of the scores of teacher groups which could make the board move.

But Theobald still was in no mood to bargain, no matter what the school board said. When school reopened in September, there was no bargaining election in sight. Selden's bluff had been called; he had to do something. The U.F.T. called for a strike November 7, the day before election day, thereby putting into effect two more standard A.F.T. strategies—try to strike just before a school holiday, to make a one-day strike look longer and to provide enough time to get out of it respectably; and schedule a job action as close to a political event as possible (it makes politicians nervous and they make mistakes).

The board wouldn't move; the teachers struck. Throughout the day, Cogen talked to television and radio and press journalists, working up the image as *the* spokesman for all teachers. The strike was a virtual failure; only about five thousand teachers stayed out of work. But it was the city's first, and it received a lot of exposure. In a move which added even more prestige to the U.F.T., George Meany himself came to town to conduct "crisis talks" with Mayor Robert F. Wagner. That's yet another A.F.T. strategy— get local and national A.F.L.–C.I.O. leaders to work for you. Selden called off the strike after a three-member labor panel was created to make recommendations to the city on the resolution of the conflict; to no one's surprise, the panel —Harry Van Arsdale, of the New York City Central Labor Council; David Dubinsky, of the International Ladies Garment Workers Union; and Jacob Potofsky, of the Amalgamated Clothing Workers of America—recommended that a collective-bargaining election be held as soon as possible, perhaps in June. And to top off the list of prestigious supporters, newly appointed Secretary of Labor Arthur Goldberg interceded for the U.F.T. to ask for an impartial panel to conduct the election.

Again the school board balked at having to formalize the U.F.T.'s apparently inevitable hold on teacher organization in New York. In an apparent effort to allow the N.E.A. time to develop an affiliate in the city, Theobald announced there would be a referendum among teachers in July to determine whether or not they wanted a collective-bargaining election. The U.F.T.'s resources were growing thin. Reuther came through with outright grants of money, loans of personnel and credit at the Amalgamated Bank maintained by the

Amalgamated Clothing Workers. It would be a difficult task to organize any campaign during the summer; but Selden, now with the help of Albert Shanker, a teacher he had persuaded to become a national organizer, got out the mailings, provided bodies for visits at summer schools and kept old fighting Charlie in the news. The teachers voted for a bargaining election, 27,000 to 9,000. The December 11, 1961, bargaining election confirmed the inevitable: the United Federation of Teachers, which, just months before, was only one of three-score teacher organizations, won 20,045 votes; the Teachers Bargaining Organization, an unashamedly hasty effort of the N.E.A. to torpedo the union, took 9,770; the old Local 5, a mere shadow of its pioneering past, settled for 2,575 (and later disbanded, with most of its members going to the U.F.T.); only 662 teachers voted for "No Representation."

No matter what the Midwestern prejudices against the development of a strong New York local were, it was impossible for any loyal union member to denounce Selden's splendid victory in New York. It had shaken the stodgy union from a debilitating apathy and within four years doubled the A.F.T.'s membership. Today, the United Federation of Teachers is the largest union local of any kind in the nation. Reuther celebrated by taking the A.F.T. under his personal care, putting it into the I.U.D. "The best assurance of a democratic school system will be the development of a strong union of teachers," he said.

But membership increases do not come automatically, simply because a union local wins a bargaining election. Something else has to happen, and that something else invariably is a strike. It was a lesson learned on the streets of New York; teachers are willing to have the advantages of militant union representation, but they're not always so willing to sign up, pay up and be called upon to engage in militant activity themselves. A teachers' strike in New York was inevitable. Negotiations were broken off March 22, 1962;

20,000 teachers struck April 11. The issue on the table, as it invariably is, was money; but the thrust was for power, for consolidation of gains and for the enrollment of all 50,000 teachers into the Federation. The denouement played itself out wondrously well for the teachers. Governor Nelson A. Rockefeller, in a role he has created for himself time and time again, was the hero. Somehow he came up with an extra thirteen million dollars in state aid to the city school system. The strike was over in a day, but it set a number of precedents, the effects of which would be felt for years. It took the school board out of negotiation and replaced it with city and state political officials (where the A.F.L.–C.I.O. lobby can get at them); it made the combination of a bargaining-election victory followed quickly by a strike a standard organizing technique, and the settlement placed the teacher union in a virtually equal role with the board as shaper of school-board policy.

The national federation itself was thrown into chaos because of the sudden growth in membership and the swinging of the scales to the New York wing of the union. It was a growth that the Chicago-dominated union could not hinder, although the whole question of "one big union" was foreign and unnerving to the old-line unionists. But the course of events ground on, forcing the A.F.T. into its future. In July of 1962, John F. Kennedy signed Executive Order No. 109882, which granted federal white-collar employees the right to organize and bargain collectively, thereby bestowing on white-collar unionism a Presidential mantle of respectability. The A.F.T. bought its own national headquarters, the Chicago mansion of Cyrus McCormick. And the 1963 national convention repealed its no-strike policy. Megel, apparently suspicious of the New York crowd, discouraged any speculation about the A.F.T. merging with the N.E.A.; like so many Chicagoans before him, he believed in militant, union-backed action. Grand and lofty designs for the future of the organization were too reminiscent of the flaming libertarian rhetoric of the 1930's New York unionists. "As long as I am a member of the American Federation of Teachers," Megel said, "I shall treasure this affiliation with the A.F.L.–C.I.O. and shall fight to keep this great organization from being disaffiliated from the A.F.L.–C.I.O. or from being defected either to a merger with the National Education Association or from becoming just another individual unit of teachers under a guise of 'professional dedication to educational theory' alone."

But the new direction of the union was in the hands of Selden, Reuther, Zonarich and Shanker—institutionalized now as the Progressive Caucus. Reuther urged a "union of a million members." Zonarich castigated the teachers for failing to tax themselves heavily enough for the struggle ahead. The dream of a truly national union of teachers appeared even closer that year when the convention of the superintendent-dominated N.E.A. humiliated its classroom teachers by overturning their resolutions calling for a desegregation of their all-black and all-white affiliates and for the imposition of sanctions against the low-paying Utah school system.

As the 1964 convention drew near, the "New York crowd" was prepared for the coup, the capture of the union presidency from the plodding hands of Chicago. Selden and Shanker were promoting old "Fighting Charlie," and they reminded the teachers in convention assembled that if it wasn't for New York, membership would still be around 50,000, instead of 100,000. Cogen won easily, pledging that "every local will be encouraged to engage in militant activity." Zonarich appeared at the convention and pulled out the surprise package—the I.U.D. would match every dollar the A.F.T. raised for organizational purposes. "We're going to put on one of the greatest organizing campaigns in the history of organizing in the United States," Zonarich shouted to the delegates. Within a year, the I.U.D. pumped $362,000 into the A.F.T. war chest; by the time the massive organizing campaign ended in 1968 with Reuther's withdrawal from the A.F.L.–C.I.O., the I.U.D. had spent more than one million dollars on the teachers. The teachers themselves had done their part—in more than two hundred strikes, and in nearly that many bargaining elections, the A.F.T. increased its membership to 170,-000. By 1970, dues-paying enrollment topped the 200,000 mark.

The field was being carefully cultivated for Selden to make his move. He had come to the A.F.T. with Cogen as his special assistant. Shanker was firmly entrenched as U.F.T. president and the most powerful A.F.T. vice-president. Teachers were looking for an organization, a program and a leader—"a man like Walter Reuther," Selden had written in 1966; and now, in 1968, he felt they had all three. The organization was the merged A.F.T.–N.E.A., a million members strong, capable of the most powerful lobbying in Washington and proprietors of the Ultimate Weapon, the nationwide teachers' strike. The program was the all-inclusive contract, based on the New York model—which Shanker had strengthened with a strike in 1967—making the union, in some ways, even more powerful than the school board in determining personnel and even curricular policy. And the leader? David Selden, of course.

Pledging the immediate opening of merger negotiations with the N.E.A., Selden won election to the A.F.T. presidency in August of 1968. On the surface, at least, it appeared that he was on his way to his dream. George Fischer, the newly elected president of the N.E.A., encouraged merger talks. Selden was able to convince the antimerger forces within his own ranks—particularly the national organizers—that the A.F.T. would not be "swallowed whole" by the larger association. The A.F.T. had won bargaining rights in nearly every major city in the country—New York, Boston, Philadelphia, Detroit, Chicago, Cleveland, Gary—and although it had only 200,000 members, it represented nearly a half million teachers at the bargaining table. No organization that large could be swallowed up. When the Flint, Michigan, local merged with the much larger N.E.A. affiliate, both Fischer and Selden reacted like doting fathers. The national merger was inevitable, they predicted.

But it has been the history of the A.F.T. that events not totally under the control of its leaders have made their best-laid plans disasters. The first was Reuther's withdrawal from the A.F.L.–C.I.O. Spiritually and politically, the A.F.T. belonged with Reuther's new American Labor Alliance, but Selden hesitated and then, in effect, turned his back on his old friend. Reuther's defection caused the I.U.D. well to run dry, and the A.F.T. began operating in the red. Secondly, Selden's friend Fischer was reminded quite forcefully on a number of occasions that he was not the sole leader of the million-member N.E.A.; Executive Secretary Sam Lambert maintained considerable power. And Lambert was not very happy with the prospects for a merger. To woo the more conservative Lambert, Selden let it be known that he was willing to repudiate his organization's affiliation with the trade-union movement. That probably was a mistake; Lambert didn't believe him, and the move may have alienated a large segment of the A.F.T. membership.

More important, Selden seemed to be losing his control over the operations of his staff—particularly the national organizers, the A.F.T. warriors who saw themselves as trade-union militants, not teachers. The organizers brought more than half of all A.F.T. members out on strike in the first year of Selden's two-year term; and many of the walkouts involved bitter jurisdictional disputes with N.E.A. affiliates. The Association members simply felt that this was no way to treat a friend. The bitterest of all these strikes was the seemingly interminable New York City dispute—a strike aimed not so much at the city school board, but at what had been considered very promising experiments in community control of the public schools. There are no indications that Selden wanted to put a lid on Shanker's strike—he probably couldn't have, if he had wanted to. But the image of a teachers' union as a reactionary force in an urban community was the inevitable result of the two-month strike; serious educators of all stripes were shocked when an independent study showed that the long New York teachers' strike may have significantly retarded the reading progress of many city children.

These were desperate times, Selden apparently felt, and they called for desperate actions. The future of a dream was at stake. While denouncing some of his own staff members as "extremists," he prepared for the major test of the merger policy, in Los Angeles. Instead of allowing his staff to work toward the usual goal, a collective-bargaining victory, he instructed the warriors to build a merged local. The Los Angeles Federation of Teachers was only a fraction of the size of the N.E.A. affiliate, but the warriors had in the past pulled off bigger upsets. They felt that they could do it again.

In February, 1970, Selden moved almost his entire staff into Newark, where union teachers were striking. There, much of the strike of the merged "United Teachers–Los Angeles" was planned and a number of national representatives made little effort to hide their unhappiness with the impending action. But Selden himself had plans which appeared to some to be designed to improve his sagging image. With considerable advance notice, he appeared on a picket line in Newark; county sheriff's officers were waiting. Once arrested, Selden refused bail. Once convicted, he refused to appeal. He was sentenced to 60 days in the county jail.

Selden was—and the A.F.T. image machine didn't fail to press the point—only the third president of an international union to serve time in jail. Eugene V. Debs of the United Railway Workers had been the first; the indomitable Michael Quill of the Transport Workers Union was the second. The A.F.T. president said he was going to jail to dramatize the inequity of laws and court actions forbidding strikes by public employees. But whatever impact his incarceration might have had on The Cause, or on the sentiments of rank-and-file teachers, his actions apparently did not impress others in the A.F.T. leadership. While Selden voluntarily languished in jail, the union's executive council resolved not to encourage any further merger attempts with the N.E.A. That association responded with a similar move. Meanwhile, the Los Angeles strike began April 13, staffed by all but one of the A.F.T.'s national representatives.

Selden was released from jail May 1—May Day—and immediately embarked on a nationwide tour, presenting himself as the honored guest at a score of "bread-and-water" receptions organized by the A.F.T. to dramatize, theoretically, the need for right-to-strike legislation. Through the union's own ritual of transubstantiation, however, the bread and water were invariably transformed into hors d'oeuvres and Scotch, and the solemn receptions became back-slapping cocktail parties. To Minneapolis, to Portland, to San Francisco, to Philadelphia, to Chicago, to New York, to Boston, Selden the jailed hero, traveled. He even donned dungarees and a bulky sweater to march under the "Huelga" sign with Chicano grape pickers in a demonstration against the Agriculture Department in Washington. But his national exposure was overshadowed by the humiliating collapse of the strike effort in Los Angeles on May 14. The teachers won nothing; a number of the union staffers resolved never again to cooperate with the N.E.A. staffers, who, they believed, had undermined every attempt they made to negotiate "out" gracefully.

In July, National Representative Kenneth Miesen announced his candidacy for the A.F.T. presidency. Selden, in an action which belied his self-created image of civil libertarian, asked that Miesen be fired for "engaging in political activity" in violation of his contract. The executive council concurred. At the convention's opening session, Selden denounced all future merger discussions; like Jerome Davis thirty-two years earlier, Selden was putting away his most desired goals. It almost didn't work; he defeated Miesen by little more than one hundred votes, with more than three thousand cast. In fact, Selden failed to pick up a clear majority.

What followed the convention had all the appearances of a

purge. Selden charged five of the remaining eight national organizers with political activity in behalf of Miesen, charges which were later dropped. The Federation's skillful and most powerful organizer, James Mundy, resigned and then was fired from his position as director of organization.* Another rep's contract was allowed to expire and he found himself without a job. New reps were hired, reps with little national exposure and, therefore, little chance of building a powerful political opposition.

Within a year a calm had settled on the palace politics of the national union. But Miesen was expected to run again in 1972. And a new coalition of union members from smaller cities began to draw support from black, Puerto Rican and youthful teachers, and teacher aides. The coalition's objective was to bring Selden and Shanker down from the union's top positions. But the A.F.T.'s goals of controlling the profession and the schools it is paid to serve remained unchanged.

---

* More on Mundy's rather complicated separation from the national will be discussed later.

3

Warriors and Victims

JOE CASCELLA recognized at once the enormity of the two problems he faced. Unless immediate solutions could be found, he quipped, both his effectiveness as a national representative for the American Federation of Teachers and the welfare of thousands of Hartford children and their teachers would be in jeopardy. The first problem was that it was considerably past 10 P.M., and the bars in the state of Connecticut close on Sunday at nine. The second was what to tell reporters now that the members of the Hartford Federation of Teachers had refused, for the second consecutive week, to vote the strike he had warned two weeks ago was absolutely necessary for the salvation of the schools in the New England city.

Beneath the dark fedora he always wore to impress ally and foe alike of the formal and often ominous nature of his mission, his thin, angular face brooded with concern.

Suddenly, a wide toothy grin flashed. "Son of a bitch," he declared, and he padded briskly across the hotel lobby to the elevator, which carried him, much too slowly, he remarked, to the twelfth floor and his room. He rummaged impatiently through the artifacts of his gypsy existence—boxes of laundered shirts, spare ties and socks, credit cards, slips of papers bearing cryptic messages and the telephone numbers of everyone from the state education commissioner to the young and terribly bored teacher who insisted he note it down just in case he found the time to call her. Among the debris, he found the solution to his number-one problem. In seconds, he broke the plastic seal of the small, dark-green bottle and poured a generous portion into the bathroom glass.

"Now I can relax and think."

Through his memories of seven years as the Federation's chief strike strategist, through countless small towns and big cities, he rummaged again for a solution to his second-biggest problem. He wondered aloud how he had handled similar problems in Kenosha, Baltimore, Hamtramck, Washington, East St. Louis, Superior, Gary, San Juan, Newark, San Jose, Woodbridge, New Haven, Detroit, Boston, East Chicago Heights, New Orleans, St. Croix, Pittsburgh, Pawtucket, Louisville, Monterey, San Francisco and even Guam. He concluded angrily that he had never faced a similar problem. The Hartford teachers simply did not know there was a war going on; they were being unreasonable.

That's it! Again the toothy smile and unteacherlike expletive. He drew himself up to full height in the middle of the cluttered room, waited with reasoned impatience as the imaginary reporters pulled out their notebooks and the technicians made last-minute adjustments on their cameras, tape recorders and lights.

"Hartford teachers," he finally announced in the short, clipped tones that somehow have infected the voices of all of the Federation's warriors, "will go to unreasonable lengths to be reasonable." He flashed his yokel-like grin and congratulated himself with another gulp of Scotch. Cascella put the glass down quickly, reminding himself of the television cameras that weren't there. He continued:

"The teachers are the only people in this town concerned with the education of the children. They are angry because the school board has failed to come up with the benefits necessary for quality education in Hartford. They're ready to go out tomorrow if it means making the schools more effective.

"But these people—and I am, too—these people are teachers. They do not want to be separated from their children. They know that the school board will endanger the welfare of these kids by keeping the schools open without teachers. So they'll make whatever sacrifices necessary to find a solution to this problem without resorting to strike.

"This shows, I believe, that if there is a strike, the school board must take the full responsibility. We've tried. As I've always said, we expect the worst and hope for the best."

With a perfunctory wave of his hand, he dismissed the imaginary press conference and allowed that he had once again overcome another of the obstacles that governors, mayors, school-board members, reporters and, at times, union teachers themselves, were wont to place in his way. "You know," he confided with a sense of modesty enhanced by the almost un-interrupted flow of Scotch, "there are times I've performed miracles."

He lapsed into a period of uncharacteristic silence, a vacant stare belying the forced buoyancy of his smile. Joe Cascella was far away from Hartford now, perhaps back in Belleville, New Jersey, in the home his wife had left because she simply could not stand being alone all the time; perhaps in Washington, D.C., where, he knew, his boss, Federation President David Selden, was discussing freely the reasons he had for firing Cascella; perhaps in Bangkok, Thailand, where, of all places, he had been when he had *not* begun to do those things—namely, instigating a "dump Selden" movement—for which Selden wanted him fired; perhaps in New Brunswick, New Jersey, removing chicken leavings from the coops of the Middlesex County workhouse, where he had spent seventy-two days of his life for leading a strike in Woodbridge. Cascella looked too tired, his face too old, his slicked hair too gray, to be only forty years old. Although he resisted, the levity with which he had conducted the imaginary press conference only minutes before ineluctably drained away. Instead of the caustic and self-assured union organizer he so desperately portrayed, he resembled more and more a lonely, middle-aged man, drinking warm Scotch from a bathroom tumbler, a career transient, alone in a hotel room stinking with bathroom disinfectant and stale tobacco smoke. "You know," he said with a gravity which appeared to make him uncomfortable, "this really is a pretty shitty life."

The phone rang. A newspaper. The smile returned. The dreadful peace between battles was over. Hardly for the benefit of the caller, he buttoned collar and cuff, smoothed the rumples from his silk suit.

"A strike?" he answered the caller's first question with mixed anger and pained concern.

"Look, I hope you tell your readers tomorrow—and I really mean this and you know I've always given you straight answers—I hope you write tomorrow that I said Hartford teachers will go to unreasonable lengths to be reasonable. . . ."

And, the following day, Joe Cascella, veteran and renewed warrior, set out to prove the sincerity of his remarks by appearing to sabotage efforts to mediate the salary dispute. He said he rejected every suggested mediator offered by the State Education Commissioner, including the State Education Commissioner—"He's top management"—and managed to plant a story in a local newspaper that the school board had rejected out of hand every mediator suggested by the State Education Commissioner, including the State Education Commissioner himself. The following Sunday, the Hartford Federation of Teachers decided the best way to save the schools of the city was to close them with a strike. As expected, the local courts took exception and began levying disastrously high fines against the union local and its leadership. Three weeks later, with nothing gained, the Hartford Federation of Teachers decided the best way to save the schools of the city was to return to work.

"Once again," Cascella told a press conference convened hours before his plane to Washington was scheduled to leave, "the teachers of Hartford have proven their first concern is with the children of this city."

So the Movement endures, the struggle to smash the power of the National Education Association, to make every teacher a dues-paying union member, to institutionalize the American Federation of Teachers as a more-than-equal partner in the operation of public schools—in fine, to control the education profession—continues, by leaps and by stumbles. While Joe Cascella was exercising the magic of double-think in Hartford, Connecticut, by explaining that only teachers concerned enough about education to strike are concerned enough about education to return to work, his fellow comrades in arms, the "traveling troupe of circus clowns," as one of their number described the group with rare candor, were spread throughout the land, answering the call to battle.

This small band of men, ten or twelve at maximum strength, driven by their own egos, a sense of loyalty to "the Movement"—it is not a union only, it is a *movement*—and a fanaticism for battle which blurs not only their sense of time and location but also the routine ties to family and home, leads, follows and, at times, creates the teacher militancy which is changing the face of American education in the last third of the twentieth century. Yes, Shanker may be responsible for the 60,000 union teachers and paraprofessionals in New York City; yes, he, through his power over Selden and the union's executive council, can wield the ax in the national organization whenever he is sufficiently provoked. But, contrary to the opinion of many, New York City is not the country. There are nearly 200,000 teachers in the union outside New York City, and these are the ones whose attitudes toward the trade-union movement, whose willingness to strike, are molded by the A.F.T.'s staff of national representatives.

To understand these men, however, it is necessary to know James Mundy. In the sixties he was the Federation's chief organizer; he is no longer with the Federation, primarily, he said later, because Albert Shanker still is. After abandoning a law career to become the A.F.T.'s director of organization, after prodding, inspiring, bullying the national representatives —and through them hundreds of thousands of teachers—into an activism unmatched by public employees in any other field, after losing his home life to what has been described as the "fever of the Movement," Mundy was fired.* He now practices law in Washington. And he wonders whether the seven years of battle, the seven years of urging his best friends on the national staff to resign from the monotonously cheerful human community to become knights—or perhaps pawns—in the game was really worth it.

In the sparsely furnished apartment which served as both home and office on Washington's renewed East Capitol Street, Mundy drank low-calorie beer and surveyed the wreckage. "I often think of the Sunday nights I've called these guys at home and ordered them to catch the first plane to some Godforsaken spot thousands of miles away. And they went, sometimes followed out by the pleas of their wives to stay home, just this one weekend. But the Movement wasn't built by people who stayed home on weekends." They went because the organizational system which Mundy built for the A.F.T. puts the national representatives into positions of inordinate power over the destinies of entire communities, their children, their teachers, their local property taxes. It is a heady feeling, and Mundy knew it as he traveled the country, carefully re-

---

* Albert Shanker, angered over what he termed Mundy's unauthorized use of a U.F.T. organizer, had asked the A.F.T. executive council to dismiss Mundy. The council refused, primarily because it is poor labor—and, probably, public—relations to fire such a high officer outright; it is better to afford someone whose services are no longer desired the opportunity to resign now that he knows a power as strong as Shanker no longer wants him. Mundy did submit his resignation, he says, effective December 31, 1970. The council accepted it— effective immediately. Mundy then withdrew the resignation, charging its terms had been violated. The council then moved to fire him, anyway. The feud is likely to end up in the courts.

cruiting warriors for the battle. All these men, after all, were
teachers, whose daily lives were marked off in 45- or 50-
minute periods, who believed their horizons to be circum-
scribed by the inevitable squareness of a classroom, whose
entire year was laid out in advance in the yearly lesson plan
which a principal might reject and ask to have rewritten to
conform to some bureaucratic ideal. Mundy played on the
essential boredom of some aspects of a teaching career, inviting a potential organizer to the best hotel in the biggest nearby
city, ordering the most expensive meal, talking incessantly of
his travels throughout the country, his discussions with people
in the highest circles of government and, most important, his
ability to defy, without particular concern, principals, superintendents, school boards, even courts and governors. The
arguments can be irresistible. The slow disintegration of family
life, the incredible boredom of constant travel and hotel living,
the drain on health, appear only gradually and then it is too
late. The organizer is now a warrior; and it is difficult to return to the classroom, to give up the press coverage, the
speeches, the infighting with famous men. It is, above all, a
trap.

Mundy himself made that discovery shortly after he mi-
grated from Pennsylvania to New Jersey in the late 1950's to
take a teaching position in Woodbridge, an "all-American
city," whose mayor was indicted for extortion. He was a chem-
istry teacher, working to earn the tuition for the evening law
classes he attended at nearby Seton Hall University. Convinced that someday he would leave all that behind to become
a rich and famous lawyer—he would settle for just rich—he
had little understanding of, and even less patience with, the
intimidation felt by his fellow teachers when it came time to
discuss and to accept (not to negotiate) the salary schedule
adopted by the board of education. Members of the union—
Woodbridge has been a "Federation town" for years, even
when there was no national federation to speak of—urged the
young, defiant law student to join its salary committee. He

did and promptly told the school board he did not accept the salary schedule and would be busy within the next few weeks fomenting a strike. Now, Woodbridge was preparing at the time to accept the uncoveted All-American City Award, even to the point of making stencils of the national emblem for local garbage trucks, so such an un-American transgression as a teachers' strike was hardly acceptable. The teachers won a bigger raise and Mundy won at least countywide recognition as a teacher unafraid to fight school boards.

Despite his practiced aversion to people in groups—Mundy's face flushes a high-blood-pressure crimson when he is in a crowd—the aspiring attorney received numerous invitations to speak to stumbling union locals throughout the state. And one day he received an invitation to meet privately with A.F.T. President Carl Megel in a hotel in downtown Newark. That the hotel is still more famous for vice raids than for this 1962 parley is probably some indication that the A.F.T. has not had the impact on the public that some of its members believe. Nonetheless, it was a fateful meeting for the hundreds of towns and cities which faced teacher strikes in the 1960's and, no doubt, for the hundreds more which will face such walkouts in the future.

Megel knew he was retiring in 1964. He also was aware that the Midwestern coalition—the National Caucus—which had kept the union together since the Depression could not face the challenge offered by David Selden and Albert Shanker in New York. Still, he had enough time to pick his staff to ensure that the interests of the Western and Midwestern unions would be cared for. (He also managed to get himself a contract-bound job as Washington legislative representative.) Megel needed a loyal, essentially apolitical, yet cunning man to run the organization once the New York crowd took over. Although Megel hardly knew Mundy well enough to determine whether the twenty-seven-year-old law student had any of these qualifications, he did know that the only other union member who wanted the job was Selden. That apparently was sufficient qualification for Mundy. In his private hotel suite, Megel offered Mundy the job.

"No," said Mundy, "I'm going to law school."

Megel, who anticipated the purge Selden and Shanker would surely execute as soon as control passed into their hands, insisted. If travel was a problem, Mundy would be assigned to New Jersey. If night work was a problem, or study, he could have his evenings and weekends free. He could even have an office within a few minutes' ride of the law school's campus. When pressed, Mundy assumes all the appearances of a man ready for a stroke, because he cannot stand to be pressed. A particularly discomfiting situation must be ended quickly. Mundy said Yes; Megel felt the future of his kind of unionism appeared bright indeed. His man was in a key position.

While he remained in New Jersey to complete his law-schooling, Mundy could do little for the union. He did, however, befriend Cascella, then executive secretary of the Newark Teachers Union, an organization which the local press had branded as at least Communist-led in the 1950's. This was primarily because the New York press had branded the New York teacher union with the same charge. Mundy also managed to keep money flowing in from Walter Reuther's Industrial Union Department by having Cascella exercise his rhetoric in writing official recruitment reports. It was the first indication that truth could always be "improved" by Cascella's imagination, and Mundy liked it. One of Mundy's first official actions after his elevation to D.O. (Director of Organization) was to hire Cascella as a national organizer. It wasn't easy; the executive council was convinced that anyone from Newark was a Communist and it took days to have the assuredly non-Communist, essentially conservative Cascella formally appointed.

Another problem Mundy faced upon taking the job as the Federation's chief strategist was how to keep his job. It would not be easy; when he moved into his office in Chicago—the

law career, he reasoned, would be enhanced by a few years at the top of an international union—Mundy knew his appointment had dashed Selden's dream of being the court intriguer, a dream he had described to nearly everyone he met. But Megel held a different view of the D.O.'s job and was not likely to allow Selden to subvert it. To assuage Mundy's fears of an unnaturally short career with the Federation, Megel managed to convince Nicholas Zonarich, the I.U.D.'s distributor of money and patronage, to let Selden and Shanker know that the money might cease to flow if there was a disruptive purge. Selden never let Mundy forget the incident. When Mundy finally let go in 1970, the A.F.T. president himself took over the job of Director of Organization.

When Selden and Shanker gained the leadership of the national union in 1964, through the candidacy of Charles Cogen, the retiring president of the New York local, Mundy found himself with a secure job and the freedom to develop the Federation with just about as much A.F.L.–C.I.O. money as he needed. There were difficulties at first. He was constantly called upon to follow leads from organizers of other A.F.L.–C.I.O. unions who would call, sometimes in the middle of the night, to insist that he send organizers to the most unlikely areas. After disastrous and expensive attempts at organizing teachers in West Virginia, Kentucky and Florida, Mundy gave up following the leads of the A.F.L.–C.I.O. "Our men," he recalled, "were consistently being arrested and brought to state lines. Or they would wake up in their hotel rooms to find strange, although amiably undressed, girls in their rooms, along with photographers. They didn't like us in the South." No, indeed. Several of the temps (temporary organizers) Mundy had hired to recruit in the South were roughed up by local anti-union people.

Still, Reuther's I.U.D. was financing the unimpressive union and there were indications that he was unhappy with the A.F.T.'s progress. Selden, now assistant to Cogen, wanted something "big" to happen, he wanted a nationwide organizing thrust, the kind of action which he, Shanker and the fortunate political climate in New York City had produced to create the U.F.T. Although Selden was a good "idea" man— he still writes down ideas concerning the utopian future of a national teachers' union and shows them to his most loyal comrades—he did not have the kind of organizational skill Mundy possessed. Moreover, he did not have the job Mundy possessed. So to James Mundy, a nervous twenty-eight-year-old who would rather have been a rich lawyer, fell the job of organizing America's two million teachers as the core of the A.F.L.–C.I.O.'s multimillion-member white-collar-union dream.

It was an odd, although characteristic choice. Mundy expressed very little interest in education, has little now. He wrote very little, although the pages of *The American Teacher* were open to him on request. He had no dream of a unified teaching force, marching, in integrated pageantry, under the banner of trade-unionism, setting right the educational, economic and social flaws of a nation. He took during his tenure no particular view of innovation in the classroom, of educational reform, of what the future of the schools should be. Silberman, Dewey, Childs, Counts, Kozol, Kohl, Holt, Herndon, Coleman, Clark, Reisman, Woodring, Mann—he had little interest in what these men or any others had written or were writing. Although his position and the actions he took during his seven-year tenure as the organizational architect of the union were inextricably bound to the daily operations of thousands of American schools, Jim Mundy was not an educator, not a critic, not a reformer, not a philosopher. He was an organizer.

And he did it well. To do more was, within the context of the Federation, to engage in "politics." Mundy and the staff he assembled through the 1960's left that to the politicians—as long as the organizing was left to him. His mission was to make every teacher a union member, to eliminate the power of the National Education Association, and to shore up the position of teacher-union locals in communities throughout the United States through bigger and better contracts. In 1964, only months after Selden and Shanker assumed control, the broad outlines of the position were handed to him. It was called the "Co-Organizational Plan," or "Co-Org." Theoretically, each state federation—whether or not a state had a federation—was to develop an organizing cadre for use in collective-bargaining elections, strikes and contract negotiations. Technical help was to come from a national staff. It was an effort to decentralize the union, to offset the N.E.A.'s criticism that the Federation was controlled by a small group of men at the top and to bring the union presence to as many local communities as possible. In addition, "Co-Org" was designed to counter the superior resources and power of state affiliates of the N.E.A., historically the base of power for the older and larger organization.* This grand design was Selden's idea and, expectedly, Mundy generally ignored it, although official union publications keep alive its ghost.

Mundy believed the exercise of power could not be entrusted to the many, particularly the many who were closely associated with local communities. They were too vulnerable to pressure from their neighbors, from local politicians, from irate citizens. No, the union warriors had to be national in their outlook, ubiquitous in their operations, fast in their escape. They should have no ties to the town they were destined to disrupt. If, for example, a state organizer was placed on probation and facing a prison sentence in his state for having led an illegal strike—and teachers' strikes continue to be of questionable legality—he would be very reluctant to call another one in the future if that was "necessary." He would, in effect, be neutralized. However, if a national organizer faces

---

* Ironically, in 1970, the N.E.A. adopted the "unified service plan," or "Uni-Serv," designed to eliminate the power of its own state associations and to provide more skilled labor technicians to local affiliates for use in strikes, collective-bargaining campaigns and contract negotiations. Selden charged the move was designed to crush the union, a "rule or ruin" step.

arrest for contempt of court in, say, Rhode Island, he is simply kept out of Rhode Island and another national representative can be sent in. Cascella spent seventy-two days in jail in New Jersey, because he lived in the state and refused to migrate in order to avoid the sentencing.

The approach, of course, leaves the Federation open to charges of "outside agitation." The charges are true. But Mundy's job was not to answer criticism; that, again, was up to the politicians. Instead of developing a system of strong state federations, Mundy "stole"—his word—the best talent he could find in the local organizations for his own national staff. By the time the era of teacher militancy was peaking, he controlled a personally loyal cadre of men, each a specialist in one or more of the duties of an organizer—striking, recruiting, negotiating—ready to go anywhere, alone or in teams, at any time, prepared to stay as long as necessary. They were, and are, highly mobile and have been known to settle and to begin strikes in two different communities on the same day. Within a few months of taking their positions, most national representatives become members of United Air Line's "100,000-mile Club."

Technically, the decision whether to strike, or not to strike, to engage the association in an election or to await a better time, is a political one, to be decided upon by the president, the executive council and Albert Shanker. Mundy and members of his staff were permitted to advise the elected officials of the A.F.T. on the chances of coming out of a walkout relatively unbloodied, or out of a bargaining election with a new "union town." The advice, however, was invariably ignored, for two reasons—because the staff hardly ever advises against strong action (that is the nature of the military) and because militant action is based on more important things than its tactical feasibility. New Orleans, for example, was struck twice in three years primarily because, in Mundy's words, "it was our Bastille of the South. If it fell, we believed, the South would fall." Hundreds of thousands of dollars and the entire A.F.T. staff were poured into Los Angeles in 1970, not because anyone but Selden believed it would be successful, but because Selden wanted to show that the United Teachers–Los Angeles, a merger of the union and an Association affiliate, could work together in a job action. They couldn't; the strike failed miserably. Baltimore was selected for a strike, as was Newark, primarily to rid the East Coast cities of N.E.A. presence; Washington because it was felt that a successful collective-bargaining election for the A.F.T. in the nation's capital—where the N.E.A. had spent millions to prove architecturally, as well as legislatively, that it was one of the most powerful lobbies in the country—would be, again in Mundy's words, "psychologically devastating" to the N.E.A. The union's success in Washington may not have devastated the N.E.A.; but it made the historically administrator-dominated association act more and more like a trade-union. "The general philosophy," explained Mundy, "was that if you beat the N.E.A. over the head long enough, it has to start looking like a loser."

Once the decision is made, it is then up to the staff of representatives to execute the policy. The representatives usually decide the timing of the action, its intensity and when to call it off. This power is considerable, and the object of intense competition between the warriors and the politicians. The warriors can usually win because of their superior knowledge of the local situation and because of the intimate contact they maintain with local teachers, who do, after all, vote for the politicians. The Minneapolis Federation of Teachers, for example, struck early in 1970, providing Kenneth Miesen with considerable exposure and support in his nearly successful attempt to knock Selden from the presidency. The New Jersey delegation voted with the anti-Selden, anti-Shanker coalition, primarily because of the loyalties engendered by the staff members who ran the Newark strike. (Selden has since taken to visiting the scene of every major A.F.T. action, just to keep in touch.)

The reader, no doubt, is aware by now that nothing has been said about the local issues surrounding a strike or the less disruptive though ominous collective-bargaining campaign. The local media often do cover the meeting at which the strike is voted, and it is readily apparent the teachers present *want* to strike, they are not being coerced. And any national A.F.T. staff member who happens to be present will pale if even a suggestion is made that people or events outside the local community have decided the fate, for several weeks, of the local schools and children. Indeed, teachers have struck without the knowledge or the approval of national headquarters. Invariably, however, a town fated to have a strike will have as its guests one or more A.F.T. staff members weeks *before* a walkout is hinted. Through a carefully organized "prepping," the reps will, if not create the issues, at least intensify them in the minds of the local teachers. They can then wait until the support of a strike reaches a zenith, quickly call a meeting, carefully plant loyal (prostrike) teachers in the audience, and the hand has been played. "A rep doesn't call a meeting—or at least a public one—unless he knows he has the votes," explained Cascella, the staff's strike man. (He was, of course, wrong in Hartford in 1970, but he kept at it until the teachers did strike.) As for the teachers who strike without official sanction, they have to be prepared, in many cases, to suffer alone, or with a minimum of A.F.T. support. There are 125 former Minot, North Dakota, teachers who have learned that lesson well; they struck, called for A.F.T. help and, several weeks later, found themselves without jobs and the A.F.T. rep on his way back to Washington, convinced as never before that strikes are impossible without advance planning.

The nature of the reps' work changed somewhat in the late 1960's, with more energies and planning put into collective-bargaining elections than into strikes. This did not mean, however, an end to the strike; in fact, teachers were striking either to force a collective-bargaining election or to crystallize the support gained from a successful election. But prepping for an election is similar to prepping for a strike (in some cases it is the same thing), so Mundy and his staff coordinated the planning into one major package. (Once a strike occurs, of course, a whole line of strategy goes into effect— of which more later.)

During the 1960's communities to be singled out for a collective-bargaining campaign were determined by the A.F.T.'s urban strategy: every major city in the United States was to be a union town. (At this writing, there are, of course, exceptions, Los Angeles being the most important.) As the union's control over the metropolitan areas grew, however, the qualifications for a target city became muddled. A local federation would have a better chance for national support if its delegates supported Selden in the 1970 convention. Or if it was located in an area represented by a more ambitious A.F.T. vice-president. Albert Shanker, for example. Or if it made a lot of noise through its Central Labor Council. One cannot always expect such important decisions to be based on the idea that local teachers feel union representation would be of benefit to them, their school children and the community.

Whatever the reason, a carefully prescribed plan goes into effect once the A.F.T. decides to act. Months before a scheduled election, one representative takes up residence in the town, making contact with local Federation leaders and trying desperately to stay away from the regional A.F.T. vice-president and local A.F.L.–C.I.O. leadership. (These last are usually so connected to the political power structure, they are to be kept at a distance.) The first formal step is taken when the representative orders the union literature and informs national headquarters he needs at least three or four more staff members to conduct the campaign. John Converse, a kind of utility-infielder rep, supplies the literature; George Brickhouse, the A.F.T.'s director of field services, is supposed to supply personnel.

The literature is standard, written in Washington with blank spaces left for local color. The first of these testaments is the "menu." It is called the menu because someone on Mundy's staff—the import of the achievement has assigned him to obscurity—fell in love with the dinner menu on the typical United Airlines flight. So now prospective union teachers have "Issues which face all teachers" for appetizers on the red-white-and-blue (United's colors) fold-out card. As the masterpiece of pop art is unfolded, the issues become more selective. Tidbits for the special-education teachers might be found in the hors-d'oeuvres section; physical-education teachers may have their interests dished up with dessert. As with many ideas which somehow find their way into A.F.T. operations, you had to be there at the time to understand the reason for printing a million of them.

Then, of course, there is the "beautiful people" flier, a description given to it by the people whose faces and brief, often glowing, biographies appear on the pamphlet. Selden, Shanker, the regional vice-president, Mundy—until he left the union—and some of the representatives are pictured in the fliers with the pronouncement: "Just some of the people who will be fighting for you." Blank space is left, of course, for pictures of local A.F.T. leaders and A.F.L.–C.I.O. chieftains, who also are, in A.F.T. demonology, "beautiful people," particularly when they can help drum up per capita dues.

Third in the pile of inevitable paper which flows into a town just prior to a bargaining election is the "endorsement flier," containing reviews of the union given by such old stand-bys as Bayard Rustin and Hubert Humphrey. Very often, the nice telegram which is sent to the national convention of the A.F.T. every year by the incumbent president is included. It is not always politic, however, and can be discarded at the option of the local rep. In fact, the A.F.T. is very careful to make sure endorsements will not offend anyone. Martin Luther King may have been good in Philadelphia, but not in the South. An organization, after all, can have too many friends.

The endorsement fliers of Federation locals have been vaguely suspect ever since that day in 1968 when John Schmid was charged with producing a letter supporting the Kansas City Federation of Teachers which was *not* written by Ralph David Abernathy of the Southern Christian Leadership Conference. Schmid, who is from Brooklyn and considers Newark rural, was having trouble convincing even his own members that they should vote out the local affiliate of the N.E.A. Such desperate times call for desperate means. In the pile of old literature used in a collective-bargaining election, he found a typical endorsement flier bearing a letter from Abernathy mildly praising the Pittsburgh Federation of Teachers. According to charges brought by the N.E.A., Schmid very carefully cut out the word "Pittsburgh" and replaced it with "Kansas City." With which he busied himself for the next few days, reprinting the letter and stuffing it very carefully into the mailboxes of black teachers in Kansas City. Leave it to the humorless members of the Education Association to charge the A.F.T., which ultimately won the election, with an unfair labor practice. Schmid's imagination was rewarded with an appointment to the position of director of state federations, from which he will have little chance to get the A.F.T. into that kind of trouble.

Finally, "issue" fliers are prepared for each target town. These are carefully tailored to meet the problems of the local community by John Converse, who works in Washington and may never see the local community whose problems he is solving. His work is based on certain assumptions: that teachers are underpaid and desperate, that the children are suffering, that the school board is unresponsive, that the school buildings are archaic, that the textbooks are out-of-date, that the curriculum is irrelevant, that tensions are high and morale is low, that integration is proceeding too slowly, that education is underfinanced, that politicians are corrupt and/or insensitive, that class sizes are too big, that faculty lounges are too small (or are nonexistent), that the Education Association is (1) too unwilling to sit down with the board to negotiate, or (2) too willing to make a deal with the board, that benefits are virtually nonexistent, and that teachers should be raised to a level of respect and dignity befitting their high calling in every town in the United States not covered by a union contract. (And in every town so covered, too, if it is negotiating season or prestrike prepping time.)

The local rep has the option of distributing these position papers directly to the teachers, sending them to the press, or having them read by an A.F.T. politician when he comes to town to cheer on the troops "in this vital battle on which hinges the educational future of the (a) hundreds, (b) thousands of children who attend school here in _____." The reps have been very cautious about making sure that the A.F.T. politician has something to read when he addresses union recruits. This is done to prevent incidents such as one described by John Converse when Charles Cogen—Fighting Charlie from New York—urged all the teachers to go out and join the "Big Leagues" in New Haven, Connecticut. They did. However, the "Big Leagues" was the name adopted by the rival Education Association affiliate, the New Haven Teachers League. And Converse, then the local rep, and now public-relations director for the A.F.T., promised never again to leave a national president without a pre-written speech.

A number of local teachers are recruited to form "delivery crews" for the hundreds of thousands or millions of pieces of literature which must be distributed to the teachers. While this is being done, Mundy—or Brickhouse—would fly in with the coffee percolators and without the extra staff help promised by national headquarters. (Brickhouse has the nickname "Promises, Promises" for that very reason.) Negotiations are then opened, not with the school board, but with the local bakery and/or franchise quick-food shop—Gino's,

Wetson's, White Castle, and so on. Doughnuts for teachers in the morning, chicken or hamburgers at lunch. School meetings are then scheduled.

With all the drama of a grade-C war movie, a battle map is drawn up at local headquarters, over which Mundy, the local rep and/or local teachers can lean pensively. A city is divided into districts, usually on the basis of neighborhoods or high-school feeder patterns. If the controlling rep is good, he knows the ethnic make-up of the districts and will assign either national representatives or local teachers of the same ethnic or racial background to cover meetings in those schools. (Sometimes this is not always possible, but David Mann, a black, did make a hit with the teachers in San Francisco's Chinatown.) Each school in the district will, if the personnel is available, have five meetings a week and one Thank-God-It's-Friday "happy hour." Reps are quaint, rarely original.

At morning meetings, teachers arrive at their faculty lounge, if there is one, or the cafeteria, to find a percolator brewing fresh coffee and stacks of paper cups placed conveniently near piles of the A.F.T. material. A smiling national rep—or a friendly local teacher—is there to answer any questions concerning either the origin of the percolator or the program of the A.F.T. If previous negotiations have been successful, a truck will drive up at that moment with freshly baked doughnuts or breakfast pastries.

Three times a week, at lunchtime, the process is repeated, when a union functionary drives up with the percolator and several quarts of fried chicken or several dozen hamburgers. A.F.T. promotion is served with the relish.

On Friday afternoons at three, usually at a nearby meeting hall, the A.F.T. will sponsor a "little get-together," complete with cheap Scotch, rock, soul or popular music (depending on the nature of the recruits) and a little talk from the A.F.T. staff member. Usually, a teacher seeking a drink, companionship or escape from going home will be given a "Hi There, I'm ———" sticker for instant recognition and a dues-check-off card already made out in favor of the union. A pretty little thing invariably will man the welcoming table and quite innocently tell the unsuspecting teacher, "Just put your name on the sticker and fill out the card." It is not known just how many teachers have inadvertently joined the union this way but a plentiful flow of Scotch is almost always considered a good investment.

Each weekend during the campaign, the national staff member will hold a private strategy meeting to discuss the week's achievement. At times, when the local staff is incompetent, untrustworthy or too entangled in local "politics"— A.F.T. activities are fine social affairs, good times to get to know the young man (or woman) who will get you into trouble with your husband (or wife) and, if you happen to be a local president or other leader, a good way to lose an election because of personal entanglements—the A.F.T. warrior will meet only with Mundy and/or Selden and/or Brickhouse. Decisions of great import are made at these "briefing" sessions—like whether to take the percolator out of the school which is hopelessly N.E.A. and put it in another school, which "could go either way." When a school is written off, its flag is taken from the map and the troops are concentrated in other areas. The daily delivery of doughnuts may be stopped.

In a large percentage of campaigns, in which the N.E.A. puts up only a token battle (the A.F.T. rarely starts a campaign it expects to lose, unless it is a very important city) and the board agrees without a fight to recognize the winner as bargaining agent, only one rep—at most, two—handles the entire campaign from "menu" to election day. In larger cities—Baltimore and Newark, for example—the entire staff, Selden, Shanker, presidents of larger locals, the two-member staff of *The American Teacher,* Executive Secretary Robert Porter, Civil Rights Director Len Lewis, publicity man Converse, and several secretaries, move in to coordinate with one another, confuse the warriors and take up residence of varying degrees of permanence. This kind of immigration usually heralds a strike.

Mundy usually relied on one of four specifically trained subordinates to run an election campaign which was not likely to be too complex. (Selden has carried on the same strategy, although now he has taken to assigning reps to regions, to prevent them from getting the kind of national exposure that almost made him a former A.F.T. president.) The four—Clarence Howard Hursey, David Mann, Vinnie Russell and Chuck Richards—are trained primarily to "relate" to teachers (except Russell, who is expected to "relate" to paraprofessionals) and not to engage in the kind of bombastic rhetoric or introversion which marks, respectively, strike specialists and negotiators among A.F.T. organizers.

Once a bargaining election is won, the A.F.T. will opt either for a strike or, if resources and personnel are committed elsewhere, for a peacefully negotiated contract. The election specialists are flown out, and a negotiator—usually Robert Bates—is flown in to begin contract talks. Bates usually is not used to conduct a strike, but rather to end one or to prevent one altogether if the local, despite angry sentiments against the school board for cooperating with the N.E.A. affiliate during the collective-bargaining campaign, simply is "not ready" to strike, or if the A.F.T. is not ready to support one.

A good way to tell if a strike is in the flash cards is to check the local newspaper for stories about the union immediately after the collective-bargaining election. If there are "mass" demonstrations in front of school-board headquarters, this means a national rep is testing the strength of his power over the local and there are likely to be problems. If there are no stories (exaggerated diatribes against the president of the school board or the mayor do not count; this usually reflects a local union publicity director with a hyperactive thyroid) about all-night vigils or prayer meetings or marches for educational quality—all tests of organizational readiness

—you, your children's education and your tax rate are probably safe. For a while.

Bates and the other A.F.T. staff members used as negotiators never conduct serious negotiation in the press. Never. If the membership ever knew what was being callously thrown away, particularly in terms of "educational improvements," for a few more shekels, the association could lay off all its organizers. The negotiation phase of A.F.T. activity is a quiet one, and less expensive (unless a strike happens to be going on at the same time). The rep in charge of negotiations is usually left in complete control of the talks and the local union's negotiating committee. Although the standard A.F.T. contract and its relation to control is discussed later, it should be emphasized here that the unimpressive document is the key to the A.F.T.'s future. In one pile of papers, the union's partnership with the board, its recruitment drive and its ability to lock into every phase of the operations of a school district is institutionalized in a binding contract which will, if negotiated by a competent rep, stand up not only in court but against the drives of the "outs"—particularly in urban school systems—who want in.

Every A.F.T. rep, whether he is used for negotiation or not, is thoroughly versed in the six sine-qua-nonical elements of a union contract:

1. A statement recognizing the A.F.T. local as the sole bargaining agent at least for the teachers, but also, if possible, for the permanent substitute teachers, the per-diem teachers, teacher, school and community aides, home teachers, special-education teachers, transient music, art and health teachers, psychologists, social workers, coaches, clerks, secretaries, security guards, custodians, and school-crossing guards.

2. An extensive statement of union rights in the operation of the school district.

3. A grievance procedure, ending in binding arbitration.

4. The Welfare Package—in a word, *money*.
5. Duration of the contract—preferably one year, except, as in New York, if the mayor is buying labor peace and is willing to pay a high price, or if there is a provision for a salary reopener.
6. The "savings clause," a routine paragraph which states that no provision of the contract shall be so construed as to conflict with any existing law. This gets sticky only if the school board wants to add "and existing board policy"—of which more later.

Generally speaking, the local Federation leadership, with information on "model contracts" supplied by friends in Washington or New York, compiles the list of demands. (National headquarters usually sets the starting-salary demand; in 1970 it was $10,000. Of course, no local won that, but they can dream.) The locals also go through the motions of appointing their own negotiating committee, whose main purpose is to maintain the myth that it's "just teachers like yourself" who are doing the bargaining and to catch the brickbats when the charges are made that an "outside agitator" has (a) sold out (from the teachers), or (b) is only interested in the furtherance of the national, not the local, union (from the school board). Beyond that, the negotiating committee does the routine paperwork; and if a lump sum is accepted as a final settlement, it divides the spoils among local friends—"The coaches really pulled for us during the election, they should get more than the nurses."

If the contract is an important one, the rep in charge usually will have checked the settlement out with Mundy (or, as now, Selden). If not, usually any good settlement will do, and a copy of it is filed with the national after acceptance. Particularly good grievance procedures or benefit packages are written into model contracts and distributed by Converse to local unions for help in developing their own contract demands.

The first step in opening negotiations is the formal delivery of the demands to the school board. (School boards have lately delivered to the union a set of their own demands for improved performance, extra training, et cetera. The A.F.T. is now working on that problem.) If the contract demands are first delivered to the local press, beware. The more publicity, the more chances for a strike. Then there's usually a "phony war," while the local teachers wait for A.F.T. help and the board decides whether it will say "no" nicely or hire an outside specialist to do it. When the rep arrives in town—again, usually Bates—serious negotiation can begin. "Serious negotiation" invariably means Bates will jettison the "silly demands"—a two-week paid honeymoon for all newly married teachers is one example. Another, not considered so silly by the local teachers who thought they wrote the proposals, is the laundry list of educational improvements, the improvements promised to teachers during the bargaining campaign. The abandonment of these items has to be done tactfully, often by setting up a committee to make a further study of these improvements, to report back no later than April of 2745. (The missing-persons list compiled by the San Francisco and New York police departments together would likely not match the list of members of disappearing joint board-and-union educational-improvement-study committees.) Having trampled on the ideals of the less experienced union members, Bates then exacts complete discipline from the remaining local members of the negotiating committee. No talking. No smiling—smiling is weakness. No drinking. No noise. No fidgeting. Board members usually are unnerved when faced with six or eight expressionless automatons who they know will give no quarter to human frailties, family problems, illness, death or the impending financial collapse of the town in which the action is taking place. (Bates is known throughout the union, and in the towns he has worked, as "Mr. Warm.")

Bates's arrogance is a cosmetic. He has, one of his fellow reps noted, a "built-in sneer." Or, as a board member who has faced him across the negotiating table allowed, in considerably less complimentary terms, "he looks like a snotty punk with a chip on his shoulder." But it is part of the role he plays, part of the weaponry of the A.F.T. warriors. Bates uses it, he explains, to avoid any lapse in strictly correct relations on the part of the school-board negotiators, and thus to prevent any "joking" intimidation, any "emotional" appeal to common interest, or, worse still, the kind of patronizing "we'll-do-the-best-we-can-for-you" attitude which marked much of what passed for negotiation for many years. Bates's insistence that the collective-bargaining process can be the only means and end during formal negotiating sessions creates entirely new attitudes between the school board and the teachers. To some it means something is lost of the tranquil cooperation between the publicly elected school board and its instructional staff. But that "some" are primarily board members. To others, mostly teachers, it means something is gained, the replacement of the hit-and-usually-miss appeals to the conscience of a public body often more concerned with its own political power than with teacher's salaries by an impersonal procedure which carries its own dynamic—the give and take of bargaining. It is simply more difficult for a school board to single out for special harassment members of a businesslike group of teachers following a well-established line of reasoning and argument than it would be for the board to find cause for eliminating one or two "troublemaking" teachers who are constantly demanding higher salaries and better working conditions.

If it is a process which angers some, baffles most and bores many, it obsesses negotiators like Bates. For reasons related to his conception of himself as someone more than a mere teacher, he has become a true student of negotiating. Bates has read every text he could find on the subject—discovering a new one is practically reason for a holiday. For relaxation, he often acts out new negotiating techniques; for doodling, he'll write over and over again new contract language. His fellow reps consider him something of an ascetic —or as close to an ascetic as a union organizer can be— who will forgo eating, sleeping and even drinking, just pacing the floor of his hotel room or the bedroom of his Perth Amboy home, contemplating collective bargaining. Mundy recalls sharing a room with him during one of Bates's negotiating assignments: "He hadn't slept for days because of round-the-clock talks. Finally, there was a break. But he sat down at the hotel room desk for hours, poring over one or two sentences of a contract proposal. He went back to the table, without sleep but with the new language and broke the deadlock." Two ultimate ends are involved—to prove himself the best contract negotiator in the A.F.L.–C.I.O. (he already is the best in the A.F.T.; even the politicians who shrink from his ambition and energy will concede that); and some day to develop a contract so tight that, in his words, "the teachers will be able to have as much control over education as the American Medical Association has over medicine."

At the table, he appears phlegmatic, indifferent, almost as if he felt imposed upon just being there. But the sandy-haired and befreckled Bates simmers with a kind of kinetic energy which enables him to outlast the most durable board negotiator. Away from the table, he constantly moves nervously, unable to relax, talking, swirling the swizzle stick in his martini, clutching the lapels of his jacket, tapping his fingers on the table, fidgeting with his cuff links, glancing again at his watch —driving anyone with him bananas. With that kind of personality, with his brand of ego, teaching was a poor choice for a profession—which is why he taught for only a few years. Bates's brand of negotiating can be a tiresome process. He presents those demands he believes are necessary to end a strike or gain a settlement. (Not necessarily those the teachers have decided are necessary.) When the reply to the offered contract language is delivered, he jots down the response, asking the respondent why the demand was rejected or why it was rephrased. That response is noted. On to the next item, offer, response, questions. During the first few negotiating sessions, Bates compiles a "history" of the development of a clause, noting why it was rejected, what might be a better alternative. Both at the table and at his hotel room, he keeps his "bible" close at hand, a loose-leaf binder containing all his notes, alternative language and examples of similar clauses he has worked out in other communities. Keeping in mind his idea of what the clause should mean, rather than what the words read, he then approaches the board with varying versions, perhaps eliminating an offensive word but making additions to the clause to keep the original meaning. It is really constant repetition, although his skillful manipulation makes it appear that he is offering concessions. When, in the persistent exchange of often simple declarative sentences, he feels that he has devised a formulation that is acceptable to the board, he moves away, back to a clause on which the consensus has not been reached. And the procedure is repeated.

With financial items (which Bates feels are less important than the magic of the words that he believes someday will deliver public education to the teachers), the process is similar. Present the most outrageous, listen carefully to the reasons for rejection. Put the money in somewhere else. (Since most teachers are paid according to a graduated scale based on years of experience, large increases can be skillfully hidden or spread out on different levels. A simple example might be: instead of a $2,000 increase at the first year, why not two $1,000 increases in, say, the fifth and eighth steps.) At the same time, lower the amount of time needed to reach maximum salary, or put the largest increases in those salary levels at which most teachers in town are employed. Give away nothing, manipulate the figures. Find out what will settle—but don't reveal it—and stick to the best possible deal. Most important, never act as if agreement has been reached on any item.

Bates may then suddenly create a sense of urgency and

come back hard with what he likes to call the "need to settle," those items upon which final agreement has not been reached (although Bates, by that time, knows what the board will buy). But he doesn't come back with the tentatively agreed-upon language and costs but something better. The board just might accept, or it might become so angered that it will lose the attention it might have previously paid to the development of language and salary terms. If the latter, board members are likely to be angry and accuse Bates of not bargaining in good faith. Time to act snotty, good time to walk out, charging the board with sabotaging negotiations by refusing to stick by the terms it had already agreed to in previous negotiation. Agreement to return to the bargaining table may cost the board acceptance of the "best possible," or original, language of an item, rather than the language Bates probably would have accepted. As a concession, Bates may then, to wrap it up, agree to those points he knows he and the board already have accepted.

Bates is deadly serious about negotiating, treating nearly every word of a clause on grievance procedure, union rights and recognition or transfer and assignment policy with almost as much attention as Allen Ginsberg might give to *Om.* Some on the staff feel Bates is too serious and therefore unable to settle contract disputes with the time-tested "adjoining urinal" method, also known as the "closet" method or the "Look-Joe-why-don't-we-get-a-bottle-and-go-back-to-my-room-and-settle-this-thing" syndrome. In such a process, the front of negotiation is kept, with subordinates going over already agreed-upon contract language, while the people with the power—the rep for the union, either the mayor or the paid negotiator for the school board—are elsewhere making a deal to end the strike. "No strike is ever settled at the bargaining table" is an axiom of some more seasoned reps. It might, however, be settled at "adjoining urinals," as the name suggests, when the two chief negotiators leave the room, ostensibly to relieve nature but really to reach agreement. Exotic variations have occurred. In one major city, for example, talks had reached an impasse—primarily because of Joe Cascella's insistence on calling the board's negotiator a "son of a bitch" to his face. A break was called to give both sides a chance to calm down; the two negotiating teams retired to caucus rooms. Cascella wandered around the unfamiliar hotel, looking for a bathroom. He found a likely door and opened it. Inside the clothes closet were a union officer (female) and the board's paid negotiator (male), huddled uncomfortably under some overcoats, working out an end to the strike. While suspected "adjoining urinal" settlements are more difficult than conventionally negotiated pacts to sell to teachers (the making of deals always is righteously suspected), in one way it makes little difference. The power to determine the operation of the schools and the local tax rate are in both cases vested in the smallest number of hands, and the public—these are, remember, at least theoretically public schools—has absolutely nothing to say. There simply are not enough urinals to go around.

Of course, some die-hard board members and mayors have insisted in the past that negotiation not be secret or lead to secret agreements. John Converse, the A.F.T.'s second-best —he believes he is the best, but is too much of a gentleman to contradict Bates—confronted such a "board trick" in Lawrence, Massachusetts. The mayor simply refused to meet him in the bathroom, to sit down over a bottle of Scotch, cuddle in a closet or even sit across the table from him, if the table was not in full view of the public. Converse agreed to the open negotiations and proceeded to pack the high-school auditorium with teachers and other sympathizers. Each time the mayor or the board member made a point, the audience jeered; each time Converse made a speech, he was given a standing ovation which lasted several minutes. For hours, the process continued until the board caved in and agreed to private talks. "It is impossible to negotiate in public," Converse says. Perhaps so. If it isn't, Converse, or whoever the rep is, will make it impossible. Sometimes you just cannot win.

If the A.F.T.—or the local—opts for strike first, contract later, the major task of the reps trained as strike specialists is finding something to say—to teachers, to the press, to angry parents. The strike, of course, is an action taken only when more reasonable efforts to settle a dispute have failed; or, more likely, when more reasonable efforts have not been attempted. The warriors involved always have little patience with parents who are angered because their children's education has been interrupted, or because now they have to put up with their kids for more hours every day, or, much more seriously, because chances at college have been endangered and opportunities to learn have been thrown away, or, more prosaic perhaps, but very important if you happen to be poor, because the only hot meal your kid gets each day is at school. They have little patience, because those parents just don't understand the kind of work put into a strike, the hours and days of prepping, the morale building, the administrative work. "We're not striking," said one rep, "we're working."

There is, of course, only one reason why teachers strike: "to improve education"—unless we're talking about New York in 1968, when the U.F.T. struck for 'justice.' Since not even teachers really believe those reasons, let us pass on quickly to the other real reasons why teachers strike.* Teachers strike to make life a little more tolerable by gaining one or more of the following: money; more free time; less administrative or board interference; less parental interference; more insurance, health care and pension benefits (money); shorter working hours (the "more free time" noted above is *during* the school day); job security; the freedom to be (or to refuse to be) creative, troublesome, ultraconservative, radical, moderate, chic, sloppy, concerned, indifferent, excellent or mediocre (sometimes known as *academic freedom*); a temporary es-

---

* There are, of course, exceptions. Some people always will believe we had to destroy Hué in order to save it, drop the atom bomb to save lives, and execute people to deter murders.

cape from boredom; and, when the bureaucracy becomes overwhelming, just a chance to kick the whole goddam system in the you-know-what. Or at least, ask any striking teacher why he or she is striking, and the answer will be one or more of the above. To be fair, many teachers do strike for those reasons. To be perfectly accurate, however, many teachers, if not most, strike to make life while they are working a little more tolerable, because if they did not, life with their fellow teachers would be less than tolerable. I have not, of course, had a revelation; *every* strike, in *every* industry, carries along with it the dynamic of gentle (sometimes not so gentle) intimidation, and the lot of workers throughout the country, blue-, white- or paisley-collar, are the better for it. However, when you scab on a teachers' strike, you are often accused of scabbing on the Movement, you are undermining The Only Way to Improve Education, The Only Way to Bring Dignity to the Profession; and, by the way, you are resisting one of the most compelling psychological softening campaigns ever devised by organized labor. That is the sole task of the A.F.T. strike strategist—to devise methods by which even thinking about abandoning the Movement in order to pay the mortgage is different from being a loyal member of the Vichy government only in circumstance and degree. (The A.F.T., however, never gives up on "scabs" or "collaborators." There's the old saying, you know: "Today's scab is tomorrow's picket captain." That's the old saying, but I would not believe it.)

This is not a simple task, however. For a number of reasons. First, teachers are at least nominally educated and do have, the literature said somewhere, the pursuit of truth as one of their prime functions. Theoretically, at least, this would prevent them from following their rep blindly into battle. Mass action should not exactly be their style, since such action does not require so much intellectual participation, but rather just having your body out of that classroom and, if possible, on that picket line. (There are, of course, extremes, and this is usually what makes faculty meetings at large universities so dreadfully boring; no professor ever wants to believe he has been convinced of the truth, since truth is only approachable; it also is probably the true strength of the legitimate academic community.) Secondly, many teachers confront in most strikes serious moral questions concerning whether or not children should be abandoned for any substantial length of time—particularly in the urban areas. Thirdly, many teachers somehow equate professionalism with not withdrawing their services. (The A.F.T. is working on that, equating professionalism with withdrawing of services; in both cases, however, logic becomes a pretzel.)

For these reasons, and for the traditional deterrents connected with not being paid, the conduct of a successful teachers' strike demands considerable planning and expertise. Which leads us to the *real* reason why teachers strike, or, at least, why union teachers strike—because the A.F.T., either the politicians or the reps, planned it that way. No A.F.T. strike that has been even moderately successful has ever been conducted, or sustained for more than two or three days, without substantial help from national staff, assistance which might be sent in weeks *before* the teachers vote to walk out. And no substantial contribution of time and effort is ever made by the national unless it somehow will fit into national plans. In fact, considerable effort is made by reps to squelch the strike plans of locals if the staff is spread so thin that no assistance is available. Teachers in Bayonne, New Jersey, did not strike in 1970, because the A.F.T. was too wrapped up in nearby Newark. The Los Angeles strike was delayed for the same reason. True, teachers, in frustration and anger, have walked off their jobs without prior planning. They also walk back in a matter of days with very little, if anything, gained and probably a great deal lost.

Once war has begun, truth, thought and dissent are the first victims. The reps must keep the teachers occupied; if the preparation has been successful, organized activity—picketing, meetings, calling parents, marching—will begin immediately. The reps must keep them from thinking about payless paydays; about angry parents, principals, board members, politicians, governors, newspaper editorials; about court injunctions, fines and jail; about being fired; about scabbing substitutes; about the children. It's difficult to stop thinking about the children, because everybody is talking about the children during a strike. The rep says the teachers are doing it *for* the children; the school board says they are doing it *against* the children; the editorial says, "The children are the only losers; they will be the ones to suffer most from this illegal action." It is easier if the teacher just remembers what the rep said about children—"Who thinks about *your* children when you don't come home with enough money to buy them proper clothes?"

In nearly all strikes until he was fired, Mundy would fly in to help. Now it might be Selden, Brickhouse or Converse. With a little luck, one or two more reps, perhaps a few state Federation people, will come into town. Now it's time, as Mundy puts it, for one bottle of bourbon, one bottle of gin, one bottle of Scotch and a session on what to do next. The "inside man" (negotiator) already has made formal or informal contact with the school board, or should have done so; negotiations should be resumed as soon as possible—particularly if the first day of the strike didn't go well. If it did go well, the momentum, the newspaper headlines and the regularly scheduled pattern of picketing, meetings and rallies will keep the teachers out until the weekend. Sunday there's a membership meeting. No need now for anything dramatic; maybe Selden will appear at tomorrow's noontime rally; let's just sit tight.

When Selden comes in on the following day, he'll bring with him, as Mundy always did, "left-hand pocket money." For the first few days of the strike, these funds will buy teachers beer at the hotel bar where the noontime rally is held. Later on in the strike, it might be needed for food for the teachers. (Mundy kept it in his left-hand pocket, separated from his personal funds, which he keeps in the right. It is the closest thing the A.F.T. has to a strike fund. When things really go bad, interest-free loans are granted by the A.F.T. In Los Angeles in 1970, "left-hand pocket money" was spent at the rate of $3,000 a week.)

It is essential for the "outside man" to stay in the papers, on the radio, on the television, even at the risk of arrest for contempt. He must be there to reassure the teachers that what they are doing is important, that it is making people listen, that it is having an impact. In Baltimore, as the strike was fizzling, Cascella appeared on television to announce the schools of the city were "in a state of crisis." Not only the teachers, but the school board, believed him. That is his strength. "He comes over well on the tube," says a fellow rep.

If the strike is successful those first days, the inside man need be in no real hurry to settle. Converse said he kept teachers out longer in Lawrence, Massachusetts, even though they had gained practically everything they had demanded. "His strike was so successful," Mundy remembered, "he figured why end it when the teachers could get more." By the first weekend, informal talks are usually under way. But the outside man tells the membership meeting that Sunday, "The board has refused to sit down and bargain in good faith." Most teachers are led to believe the outside man is on the negotiating team—so how could there be negotiations while he is there at the membership meeting? The press, of course, is "lying" when it discloses talks have begun.

Into the second week of the strike. If the board hasn't broken, there is trouble. The contempt actions and arrests will no doubt begin, and while these antistrike tactics strengthen the will of the more adamant teachers, they can destroy morale. The outside man schedules several mass marches— down the main street, in front of city hall or the school-board building. He announces "freedom schools," where teachers can volunteer to tutor seniors for the college boards. Community meetings are set up. There's a bus caravan to the state capital to protest to the governor, another to a neighboring city to apply for jobs. (All for publicity—the teachers must keep seeing themselves in the press, having an impact.) The board begins to send telegrams to teachers notifying them that they may be fired if they do not return within the week, or it begins to call on nonteaching professionals to help with the schools. The arrests and the court actions begin, the judge warns of heavy fines. If the strike is on the East Coast, Shanker may come in to save the day—"You are fighting for the same dignity the teachers of New York have won in their many, long battles." Shanker's presence might turn off some black teachers, but those who are feeling persecuted see in him the symbol of defiant success. The outside man reads the same absentee reports with which he began the strike. The newspapers are talking about massive returns to the schools; the press is "lying."

As the outside man is declaring that negotiations will never be resumed while teachers are being arrested, the inside man is calling everyone from the governor to the local political boss trying to restart the talks. An "anarchy committee" may be activated by local Federation loyalists, and returning teachers may receive threatening telephone calls, broken car-radio antennas, flat tires. Local ministers, civil-rights workers, businessmen are being asked to intervene to get the board talking again. If it is a town with a strong central labor council, political pressure is applied; if that is lacking, parent groups are organized by the union. In Woodbridge, New Jersey, angry parents kept board and union negotiators barricaded inside the school-board offices, only appeals for sleep persuaded them to allow escape.

In a "good strike," the board relents and begins negotiation. (Usually with the help of a prominent mediator—someone like Theodore Kheel or Lewis Kaden is always a victory for the union, but it might be a local judge or college professor—the school board finds a way out.) Local political pressure may erode the school board's insistence on ensuring that the contract language does not guarantee joint ownership of the schools by the union. The mayor invariably thinks only in terms of money, pressing the board not to keep the schools closed "just because of a matter of semantics." The board gives in, the teachers get only half the money they were promised, none of the educational improvements—a committee will study those—but they do get a union-recognition clause and a grievance procedure which entrenches the power of the A.F.T. The last task for the rep is to "sell" the package to the membership.

In a "bad strike," the school board may await the inevitable cave-in. As the 1970's opened, more and more school boards, usually because of professional help, learned that a teachers' strike can, in fact, be ridden out; that strong countermeasures against the teachers—like those taken in Newark in 1970 and 1971—will soften morale. If the schools can somehow be kept open with supervisory and substitute help, the teachers, in the third or fourth week, will find their passion for the battle cooled, their financial positions gravely undermined; the newspapers will lose interest. Worse yet, when the outside man begins to run out of busy-work gimmicks to keep the teachers' minds occupied, they begin to think, they begin to wonder if it all is worth it. Antistrike factions develop, usually around the local president, who will, after all, still be there when the reps return to Washington.

As dissatisfaction increases, the number of returning teachers increases, and strength at the bargaining table erodes. The A.F.T. is working at the problem, of course, seriously considering whether the work of the anarchy committee should be broadened and strengthened, wondering whether high-school students should not be enlisted in the Movement. Whatever the response to an increasing board tendency to "let them strike" turns out to be, it will have to be an escalation. The school board may come out of longer strikes with more of its power intact; the A.F.T. may be the loser in more and more strikes until they find ways to counter "board militancy." But one thing is certain: the kids will be pawns in the game, as they always have been. Now, however, more and more of them will be called on to sacrifice more and more of the precious little education they receive anyway. For the good of the board's power. For the good of the union's power. For no good reason at all. As the editorials say, the children are the only losers.

With the possible exception of Albert Shanker, perhaps no one Federation member is responsible for more struck school systems, for more time lost from the delicate educational experience, than Joe Cascella. Thin, wiry, arrogant, willing to sacrifice not only hundreds of teachers but also himself to the fires of battle, Cascella, outside New York, has become the personification of angry teacher unionism. Perhaps even militancy run amok. From San Francisco State to Woonsocket, Rhode Island, from Kenosha, Wisconsin, to St. Croix, in the Virgin Islands, from Guam to Newark, Cascella has organized, harangued, negotiated, raising teachers from a stifling timidity to an often equally stifling anger.

Somewhere there is a retired high-school English teacher who can be thanked for all this. Cascella doesn't even remember his name, but that teacher handed the scrawny tough guy from Newark's Central Ward an application to Montclair State Teachers College in New Jersey. Cascella, who imagined himself "looking for some kind of job after the service," protested he had no idea of what he would do with a college education or, really, what he ever wanted to do. "If you can't think of anything," said the sage teacher, "be a teacher." The thought did not exactly produce ripples of electric excitement, but he did go to college, was graduated and started a career as a salesman, vacuum cleaners his specialty. When times were slow, he worked as a substitute teacher in Newark. After two years of subbing and selling, he took a permanent teaching position in a wealthy bedroom suburb in New Jersey. The Education Association there made him chairman of its salary committee, a representative group of teachers who an-

nually were told how much they would receive the following
year. They were expected to say "Thank you" and collectively
contribute to the N.E.A. myth that something called "professional negotiation" would ever have an impact on teachers'
deplorably low salaries. Teachers were invariably trapped in
the administration-dominated Association.

Cascella had caught wind of an unexpected tax cut in the
Bergen County community. He offered the suggestion that
part of the reduction in property taxes might be diverted into
a two-hundred-dollar across-the-board raise for teachers.
Everyone in the negotiation room, teachers, board members
and the superintendent, wriggled with embarrassment; Cascella wondered who had been flatulent—everyone was so
uncomfortable. The president of the board promised—ahem
—to take the matter under advisement and called a quick end
to the session. The following day Cascella was called in to see
the superintendent. "Look, Joe," he said, with paternal fa-
miliarity, "I'm an armchair Communist myself." Now it was
Cascella's turn to wriggle. "But when I buy my copy of the
New York Post, I drive over to Montvale" (a neighboring,
theoretically more liberal town) "if you see what I mean." Joe
didn't, but it soon became clear. He was fired.

He returned to the Newark schools, where, if you believed
the local Republican politicians, there were more card-carry-
ing Communists than in the entire 21st All-Party Congress.
Particularly in the Newark Teachers Union, which he joined
immediately. In a few years he was the N.T.U.'s executive
secretary, a job which, at the time, carried about as much
power and prestige as third vice-president of the Flat-World
Society does today. But into his office one day walked James
Mundy, national representative of the American Federation
of Teachers, A.F.L.–C.I.O., and Cascella's national career
began.

Cascella's first assignment was to protest the firing of a
teacher who, by his accounts, deserved to be fired. He failed,
but a local newspaper reporter was fascinated by the idea

of a traveling teacher-organizer and wrote a story. The jolt to Cascella's ego was devastating; he read and reread the piece. It was the first time he had been interviewed, and he had expected to be blasted as a "labor goon." He wasn't, and he decided to seek out the help of the press no matter where he was. He was in Louisville, Kentucky, in a few days, sent there by Mundy because the teachers had walked out and were about to lose everything, including their jobs. They had walked out in anger when the Louisville electorate rejected a tax increase which would have meant a pay increase for the city's 1,900 teachers whose salaries were $800 below national average. Only two hundred were striking, all members of the tiny and ineffective Federation local. If the strike continued at that level, the two hundred would have lost their jobs. Cascella called a general meeting of all teachers, union and Association, and most of them showed up.

"My name," he said humbly to the audience of two thousand, "is Joseph Cascella, a national representative for the American Federation of Teachers, A.F.L.–C.I.O. That is, and think about it, the American Federation of Labor and the Congress of Industrial Organizations, America's working force concerned enough about the plight of school children in Louisville, Kentucky, to ask me to come down here and do what I could." He rambled on, raising his voice from the depths of humility to the peak of anger that he knew the teachers felt, back down to a reasoned, considered tone of defiance on the side of justice. America, he declared, was looking at Louisville. This was to be the site of the beginning of the end of poorly financed education not only for Kentucky but for the country. Louisville would lead the nation if only the teachers would take up the cause. He then read a telegram from Mayor William Cowger asking him to leave Louisville. "What is he afraid of?" The Louisville Education Association proceeded to vote support of the strike and, for one day—until the Kentucky Education Association reminded its local affiliate it does not take orders from the A.F.T.—

the schools of Louisville were completely closed. When the L.E.A. withdrew its support, the A.F.T. limped on, finally calling an end to the strike when all, apparently, was lost. Cascella called a press conference. The union teachers were going back, he said, to begin an organizing drive to defeat the Association's primary role in the representation of teachers. And that's precisely what the newspaper said, turning a complete rout into, well, an orderly retreat.

The sharp, but always darkly dressed Cascella ended his first year as a warrior in Pawtucket, Rhode Island, a town so used to teacher strikes that the local Federation's walkout was all but ignored. An ignored strike, a strike with little or no impact, creating little or no inconvenience, is worse than no strike at all. So it was in Pawtucket that Cascella developed those gimmicks which were to mark him as the A.F.T.'s "showman." As expected, the board obtained an antistrike injunction. But to keep down a sense of urgency, it decided not to push efforts to deliver copies of the injunction to the teachers. Cascella gathered the teachers for a march on City Hall, demanding to be served with the injunction. The television crews were there as Pawtucket's teachers solemnly accepted the court papers, the City Hall façade looming behind them. Then Cascella asked the TV crewmen to stay a while. Since the injunction banned picketing, he had every teacher lay down his picket sign in a pile before the steps of the Municipal Building. The camera was trained on the pile as it grew into a considerable heap and teacher after teacher, like a defeated soldier, laid his weapon down. The picture of the massive pile of signs appeared in every local and regional newspaper, and the people of Pawtucket were not about to forget that their teachers were on strike. (Cascella was absent from the contempt hearings, and an order was issued for his appearance in court. But he moved his strike headquarters across the state line to South Attleboro, Massachusetts. Only recently has he been able to walk free in Rhode Island.)

In Pawtucket, Cascella believed in "a story a day" in the

local press, whether or not anything of substance happened. With the picket signs sacrificed for one day's story, he ordered teachers to walk back and forth in front of the schools as "picketless pickets," wringing their hands, feigning indecision. "They are agonizing," he told reporters, "about whether they should return to class." They didn't; and that in itself was a measure of his strength as an outside man. The following day he called a press conference to announce the creation of "freedom schools," in which high-school seniors could receive college-board prepping by volunteer strikers. He never bothered to tell anyone of his plan—"It just came to me," he explained—but it made good copy. The "schools" eventually were established, but never amounted to more than a token gesture.

Cascella organized volunteers to come to headquarters to print up and to deliver "Crisis Bulletins," modest fliers which kept the striking teachers busy as well as "informed" and invariably got into the hands of the newspapers. Typical bulletins ran something like this:

"Crisis Bulletin—Day Number Three. Pawtucket schools are on the verge of collapse as board does nothing. [Governor John H.] Chafee seeks personal intervention."

The stories, of course, were usually fabrications, but that was not the point; the point was to make the strike the most dramatic thing to hit Rhode Island since Roger Williams. Cascella made small but adequate inroads into parents' organizations, telling teachers through his bulletins: "Angry parents are rising up against the school board to demand talks with teachers." Cascella held the Pawtucket teachers out for two weeks that year, just long enough to get Governor Chafee involved and the teachers a solid, powerful contract.

Back out into the Midwest to East St. Louis, Hamtramck, East Chicago Heights, small towns, generating strikes and membership with quick but headline-making actions. In 1965, he was sent into New Jersey to develop a desire for collective bargaining among teachers. (Contrary to union doctrine, not

all teachers are born with a desire for collective bargaining.)
The town selected for a "hit," Perth Amboy, was a rare town
with a union majority and a strong young president, Robert
Bates. Cascella conducted the entire affair in the press and,
because it was the first major teacher strike in New Jersey, it
was front page everywhere in the state. He arranged for talks
with the school board and invited reporters. One of the school-
board members stood up to make his way, the story goes, to
the bathroom. Cascella leaped up without warning: "Why are
you running? Why are you afraid of your teachers? You saw
it"—he turned to the reporters—"the school board is running
from its responsibility. There's a crisis out on the streets and
they are running away from it. We won't put up with this!"
And he, Bates, and several other teachers walked out, charging the board with torpedoing the negotiation. The following
night Cascella appeared at a City Commission meeting, using
the forum to charge that the school board had "run out on the
children of Perth Amboy." While he was waiting to speak,
someone asked for information on how to apply for a parade
permit. It was enough for Cascella. The following night, all
of Perth Amboy's teachers marched on the school-board
offices, Bates at the helm, crying: "Why is the school board
afraid of its teachers?" Perth Amboy gave in, tendering as
much recognition as possible under the state law to the
Federation as bargaining agent.

In 1966, Cascella's orders were to capture Baltimore "by
any means necessary." The city was then the largest controlled
by an N.E.A. affiliate and it had to go if the A.F.T.'s urban
strategy was to prove successful. At the first membership
meeting, early in 1966, fewer than twenty union teachers
showed up; sixteen months later the Public School Teachers
Association of Baltimore (the N.E.A. local) was defeated by
the A.F.T. in a bargaining election, 3,687 to 3,358. "I can
say," Cascella says now with little modesty, "that in all
modesty, I performed a miracle in Baltimore." The key, again,

was the press. The daily newspapers and the considerable television and radio coverage enjoyed by the city initially looked upon the Federation as little more than a bad "in" joke among teachers. It was. Cascella had to begin with less than an established union, because the union members wanted little to do with collective bargaining. Although he formed a fast and lasting friendship with the *Baltimore Sun*'s Gene Aoishi—Spiro Agnew's "Fat Jap"—it took more than friendship to get the Federation into the press. But what was demanding coverage was a growing open-housing movement, led by the Congress of Racial Equality (CORE). CORE had been engaged in persistent demonstrations, some of them leading to outbreaks of violence. "If we couldn't make an impact ourselves," recalled Cascella, "we had to join up with those who could." The N.E.A. affiliate deliberately stayed away from the city's boiling racial politics. But Cascella saw the chance; he announced to the press that there would be a conference with CORE to discuss "possible joint action" to relieve the city's housing problems.

Those members of the union who see the A.F.T.'s only chance of lasting success in the cities as a permanent alliance with the activist black community were heartened as the denim-clad CORE officers arrived at a downtown hotel to meet Cascella and other union officials. All of the city's media were there, awaiting the announcement of some form of joint strike against landlords and the school board. But they should have saved their hopes. It was only an arrangement of expedience, granting CORE the opportunity to legitimatize its campaign, giving Cascella space in the press and an identification with the city's ghetto teachers. Together they stood, after a brief conference, noting "areas of agreement" and promising "co-ordinated efforts" for some vague goal. The A.F.T. now was a reality in Baltimore. And black teachers aligned with the Education Association began to ask disturbing questions. Mundy sent in nearly every member of the national staff and

as many "temporaries" as he could muster, to make Baltimore
a union town. He divided a map of the city into ten districts
—he had ten staff members—and the battle was on.

The typical campaign was fought, the meetings, the dances,
the literature. But the N.E.A. local appeared invincible.
Every report back was the same: no way. It would take little
short of a miracle to capture the city. Cascella felt that a
strike could do it. The rest of the staff were skeptical, but
grudgingly supportive; little else could be done. The preparations were made, the organization, the meetings, the harangues;
the teachers must go out to save the city from educational collapse, was the theme. Days before the strike, the
reports from the district organizers came in: Cascella could
expect, at best, five hundred out, and not all of them willing
to picket. He went ahead. On May 10, 1967, some four hundred teachers—out of more than seven thousand—went on
strike. The leadership of the union began a sit-in in the
school-board offices. Of course, nothing substantial had happened. But the newspapers, the radio stations and the television commentators made it the city's number-one story,
featuring Cascella crying out: "Baltimore is in a state of
crisis. Unsupervised children are tearing apart the schools.
The tensions are spilling over into the street." Fortunately for
the union, the city fathers believed him. The court injunction
came fast, and the next day came the arrests; 130 pickets,
conveniently placed where the union said they could be found,
were hauled into paddy wagons and taken away. Cascella
was delighted, the coverage had gone far beyond what he had
expected. He was called into the mayor's office and was asked
to call off the strike. The union's answer was that picketing
would stop if the teachers were released. The teachers were
released, the few remaining pickets who had not been arrested
were called home. The following day, the pickets were out
again, again arrested and again released. With little more
than one hundred teachers, Cascella had managed to produce
nearly four hundred arrests. On the third day of the strike,

the tempers of the local courts growing thin with the warrior's little game, Cascella brought them back and called on the Association affiliate to join them in "one big strike for educational opportunity." Orville Berwick, the Association's executive secretary, apparently fell for the bait. Whether he sincerely believed Cascella's promise of cooperation or whether he wanted to show he could produce as much noise, Berwick called for a strike-vote meeting on June 9, 1967, exactly one week before the scheduled bargaining election. Cascella's thin but highly effective network of "passing the word" was put into effect—no teacher who thought of voting for the union should show up and, for those who still favored the Association, to vote for a strike would be suicidal, the A.F.T. would never support it. And if you thought there were a lot of arrests the last time, just wait. The message was clear. At the membership meeting, two hundred teachers showed up, out of an Association membership of more than five thousand. Berwick insisted on calling for a strike vote and, while the reporters that Cascella made sure would be there shook their heads in embarrassment, the teachers voted him down. The Education Association, unlike the gutsy, willing-to-fight union, simply could not cut the mustard. A week later, the miracle happened: Baltimore, which was, except for Newark, the last major Eastern city to run its schools without benefit of union, had gone A.F.T.

It was, of course, no mean organizational feat. That the tensions in a city already nervous about its racial problems, were exacerbated is secondary—to the union, at least. What made the achievement more formidable for Cascella was that he ran a two-week strike in Woodbridge in January, 1967, in the midst of the Baltimore campaign. The strike, replete with all the familiar Cascella gimmickry, made the Federation a power in New Jersey and created the law which gave teachers the right to choose bargaining agents. It opened the way to capturing Newark three years later. But it had an even greater impact on Cascella's personal life. For his participation in the Woodbridge walkout, the judge said he would "single Mr. Cascella out for particular rehabilitation." Your reputation as a labor agitator is widespread, he told the fidgeting Cascella in a Middlesex County courtroom. The sentence: ninety days in the workhouse. Joe never believed the A.F.T. would let him rot in jail. In his own characteristic way, he turned his sentencing into a publicity stunt, showing up in the Sheriff's office weeks before he was scheduled to begin his sentence to demand to be allowed into jail. (All reporters had been duly notified in advance, of course.) The months passed as appeal after appeal was made and denied. Cascella bought a trailer and drove across the country with his wife to set up a bargaining drive and eventually a strike at San Francisco State College. In December, 1967, however, Mundy flew to California and personally delivered the bad news. The A.F.T. would not try to bring his case before the United States Supreme Court. It was "too risky"; if the high court declared all teacher strikes illegal, the impact on some states would be devastating. Cascella blanched. "I feel shitty," he said, and he flew back to New Jersey to begin what was to be a seventy-two-day sentence, to become the first staff member of the American Federation of Teachers to go to jail for union activities. (He began his term the same day Albert Shanker was released from jail in New York City. Cascella was miffed; Shanker got more press coverage.)

Cascella returned to California after his release, trading verbal and well-publicized darts with Ronald Reagan and S. I. Hayakawa at San Francisco State. The most he achieved, however, was the creation of a fairly solid faculty union and Local 1928, an organization of radical teaching assistants, most of them young, most of them not terribly happy with the Selden-Shanker brand of power unionism. From there out to Guam, to negotiate a contract, then back to New Jersey. Thereafter he worked as a district outside man, then as Mundy's chief assistant in the Los Angeles strike, after providing some "community relations" services in Newark.

By 1970, however, his professional life began to turn sour. To forget his troubles he turned an organizing junket to Guam into a round-the-world vacation. Selden was having his troubles back at headquarters, a black faction angry at Shanker, a New Left faction angry at him, a small-local faction demanding more national service, and a staff faction, led by former rep Kenneth Miesen, after his job. For reasons best known to Selden himself, he believed that Cascella was behind the insurgent's candidacy. (Cascella was in Bangkok at the time and probably never knew what Miesen was up to.) Mundy left the union, thus breaking Cascella's closest link to national headquarters. When he arrived back in the United States, a week before the convention, he found a letter formally charging him and five other reps with "political activity" in violation of his contract. Mundy warned him he would likely be fired. To have lost his job, his obsession for six years, would have probably been too much for Cascella to bear. He feels, rightly so, he has sacrificed too much to be himself sacrificed on the altar of national union politics. And this is what he told Selden. Acquitted, but . . .

"But now to be a friend of Joe Cascella is to have an albatross neatly hung around your neck" is the way Mundy described the old warrior's place in the national staff. The reps he trained and brought on to national now disavow close ties to him, reminiscing fondly about "Joe's war stories," but rejecting him as any kind of spiritual leader on the national staff. The theory that Cascella himself one day will challenge Selden's right to rule still persists among the union's politicians. He is pictured as a dangerous man, a warrior who too freely committed the A.F.T. to strikes, long legal battles and fines. Local Federation leaders are encouraged by national to "watch Cascella" very carefully, because he is "out to capture your union." As 1970 waned, the warrior had difficulty making anything work. A strike he handled in Toledo, Ohio, fizzled out under him. After three attempts to bring the Hartford teachers out, they finally went out, but the strike caved in after three weeks. He cannot quit, because there is no place for him to go. He cannot just pack up and go home, because, practically, he has no home. He now has the choice of challenging Selden or disappearing quietly into oblivion and, perhaps, being denied another contract. It is impossible to make Joe Cascella disappear.

If Cascella is the former leader of the warriors, Robert Crosier is his heir. Portly, soft-spoken and articulate, Crosier has been more than once identified as "the dean of the reps," a title reserved for Cascella in greener years. Crosier, who now, in Selden's new "regional plan," which is designed, at least partially, to keep reps from establishing a national base, covers the Pacific Northwest and Alaska, is the closest thing the A.F.T. has to a resident intellectual. Simply stated, he sees the A.F.T. growth and militancy as the birth pangs of an institution, designed to take its place beside, and often in conflict with, other social institutions. The structure of education too is an institution, too long controlled, he believes, by the N.E.A. or, at least, those with the "N.E.A. mentality." Teachers organized within a democratic union structure are now the biggest challenge to that institution. Inevitably, the A.F.T. will itself become the educational institution.

Crosier says he rejects the yardstick rattling of Cascella and smiles patronizingly at old-fashioned, grass-roots organizing. He believes that the union is the only way for teachers to bury a system which for so many years denied them their dignity, to say nothing of reasonable livelihoods. Because that is what he identifies with teaching. His first job was in Yam Hill, Oregon, which in 1953 was treating teachers much the same as the rest of the country had treated them in the 1920's and 1930's. He was reprimanded for smoking, for buying groceries in neighboring Eugene—"We must support our local merchants; as a teacher, you must set an example." He also was required to live in the town and found an uncomfortable apartment in an old farmhouse. It became more uncomfortable when the town scavenger found liquor bottles in his trash cans. This clearly was "conduct unbecoming," and since he was very little liked anyway—he says he was the only teacher in Yam Hill to flunk anyone—Crosier moved on in 1954 to the Big City, to Gresham Union High School in Gresham (pop. 3,000).

There he and a few like-minded teachers formed a caucus within the local Association affiliate and demanded, of all things, the right to bargain collectively. There was no doubt in the mind of the town fathers that Crosier was a "Communist,"—which he was not—no one else would have asked for such a "Socialist innovation" as negotiations. From there, Crosier traveled on to the Bigger City, to Portland, where he threw himself into organizing activities for the Portland and Oregon State Federation of Teachers, just about the time "Co-Org" went into effect. Mundy borrowed him extensively for campaigns in the nation's north country— Minneapolis, Seattle, Michigan towns. In December of 1966, Mundy stole him permanently. Except for his use in Los Angeles and Baltimore, Crosier was kept in the Northwest, one of the A.F.T.'s prime target areas for the 1970's, along with the South and the Southwest.

Mundy ordered Crosier out to Minot, North Dakota, on Easter Sunday, 1969, telling him to "wrap up" a strike as soon as possible. A major war was going on in New Orleans and every rep was needed there. No one could quite understand how the A.F.T. had gotten to Minot anyhow, but the town of 30,000 with its union membership of little more than one hundred was simply not worth the bother. The local union members had vowed not to return to work until the board consented to negotiate. The board would not relent. Since the strike was having little or no impact, even a tenderfoot rep knew it was time to cave in. But caving in is impossible when the teachers refuse to do it. The other alternative, waging a massive campaign, with tons of publicity and pressure put on the political leadership, was simply impossible as long as every permanent rep, except Crosier, every temporary rep and a few large local presidents were in New Orleans at the time to get someone to notice that strike. Crosier attempted a few Cascella-like gimmicks, marches, vigils, but he need not have bothered. The local newspaper was simply not interested. And larger media took only passing and invariably unfriendly note. Without media coverage, a strike effort has about as much chance for success as brain surgery performed by a St. Bernard. It should never be attempted. But no one asked Crosier.

The strike continued, noticed only when a few pickets were beaten up in front of their schools, a score of teachers were arrested, convicted and jailed. God ultimately intervened for the school board and flooded out a third of the town with the spring thaw. While it provided some diversion to the striking teachers, it also wiped out their homes. Mixed blessing. It also served to wipe out the last hint that there was anything like a teacher strike going on, since the schools were closed to allow everyone to man the dikes. No union, no matter how strong, can strike a closed school system.

The school year evaporated and since there was no longer need for teachers, it hardly mattered who was striking. Nine weeks after the debacle began, it did not end, it simply drifted off into oblivion along with the living rooms of some ten thousand Minot residents. The school board, in a gesture of reconciliation, announced that it had fired every member of the Minot Federation of Teachers—all 125 of them. (It had wanted to put every one of them in jail.) Just to spite the school board, the union leadership kept their A.F.T. charter and every year they have a reunion.

Several weeks after the Minot experience, Crosier met with his fellow warriors for a "retreat" in Biloxi, Mississippi. It was to be a "think session," just the reps, Selden and the executive council, trying to find out why 1969, with its disasters in Minot and New Orleans, had gone wrong. It was becoming apparent that school boards were not reacting normally, they were not closing the schools, they were not anxious to negotiate to end strikes. If that was to be the trend of the future, what was the A.F.T.'s reaction to be? Crosier, always known as the staff's peacemaker, a man with a distaste even for a good strike, was asked to brief the Federation's political leadership on the staff's view of new strategies. This is how he remembered his response:

"If I knew what eventually happened to the teachers was going to happen when I first arrived in Minot, if I had any conception at all of the suffering those teachers would go through, of the beatings they would take, of the indignities they would suffer at the hands of the board, I might have recommended at the start a resort to violence, even if it meant burning down one or two school buildings to make the bastards listen to us. I believe that sincerely."

The reps were inspired; Selden and the vice-presidents almost fainted. When they recovered, the small meeting room in the Biloxi motel was a Babel of voices, every politician tripping over another's condemnation of what Crosier had just said.

The "Biloxi experience" was the turning point for the A.F.T.'s "traveling troupe." (A week after the meeting, the motel was flattened by hurricane Camille, and his fellow reps often look queerly at Crosier. First Minot's flood, and now this.) The union's politicians apparently were frightened by the implications of what Crosier had said. They began to look with mistrust at the actions of the "warriors" they had charged with the responsibility of winning the country for them. Mundy noticed it immediately; Selden's constant demand to know where his reps were and what they were doing soon made the new attitudes clear to them. Selden's insistence on going to jail in the Newark strike was yet another turning point. The reps handling the strike were against it, seeing it for what it so obviously was—the needed push for Selden to regain the presidency in 1970. The grumblings about that, about Selden's constant plea to the N.E.A. to merge, the disastrous Los Angeles strike and Selden's expressed suspicion that all the staff members had put Miesen up to running against him in the 1970 convention, Mundy's firing and Shanker's free hand with staff decisions (along with his attitude that national organizers should stay out of his New York domain) caused a spiritual split between staff and politicians. The purge following Selden's victory confirmed it.

The crisis will pass, probably by the time of the 1972 union elections. In the meantime, it is difficult to judge whether a strike action is taken at Selden's insistence, or in spite of it. As difficult to judge for Selden as it is for anyone else. Before the conflict ends, at least some school time for at least some children will be sacrificed for internal political reasons. If teacher strikes ever have justifications, and I believe they may, these certainly are not among them. When the crisis does pass and it's solidarity forever once again among the staff members of the American Federation of Teachers, the new school-board militancy will have to be faced squarely. Perhaps violently, perhaps not. But until school boards and the teachers' union stop looking at each other like opposing armies—and I'm not sure that will happen for a very long time, unless the A.F.T. wins Crosier's "institutional struggle" with American education, not an event worth counting the days to—the children will be the only losers.

4

On Not Being Albert Shanker

T HE MEETING was not going well and it obviously worried the president of the local Federation, a short, fat man loosely enveloped in a hopelessly rumpled dark suit. He had spent the first two hours of the organizational meeting perspiring, assuring restless reporters the meeting was going well indeed and struggling to shove the tails of his crumpled white shirt into the trousers which simply were not up to what his expansive waist demanded. More than one thousand invitations had been sent out, one for every teacher and paraprofessional in the district. Fewer than fifty had shown, and most of these were the city's youngest teachers, who promptly transformed this "very serious" meeting into a party, shoving aside the carefully placed tables and metal folding chairs of the community center in order to make room for dancing, turning up the volume of the scratchy stereo and taking full advantage of the overstocked supply of cheap Scotch. The fat man darted aimlessly around the room, dabbing his forehead with a limply folded handkerchief. "We'll get started in a minute, just as soon as the rest get here," he said without conviction to his honored guest, and he quickly darted away again, as if fearful that his guest would mention something about the obvious.

But if the guest had heard or even seen his fretful host, he made no outward sign. His thoughts apparently were elsewhere, his emotionless eyes fixed blankly on one leg, which he had crossed over the other. The loud disharmony of the music, the possessed stomping and sliding of what passed for dancing, his own personal failure to act as a draw for the recruitment efforts of the local's leadership—all this might as well have taken place in a dimension apart from where the guest sat now.

He is handsome in late middle age, with blond-and-white hair falling jauntily over his forehead, reaching carelessly down past the collar of his pajama-striped shirt. His dress is an easy blend of hick and mod, a shirt to make Joseph proud, a conventional bow tie, straight and carefully tailored gray slacks, canvas shoes and a dark blazer. At first, his thin frame and lined face appear athletic, rugged, tempered and trimmed from constant activity in the sun and the wind. But no, come closer, and the frame is delicate and the facial lines appear more testament to worry and age than to exposure to weather. They are tracings, not carvings. But it is an agreeable face just the same.

He is older than nearly every one else in the meeting hall and perhaps that accounts for his preference for reverie over participation. Perhaps he is recalling what he was doing when he was the age of the young teachers who now are working out the most frantic rituals of dance just a few feet away . . .

It is Michigan's industrial southeast and the time is late 1930's. The cities of Dearborn and Detroit, like cities across the wretched land, are electric with anger, frustration and bewilderment. Work is scarce, money is scarcer, debts mount. For many, perhaps most, it is not a time for contemplation, for checking reality against doctrine and discussing the social and economic forces which have put you into the frightening

hole you are in. Unless, of course, you are fortunate enough
not to be among the financially devastated, fortunate enough
to have been born into the relative comfort of the educated
middle class, to be educated yourself and to be able to consider the madness around you from the distance a full stomach
can provide. Then, these are ultimately exciting times and
the cities are exciting places. Like Boston in 1775, or Paris in
1789, or St. Petersburg (no, not Florida) in 1917, or Chicago
in August, 1968. There is pain here, and anguish and death.
But if you are far enough away from the suffering, the very
air is filled with the piquant odor of dying institutions, the
wind is the thrill of adversity defied. If your lot permits ab-
stract thinking, these are exciting times indeed.

From a window in a fortresslike school in Dearborn, a
young teacher strains his eyes to see across the sooty horizon.
Behind him, with varying degrees of intensity some thirty or
forty children, most of whom are black or East European,
attend to their classroom work. Before him the monotony of
Dearborn's freight yards stretch out to the huge, half-empty
employee parking lot of the Ford Motor Company. Then,
barely visible, an overpass hangs over a wide highway and
leads to the plant itself, a flint-colored Buddha dominating
River Rouge. For weeks David Selden had been interrupting
his class to peer out of that window, because for weeks many
people he knew had been flinging themselves against the corporate machinery of the Ford Motor Company, demanding
recognition of the United Auto Workers as bargaining agent
for its assembly-line workers. All of what the teacher had read
in Shaw and Wells was now being acted out down there in
River Rouge and up here he stood in his classroom, too far
away to catch the play, much less be listed in its cast. He
brooded over his impotence. "I couldn't stand being father
to all those kids," he recalled thirty years later; "I couldn't
stand their dependence on me."

That day, however, he could sense trouble at River Rouge.
There was an inordinate amount of activity focused near the

overpass where the pickets, led by Walter (he says he knew him well enough then to call him "Red") Reuther, would gather before spreading out around the gates of the plant. There were crowds and speeding cars and running. Something had happened. When the school day finally ended, he drove down broad Michigan Avenue through Dearborn to the office of U.A.W. Local 600. He was no stranger there; as president of Dearborn's teachers' federation, the young teacher had operated a worker-education project from the office. Something indeed had happened. Reuther, his brother Victor, and a number of other U.A.W. leaders had been set upon by Ford's private guards. Walter himself had been brutally beaten. He might not make it.

The young teacher returned home that night troubled by a sensation of exhilaration. He could hardly be happy that young men with whom he had worked had been clubbed. Yet the teacher could not help but feel that what had happened to Reuther and the others was a rite of intensification for the industrial labor movement, evidence that the enemy the auto workers were facing was beginning to crumble. Reuther's name surely would outlast that of Harry Bennett, the chief of the guards, who had directed the attack. The industrial labor movement would endure despite—no, maybe because of— what had happened at River Rouge. For the teacher himself, it was a personal rite of passage, a reaffirmation of his belief that he was indeed a socialist, a believer in the struggle of the workingman. His father may have been a comfortable school principal, his mother active in the Daughters of the American Revolution. It mattered little. He believed that he as a teacher, as an intellectual, could appreciate, perhaps more than even Reuther himself, the meaning of the attack at River Rouge. That the application of the intellect to the grit and the blood of . . .

"Look, I guess we'd better get started. There's a pretty good crowd here now and I'll introduce you."

The older man looked up, but the host had darted away again, this time toward a microphone which somehow had appeared near the entrance of the community center. The music had stopped and the chairs had been lined up again across what had been the dance floor. The guest discovered that he was not alone at his table.

"When's Shanker coming?" the young girl asked, less out of interest than out of trying to find something to say now that she was sharing a table with someone.

"I don't believe Al is coming today. I think he was tied up in New York." The guest's voice bore a slow Midwestern assurance.

"You're with the A.F.T.?"

"Yes, I'm Dave Selden. I'm president of the national."

"I thought Shanker —What's he, a—"

"Albert Shanker is president of the United Federation of Teachers. That's our New York City local. And then he's vice-president of the national."

"Oh."

The two were joined by a tall black man, his head crowned with an expansive Afro cut. He straddled one of the folding chairs backwards, cowboy-style, and nodded perfunctorily in Selden's direction.

"He said Shanker's not coming today," the young girl said, by way of introduction.

Even as president of an international union, nominal leader of nearly a quarter of a million teachers, there is little David Selden can do about not being Albert Shanker. God knows he's tried. He's even gone to jail for forty-five days to create nationwide sympathy and focus nationwide attention on the abuse of antistrike injunctions. (And possibly to provide just a little boost for his reelection hopes.) But it really doesn't work, none of it. Not being Albert Shanker persists as David Selden's number-one leadership problem. There is evidence that most teachers, as well as most other people who are vaguely interested, look upon Albert Shanker, for what he does with unabashed regularity to the schools of New York City, as symbol and personification of teacher militancy unchained. These people have forgotten or, most likely, never have known, that Selden, much more than Shanker, was responsible for bringing the A.F.T. to New York in the early 1960's. Or that Selden campaigned for a nationwide teacher strike as part of his election campaign in 1968. The more involved union teacher, the one who might serve as a delegate to the national convention, for example, often believes, rightly or wrongly, that Selden might just as well be Albert Shanker, because there is little the sandy-haired Midwesterner can do without Shanker's active support. Shanker, after all, runs the Progressive Caucus (the intra-A.F.T. "political party" to which Selden belongs); as a result, he runs the executive committee of the policy-making executive council of the A.F.T.; he runs the organization committee of the council; he runs the executive council itself; and, most important, he is firmly in control of the United Federation of Teachers, which accounts for one quarter to one third of the A.F.T.'s total membership and delegate votes. A number of people on Selden's own staff have privately criticized their titular leader as little more than a shadow of Shanker. Shanker, after all, can, and has reached above (or below) Selden to direct staff operations or to determine the destinies of staff members suspected of disloyalty to Shanker or the A.F.T.

Whether or not David Selden is Shanker's "front," not being Albert Shanker prevents Selden from leading the national teachers' union in the glorious manner to which he aspires. "I want to be thought of primarily as a social reformer," Selden once said. "I want to be considered a creative person who leads the way for the country's teachers to become more dignified professionals, to make an impact on American education far more significant than they ever have in the past." But the prospects simply are not that promising. Anonymity is not one of the characteristics assigned to America's most famous social reformers. And the name David Selden is not a common, household word. (Nor, if it means anything, is it listed in either *Who's Who* or *Current Biography*.)

Selden's failure to realize long-range goals is his most serious career problem; his best-laid schemes gang agley with sowhat regularity. Ironically, a number of people who claim to know him well (few venture to know him intimately) cite his ability to plan in long-range terms as one of his major contributions to the A.F.T. Shanker himself has remarked: "Dave is always thinking twenty years ahead."

Selden's first plan had him laboring among the poor working class of his Michigan home town, Dearborn. The Selden family—he is the oldest of four brothers—lived "comfortably," by his accounts, through the Depression. His father managed to hold on to his school principalship with only a one-third cut in pay from 1929 to 1934. Selden himself took a teaching degree at Michigan State Normal College (now Eastern Michigan University) in nearby Ypsilanti and found work in a junior high school as a social-studies instructor. He called himself a Deweyite and joined the Progressive Education Association, but his performance in the classroom was, to use his words, "paternalistic" with "only the pretense of democracy." Selden found himself dominating the classroom routine and joining more extracurricular activities than Archie— swimming, drama, music, government, et cetera. After a few years, he explained, he found himself dominated by that which he sought to control—his classroom charges, he says, became his children; he, their father. "I wasn't prepared for that."

Disenchanted with teaching, Selden turned toward unionism as the core, perhaps, of his next personal twenty-year plan. He had worked in the Ford plant at River Rouge before it was unionized, and he remembers the "excitement and vitality" of what would become the hazardous task of organizing the assembly-line workers. It was at this time that Selden said he began calling himself a Socialist and began having visions of The Triumph of the Enlightened Working Class, a triumph which would, no doubt, be given a boost along the way by David Selden himself. (Selden never formally joined the Socialist party until 1969. "No one ever asked me to join," he explains.) But he stayed away from the industrial-unionism championed by the Reuthers and turned his attention to teacher-unionism in Dearborn. "When I joined the Federation, there were only seven members. By the time I left, we had four hundred and had voted the local N.E.A. affiliate out of existence. Dearborn today has one of the strongest local federations in the nation." It was an accomplishment, and a decade later the reputation he had won in Dearborn as an organizer would provide the circumstances for his reentry into the labor movement. Despite his stated leanings toward the intellectual justifications for unionism and his flirtation with Socialist doctrine, Selden, as an early teacher-unionist, followed the Fewkes-Green line in the A.F.T.'s schism. Reuther may have been young and vital, but "labor unity" was, after all, "labor unity." (Selden used essentially the same argument when he fought against moving the A.F.T. into the newly formed American Labor Alliance, the organization Reuther formed with the Teamsters when he took the U.A.W. out of the arteriosclerotic A.F.L.–C.I.O.)

But the war took the animus out of the labor movement, and Selden out of both teaching and teacher-unionism. He joined the Navy in 1943, became a crewman on a destroyer, and suddenly the plans again changed. David Selden, denizen of industrial Detroit, teacher of the wretched of the ghetto, became a water gazer. Like another famous sailor, he found himself absent-mindedly blending the cadence of the waves with his own thoughts. When he was discharged, he resolved to forsake teaching for the remainder of his life, to move to anywhere near the mystic ocean and to devote himself to art, to drama, to writing fiction and poetry.

In Jacksonville, Florida, he found a job selling and servicing X-ray machines. He reasoned that he could take "just an

ordinary job" during the day and spend his nights creating
and his weekends fixed in ocean reveries. He was drawn to the
Atlantic, he recalled, by the romance of the sea. And the fact
that his wife (his first—he has had three) had relatives in the
state. But somehow, something went wrong—again.

This as-yet-incalculable blow to culture occurred because
Selden adopted yet another long-range plan, a truly ambitious
one. David Selden set out to found himself a college.* According to his plan, the college was to be an experimental
cooperative, requiring its students to work as well as to study.
There would be a modest tuition fee, and the room and board
would be "worked off." There was included a scheme, Selden
recalls, "for a student-controlled labor bank which would
assign jobs and give credits for hours, working hours, not
study hours." He says he intended to pattern the school after
Blackburn and Antioch colleges, and he wrote to the administrations of both schools seeking advice.

But the project was contingent on acquiring an abandoned
Army camp in Carrabelle, a small town on U.S. Route 319
between Apalachicola and Sopchoppy on the northern Gulf
Coast. The rights to the camp were awarded by the federal
government to another private group who, according to Selden, sold it to Du Pont, which owned the surrounding pine-
lands. To Selden, it was some sort of tacit conspiracy between
the late Senator Robert A. Taft of Ohio—the party to whom
the base was awarded was from Ohio—and the huge Du Pont
corporation. To be done in by such an array of political and

---

* Just a word about establishing institutions of higher education in
Florida. The only requirements are a modest fee for incorporation. No
campus, no buildings, no faculty, no standards, and very often, no
ethics. Florida, at this writing, remains the diploma-mill capital of the
nation despite the efforts of legitimate private colleges and universities,
along with a few conscientious legislators, to put private institutions of
higher education under the authority—for antifraud purposes, at least
—of state education officials. This is not meant to be a reflection on
his intentions.

corporate power must have been a heady sensation for the ex-teacher, ex-salesman, and now ex-college founder.

After that "fiasco" (his word), Selden traveled back across to the Atlantic side of the peninsula and found a job teaching in a small public school in Oak Hill, a U.S. Route 1 roadside stop on the Banana River, just north of what is now Cape Kennedy. He had stayed less than a year when the romance of the sea lost its magnetism to the idea of living in a comparatively rural area of New York. Selden resolved to go to the woods to live deliberately, to be a teacher in a small rural community, to dwell in—yes—a log cabin. He did not find a log cabin exactly, but he did find a job in the schools of Putnam Valley, on the east bank of the Hudson River, just north of Westchester County. It was Selden's intention to live there for the rest of his life, to devote his energies to being the best teacher in Putnam Valley and, if time permitted, to return to his dream of writing fiction and poetry.

Then he got a letter from an old friend from Michigan telling him the job of executive secretary of the state's teachers' federation was open. Would Selden be interested? Again, a change of plans. He asked for a job application, meticulously filled it out, adding marginal notes reflecting on his own substantial skill as a teacher-unionist and on his long-range plans for such unionism and mailed it back. Within days, he says, he received a telegram, not from anyone in Michigan, but from William Green, president of the A.F.L., appointing him an organizer assigned to the A.F.T. and ordering him to Kentucky the following Monday. It was Selden's reentry into the national teachers' union and the beginning of yet another long-range career plan, one which came closer to realization than any of the others.

For the next four years, from 1949 to 1953, Selden engaged in an admittedly fruitless trek across much of the country, a "fireman" he called himself, responding to A.F.L. "leads" on "teachers ripe for organizing," adding his weight to local disputes surrounding tenure rights or salary disputes, adding a spare "per cap" here and there. He chartered a large number of locals—one hundred, the official legend goes, but he can't remember just how many—and nearly all, if not all, limped along for a few months and died. By 1950, he was convinced that the carpetbagger approach to organizing a national teacher union was doomed to failure. "I had it figured out somewhere that it would take the per capita dues of one new member over ten years in order to pay the costs of making him a member," Selden recalled. The system, he believed, simply had to be changed.

His idea for a new approach was to create area organizing councils to provide continued A.F.T. service to new locals and new members instead of simply standing by while they caved in to school-board or N.E.A.-affiliate pressure. Selden went to A.F.T. President John Ecklund with the plan. The councils would be staffed by permanent reps and temporaries trained by national organizers. New councils would be developed for every 3,000 teachers. And all the union had to do was to leave it to Selden and increase per capita dues ten cents per month. Ecklund said no, and the frustrated director of organization went back out on the hustings until 1953, when A.F.T. President Carl Megel sent him to New York City.

When Selden took up permanent residence in New York City in 1953, he considered the prospects for A.F.T. growth there bleak. He was wrong, of course, but he could hardly be blamed for pessimism. The city's 45,000 teachers were represented by nearly eighty distinct organizations, many of them distrustful of the others. The A.F.T.'s Teachers Guild, one of the largest, could hardly count more than 1,500 active members. Most of these union members were suspicious of Selden's intentions and of his insistence that the Guild must grow, must adopt collective bargaining as policy. They had not joined the Guild to further the expansion of the American Federation of Labor or even of the American Federation of

Teachers. This is how Shanker characterized the attitudes of
his fellow union members when David Selden came to the
Big Town:

> Basically, the leadership of the union, many of whom are
> still in leadership positions, never envisioned the union as a
> collective bargaining agent. They felt they were part of the
> union movement because they were liberals, or Democratic
> Socialists or because of John Dewey's original reason for
> the union—that it was similar to the current notion of getting
> involved with the life of the community if you wanted to in-
> fluence the lives of the children and that, since the children
> in the public schools were of the working class, if the teachers
> wanted to identify themselves with the aspirations of the
> children and their families, the way to do it was to be part of
> this movement.
>
> Very few of them believed in, or even talked very much
> about collective bargaining. It was not the policy of the union
> prior to Selden's coming to have collective bargaining. As a
> matter of fact, he had to fight it out with the executive board.
>
> To a large extent, the membership of the Guild felt that
> the union was for those people who believed in certain things
> and it was, therefore, a sort of sectarian sort of movement.
>
> Prior to Selden's coming, the commitment was not to
> attain power or to build a mass organization. Sure, many
> talked about "Wouldn't it be great if all the teachers joined,"
> but what they meant was "Wouldn't it be great if all the
> teachers were won over to our particular ideological com-
> mitment and join it as a religion."

But collective bargaining *was* the policy of the A.F.L. and,
to a lesser extent, of the A.F.T.; and building a mass organization *was* the commitment, though at first poorly financed,
of the A.F.L. And Selden was, after all, working for the federation of labor: it was his task to build a large organization
whose members were willing to seek bargaining rights, even
if it meant a strike. From 1953 to 1956, Selden managed to

add two hundred new members to the Teachers Guild. However, he was able to attract to his view a small number of teachers who were willing to work long hours voluntarily for the expansion of the union. Among these was Albert Shanker, a mathematics teacher from Public School 126, in Queens.

At the same time, the prospects for increased help from the national labor movement were made brighter by the merger of the A.F.L. and the C.I.O. and the conversion of the C.I.O.'s substantial treasury into a fund for the Industrial Union Department, a division dedicated to the unionization of white-collar employees and led by Walter Reuther. By 1959, Selden was able to put Shanker on the A.F.T. payroll as a national rep and hire a number of temporaries. He was able to go to the press more often, to conduct school meetings, to distribute tons of literature. To impress teachers with the potential power of an organization linked to New York City's politically influential labor movement, he made certain that he was seen often with men like David Dubinsky, Michael Quill, Harry Van Arsdale, Jacob Potofsky and Paul Hall. The strategy was to create pro-Guild factions within every one of the city's myriad teacher organizations and to exploit those splits until the dissidents broke away and joined the Guild.

The most dramatic success of the strategy occurred in March 1960, when prounion members of the High School Teachers Association merged with the Guild to form the United Federation of Teachers. "The idea was for us to keep moving, to keep acting as if we were the power," Selden recalled, "and this kind of spinning would act as a magnet to people in other organizations." Within two months, Selden called for a strike, thoroughly aware such an action had little, if any chance, for success. But the "crisis" atmosphere created by the threat justified the entry of powerful labor figures in behalf of the U.F.T., figures who could exert considerable influence on Democratic Mayor Robert F. Wagner. The Federation finally did strike, on November 7, 1960, and although by today's standards it was a poor showing, the sheer gall of the union, coupled with the city's panicked reaction, catapulted it to inevitable success in the collective bargaining that was finally conducted in December of 1961. The path of teacher militancy might indeed have been very different had the city in 1960 adopted the kind of policies that many school boards throughout the country now are following, policies which dictate that teachers on strike should be allowed to stay on strike long enough to hang themselves. The U.F.T., after all, was able to draw fewer than five thousand teachers—out of an instructional staff of nearly fifty thousand—from their classrooms for the one-day walkout.

The walkout proved that antistrike legislation, like the Condin-Wadlin Act in New York, was an unfunny joke. If more evidence was needed, Selden again pulled the New York teachers out for one day in April of 1962. Like the first strike, it could hardly be counted a success in the number of teachers who walked off their jobs. But Selden managed to exploit a ready-made dispute between Democratic Mayor Wagner and Republican Governor Rockefeller, who was running for reelection that year. The strike afforded Rockefeller the opportunity to "find" thirteen million dollars for the city's schools, money which anyone vaguely connected with, or even interested in, city-state relations knew was there all the time, waiting to be used. Rockefeller gained reelection; the U.F.T. gained a recruitment drive which made it the nation's largest union local; the idea that teachers could strike with impunity, despite harsh laws, and still come out of it with a prize and no reprisals, gained national currency.

Selden now turned to the position he had wanted for more than a decade—leadership of the now rapidly growing American Federation of Teachers. As early as 1953, he had confided to friends in New York that the presidency was unquestionably in his long-range plans. According to the game plan, the New York campaign would put him in a position to take a job at national headquarters, a position from which he could step easily into the presidency. But Megel had plans for his own future and that of the A.F.T. Selden first wanted the job of organizational director; Megel gave it to an obscure New Jersey organizer named James Mundy. Selden then wanted the position of legislative representative (A.F.T. lobbyist), from which he could make both the A.F.T. and David Selden more nationally visible; Megel arranged to have the outgoing executive council name Megel to the post on his retirement. Selden finally did gain a foothold in the national as assistant to Charles Cogen, when Cogen went from U.F.T. presidency to the A.F.T. presidency in 1964.

Selden himself admits that he and Cogen had an "understanding": Cogen would serve two two-year terms and then turn the presidency over to Selden. But the understanding could hardly be an agreement between two old war comrades, fast friends who decided to share an international union between them. The two were not friends and had fought persistently over questions of U.F.T. policy while Selden was a resident in New York. No, the understanding looked more like a deal—Cogen would be supported in 1964 if Selden was given the assistantship. The first formal act of the new A.F.T. president was to request the newly elected executive council to create the position of assistant to the president and to make David Selden its first occupant.

Although his successes in New York were due largely to political circumstance, the power of labor in the city and the shock value of even unsuccessful strikes, Selden fashioned for himself the image of a vigorous and persuasive infighter. He was the "back-room" kind of power broker, he told staff members, the type who could settle intraunion difficulties or strikes through the sheer weight of his brand of personal diplomacy. Meanwhile, he would keep Cogen "up front," old Charlie's presence the confirmation of true union democracy. It was, after all, Cogen, not Selden, whom the union's delegates elected to run the union. There is merit, however, to the idea that had Selden not acted as a "shadow president" during the Cogen tenure, the A.F.T. would have been virtually leaderless. Far from being a tough, scrappy labor leader, kin in both spirit and stature to the Transport Workers' Michael Quill, Cogen was a gentle, slightly distracted union leader. He was not a well man, certainly not a young man; the strain of the New York campaign and his personal quarrels with Selden had more than once exhausted him to the point of illness. Shanker recalls that when he informed Cogen of his victory in the 1964 election, the older man nearly fainted. When he recovered his composure, he nearly went into a panic because he did not have the slightest notion how to use a credit card and he knew that the president of an international union should know how to do such things. Cogen was like that.

Selden, meanwhile, used the power of the president's office to protect both his own interests and that of the Progressive Caucus. He created an informal system of checking up on the national representatives, encouraging local Federation leaders to report any suspicion of "political activity" directly to him. Not infrequently he would phone, or even travel to, distant sectors of the nation to check up on nascent conspiracies. The behavior obviously did not endear him to the permanent traveling staff. He built his own national base by acting as "spokesman" for Cogen with the press, in conferences and seminars and in articles he wrote for various educational journals. Often a union pronouncement would be released under the names of both.

Inevitably, he announced for the presidency in 1968, but not before (according to Shanker), clearing it with Shanker. By that time it had become clear that Selden had made a tactical mistake in leaving New York. Shanker, who had remained behind to become U.F.T. president in 1964, was far more popular, far more powerful than Selden, whom Shanker still refers to as the "senior partner" in the New York campaign. Selden had not become, and was not about to become, leader of all the teachers including those in New York; Shanker adopted a policy by which, while he insisted on using his delegate strength to promote his own interests within the national Federation, the U.F.T. was to be something apart from the A.F.T. Selden still chafes at what he calls Shanker's "insularity." Shanker simply explains that his organization doesn't really need A.F.T. support. The presidency that Selden had sought for nearly twenty years was something less than he had planned. It had little inherent power, apart from its dependence on Shanker and the Shanker-controlled Progressive Caucus.

Yet Selden believed the A.F.T. could be transformed, under his tenure, into a truly national teacher union, enrolling both Federation members and the members of the Department of Classroom Teachers of the N.E.A. On the day of his election, he pledged himself to teacher unity and a nationwide teacher strike to elicit massive federal aid to education. His supporters privately predicted such a merger would take place "within a year or two." The idea, according to Selden, was to use the same tactics that he had employed to effect the merger of dissident elements of the High School Teachers Association in New York—to keep moving, to keep acting, working as a magnet to draw dissident members of the classroom teachers' group to the Federation. On that platform, he barely won election in 1968, defeating a black candidate, Mrs. Zeline Richards, of Detroit, and Edward C. Bolstad, of Minnesota, who had run on the promise of a stronger national rep staff. Far from being a harbinger of teacher unity, Selden's victory was attended by a walkout of a nascent "New Caucus" that condemned the A.F.T. leadership for racism and a failure to speak out against the war in Vietnam.

Within weeks of his victory, Selden formally asked the N.E.A. for negotiations toward "teacher unity within one or two years." The merged profession, he said, would be the "largest labor organization in the world, the most influential organization in the nation." Mrs. Elizabeth D. Koontz, N.E.A. president, icily answered, "We see no evidence of advantage to our teachers in your proposal." Selden now, much to the embarrassment of many loyal unionists, declined to believe that the refusal was final, calling on the N.E.A. again and again to start merger talks. Even an N.E.A. press release calling Selden's pleas "another desperate effort by the A.F.T. to raid our teachers" failed to cool his ardor for the "one big union."

Selden continued to encourage merger talks—at any level. When the N.E.A. affiliate in Flint, Michigan, swallowed up the smaller A.F.T. local and with tongue in cheek, called it "merger," Selden remained optimistic. He had to; pitiful as it was, it was the only promise of his being someday the leader of the nation's more than two million teachers. He completely misjudged the anti-N.E.A. sentiments of many union members and staff personnel. To them, the N.E.A. was just as much the enemy as were local school boards. Perhaps more so. Chief organizer Mundy put it this way:

> Neither Selden nor Shanker ever had any real experience dealing with local N.E.A. affiliates. In New York, the association never really mounted much of a campaign. But most union members are ex-N.E.A. members who joined the Federation to get away from the association. And they don't want to go back!
>
> Teachers everywhere know—union teachers anyway—how the N.E.A. will make deals with school boards to help crush the union. Ask the teachers in Minot or New Orleans. Black teachers in the South remember that the N.E.A. balked at desegregation while the union went forward, They don't want any part of the N.E.A.

Selden took the inevitability of the failure of merger personally. He placed the blame for opposition to teacher unity on a "peculiar" coalition of ultraconservatives and militant extremists within the A.F.T.

For the Federation, for Selden, 1969 was not a very good year. The national, historically identified with civil rights, was stained, perhaps indelibly, by its successful fight against the Ocean Hill-Brownsville school district. The disaster at Minot raised damaging suspicions that the A.F.T., which had always managed in the past to come out with at least a promise of "no reprisals," could no longer guarantee job protection for its members. If more evidence was needed, the firing of some fifty striking teachers in East Chicago Heights, Illinois, provided it. A strike in New Orleans, an arrogant display of disregard for the welfare and, indeed, the safety of school children and teachers alike, caved in. Selden came to the 1969 national convention (in New Orleans) as a champion of the antiwar, proactivist faction and was repudiated by the executive council and the Progressive Caucus, from which he resigned, determined to win the presidency the next time around as an insurgent.

Within months it became clear that he had no base beyond the Progressive Caucus. Insurgent groups—there were more than one—were determined to pick their own candidates. By March 1970, Selden had made peace with Shanker. The A.F.T. president would be supported for reelection; the embarrassing and divisive issue of merger would be, in Selden's word, "dead."

Still, there was the merger of the N.E.A. and A.F.T. affiliates in Los Angeles with which to contend. Months in advance, it had been decided that the new group—United Teachers–Los Angeles—would conduct a joint action against the schools as an experiment in "teacher unity." The national staff, preferring to engage the Association affiliate in a confrontation for membership, only reluctantly prepared for cooperation. The strike was a disaster. It further weakened Selden's image as an effective leader and produced, or rather confirmed, a strong anti-Selden faction in the permanent staff. Relations between the political leadership and the staff in the Federation approached the breaking point. The president accused a number of staff members of "personal disloyalty," a charge which surprised staff members, who were not aware that personal loyalty to Selden was a prerequisite for the job.

Finally, in June, Selden announced he had uncovered a staff

attempt to undermine his position. He accused Mundy of engaging in political activity either directly or indirectly by failing to report what he knew. Selden charged Kenneth Miesen,
one of the union's top strike strategists, with engaging in
political activity in violation of his contract. Miesen announced
his intention to run for the A.F.T. presidency at the Pittsburgh
convention in August. As the convention approached, Mundy
submitted his resignation, and the A.F.T. was rudderless as
never before.

Selden opened the convention by publicly recanting a number of the views he had promoted only months before, including merger. (He even shaved the mustache he had grown
in jail, expressly, he later explained, "for political reasons.")
The splits in the movement, so evident in 1968, were now
gaping. George Wiley, director of the National Welfare Rights
Organization, appeared to brand the entire A.F.T. "racist" because of Shanker's dumping from the Progressive Caucus
Richard Parrish, a black New York vice-president who had
supported the Ocean Hill-Brownsville experiment. Small and
medium-size locals rallied to Miesen's candidacy, accusing
Selden of paying too much attention to merger and of allowing too much of the A.F.T.'s dwindling resources to be used
by the big-city locals—New York, Chicago, Philadelphia and
Boston. William Simons, president of the Washington, D.C.,
local and an A.F.T. vice-president, refused to turn over his
bloc of votes to the Progressive Caucus. When it was over,
Selden had won, but by only 105 votes. He had failed to gain
an absolute majority in the secret-ballot election. Simons was
the top vote-getting vice-president and Shanker came in ninth.
Jules Kolodny, a U.F.T. colleague and fervid Shanker supporter, lost his seat on the executive council.

When a young teacher-delegate brought the results of the
balloting to Selden in his suite in the Pittsburgh Hilton, he
grabbed them angrily and retreated alone to his bedroom,
where he remained for nearly an hour. When he finally
emerged, the teacher said later, he was pale and shaken. He

had won, but the struggle sealed the fate of what was perhaps his last long-range plan. A poorly organized insurgent campaign had dealt a nearly fatal blow to the machine of the big-city locals. He wordlessly ignored a plea from John Converse, the A.F.T.'s public-relations man and traditional peacemaker, to grant amnesty to Miesen and the others as a gesture toward "teacher unity," Selden's biggest dream. Later that evening, a group of Boston teachers who had bolted from the big-city bloc crashed Selden's morose "victory party," bringing along a "puppet show" from a local school.

At this writing, Selden plans to run again, primarily to prove what had been almost disproved by the 1970 convention and the tragic events that had led up to it, that he is a genuine leader of teachers. Beyond that, there are no long-range plans, no more big dreams, whether of national teacher unity, of becoming a noted poet or playwright or novelist, of founding brave new institutions of learning. "I plan," he wrote recently, "to increase the amount of sailing time still left for me."

5

There Will Be No Teachers, No School

THE FIRST TIME the sheriff's men carried Albert Shanker off to jail, in December 1967, he showed all the signs of a hapless victim of some dreadful mistake: a grim man who failed in desperate attempts to prove to the powers who were putting him into Manhattan's dour Civil Jail that it was all just a misunderstanding. Now if they'd only cut the dramatics and let him go home, he'd concede that they had made their point. (Speaking of dramatics, Shanker had arranged to be taken into custody in the wings of the stage at the Manhattan Center, where he had just conducted a U.F.T. delegate assembly meeting; the show was marked by his wife's emotional dash to the stage, to throw her arms around him and cry, "I love you.") It was not so much that Shanker had grave reservations about being a fifteen-day martyr for the cause of teacher welfare; he didn't want to go at all. In fact, he had spent the preceding weeks pleading publicly and in vain for amnesty. This was bad form. Particularly because his jailing recalled the similar imprisonment, not yet two years before, of the decidedly unpenitent president of the Transport Workers' Union, Michael Quill, who not only was not bowed by the incarceration, but also managed to offer the suggestion that the judge who sentenced him should "drop dead in his black robes." It was Quill, however, who suffered a fatal heart attack while in prison. Perhaps to mark the contrast, a group of some two hundred transit workers showed up as Shanker climbed the steps of the minimum-security, maximum-boredom lockup; they sang, "For he's a jolly good fellow."

The second time, however, Shanker transformed his incarceration into a modest ritual of triumph. He did not await his captors; he drove deliberately to the lockup shortly after arriving in New York from Detroit and the funeral of Walter Reuther, where he had been singled out as a "national labor leader." George Meany himself, fresh from his knee-jerk endorsement of the United States Cambodian invasion blunder, growled about the injustice of putting Shanker away. The local members, with assistance from the A.F.T. national staff (Selden was there), had put together a grand demonstration of support (all black and Puerto Rican paraprofessionals up front to show how the U.F.T. *really* feels about minority rights). Bayard Rustin too was there; but, then, Bayard Rustin almost always is there. Shanker's manner was calm, detached, only vaguely annoyed, as if the Lilliputians had been at it again. Someone in the crowd greeted The Leader with a bouquet of flowers, and as he walked up the six steps to imprisonment he smiled and raised his hand in the "V" gesture, and the crowd sang "The Battle Hymn of the Republic."*

It had all become very serious—scary to some. In the thirty months between his two internments, Shanker rose from a

---

* The dates of Shanker's jailings and releases from prison are reverently noted in the official American Federation of Teachers poster-calendar, which, it is suggested, should be displayed prominently in the classroom. The calendar also marks such high holy days as the start of the Newark teachers' strike (February 1), the entrance of Selden into jail (March 19), the start of the St. John's University strike (January 4), the Lawrence textile strike (January 11) and the rally for A.F.T. reps jailed because of the Woodbridge strike (March 5).

chastened and reluctant hero to a labor leader no less powerful than David Dubinsky, Harry Van Arsdale, or even I. W. Abel or Walter Reuther. (None of these last set the policy of the board of directors.) By denying Mayor John V. Lindsay the public schools and all their various constituencies as a political point of reference, Shanker had become himself a formidable manipulator of power, not just the clever strategist Selden had proved to be in the early 1960's in New York. (Arthur Goldberg lamented Shanker's failure to support him for governor in 1970, and the excellent and unprecedented contract the U.F.T. gained in 1969 was probably more a function of Lindsay's political strategy than of skillful bargaining.) Reforms such as tenure, teacher certification, and examinations for supervisory personnel to a large extent removed the schools from the quicksand of politics. But Albert Shanker demonstrated that he could wield the ultimate power over public schools; he could close them down and he did, for thirty-six days in the fall of 1968, denying one million children schooling for one fifth of an educational year. And part of that catastrophic strike was almost pure pique—Shanker's—against a small group of residents, teachers and administrators in three experimental school districts. The power to inflict such awesome punishment resides with few men. His use of that power risked racial conflagration and aggravated the recurring infection of black anti-Semitism. He proved that Lindsay's popularity was something less than absolute within the city, no matter how many reassuring walks the Mayor took through the dark night of ghetto uprisings. Shanker demonstrated his ability to sway Republican, Democrat, Conservative and Liberal in the New York Legislature in his relentless efforts to kill decentralization. And he could defy the Ford Foundation's prestige and money, which had been put behind the community-control experiment.

Throughout the nation, mayors of large and medium-size cities knew they were against decentralization, no matter what it meant, because of the kind of urban brinkmanship all the heroes and villains had played in New York. School-board members saw, or imagined they saw, Albert Shankers in every one of the local union leaders. Many teachers, just then beginning to believe that they were the poor relatives of the college-educated "professional" class, saw in Shanker a way out of boredom, low pay and the harassment that they often equated with legitimate parental concern. And just plain people, parents, began to fear that the public schools, for which they were already so heavily taxed without promise of result, would become literally unsafe fortresses in the battle between special-interest groups and militants. They were helpless onlookers, and neither they nor their children could win; they weren't even in the game.

More than any recent event, the 1968 New York teachers' strike confirmed the suspicions that public-school systems were up for grabs, prizes to be taken by the strongest contestant. Shanker and the U.F.T. had the power to close the schools, and since no other person or group seemed capable of re-opening them—without his consent—he had the power *of* the schools.

But Shanker, of course, was not out to close all the schools in the nation. His notoriety alone was not enough to warrant the belief or hope that all teachers, or even all union teachers, would consider his way *the* way. What was needed for the consolidation of power was a cogent and coherent philosophy, a program, something the American Federation of Teachers, and its leaders, have been sorely lacking since its unheralded creation more than half a century earlier. In addition, a considerable measure of influence on the national organization was required so that *the* way could be executed through a nationwide staff. In the period between December, 1967, and May, 1970, Shanker had acquired that measure of control. And he had developed a philosophy.

In broad outline, Shanker's program is a wholesale adoption of the tenets of trade-unionism combined with an almost mystical belief that teachers alone are capable of understanding how children learn. On the one hand, he claims for teachers all those rights and powers won by organized labor—the right to organize and to bargain collectively through an exclusive agent, the closed or the agency shop, the right to strike, the right to make grievances and have those grievances redressed through impartial arbitration. As in private industry, teachers must be able to make demands for increased salaries and benefits without concern for how the employer shall pay for them. Just as it is U.S. Steel's problem to find the money to meet contract demands or face a strike, it is the school board's or the mayor's (ultimately the taxpayers') problem to find the funds necessary to meet teacher's salary demands or face a similar withdrawal of service. At the same time, however, the program denies the ability of the lay public to have any but the most general role in the conduct of the schools. The parents and citizens, generally, have the right to determine, in Shanker's view, "what the ends of society will be. Once they determine that, once they decide they want their kids to be able to read and count and do a lot of other things, then I think it is up to the experts to decide how you structure or organize materials in such a way it will effectively accomplish those purposes." (In case you missed it, the teachers are the experts.) In terms of what that means in bargaining, the teachers, through their union, claim the right to determine curriculum, to select textbooks, to determine, ultimately, what makes a good or an incompetent teacher, to control entry to and dismissal from the profession, and, generally, to control the teaching profession as physicians control medicine and as lawyers control the practice of law. To do otherwise is to invite the chaotic conditions he insists were rampant in Ocean Hill-Brownsville. Public schools are public in that they are financed publicly, charge no tuition, may not discriminate on the basis of race, religion, sex or national extraction—and that is all. The ends—"whether you want a computer or a renaissance man" is how Shanker puts it—may be popularly determined; the means are sacred to the profession.

And who shall control the profession? The members thereof, of course, through the American Federation of Teachers, A.F.L.–C.I.O. (Not yet, of course, but that *is* the idea.) Control of the A.F.T. technically rests with the national convention, whose delegates meet annually to pass on all manner of resolutions (they elect a president every two years). The delegates are divided into caucuses, essentially political parties, which take varying positions on issues and run their own candidates for the presidency and the twenty vice-presidencies. Patronage, money and services to local districts are channeled through the caucus in power. (Just like the Big Time.) In the months between conventions, the executive council— the twenty vice-presidents—passes on policy matters and decides which issues the convention will discuss. The council's executive committee, made up of the chairmen of various council subcommittees, generally controls the deliberations of the council as a whole. The actual power rests not so much with these constitutional committees as with the leader of the dominant caucus. In the period between his two jailings, Shanker built the Progressive Caucus from a New York– oriented insurgent group to an almost monolithic association of the leaders of all the big cities—New York, Chicago, Washington, Baltimore, Philadelphia, Boston, Cleveland and Detroit. He built it and, because of the great number of teachers he represents, he runs it.

Through the full-time president—now David Selden—the policies of the ruling caucus are executed. Theoretically, Selden's staff, primarily the national reps, are the practicing executors of policy. And the parents, the taxpayers and the children feel the impact through strikes and, less dramatically, though far more significantly, through the contract. Shanker, indeed, has come a long way.

Albert Shanker was born September 14, 1928, on New York's steamy Lower East Side. (It seems everyone who has risen to political heights in the city was born either in the Lower East Side or in Hell's Kitchen.) His father, Morris, was an immigrant who had studied to be a rabbi while in Poland. Although he did occasionally preside over religious services, he made his living delivering union newspapers. Albert's mother, Mamie Burko Shanker, was a sewing-machine operator and an active member of the Amalgamated Clothing Workers of America. In Manhattan and, a few years after his birth, in the Ravenswood section of Queens (the 1930's version of a suburb), the Shanker children, Albert and his sister, Pearl, grew up on trade-unionism and the New Deal. As a child, Albert marched in parades honoring Franklin Delano Roosevelt.

In Queens elementary schools and in the academically superior Stuyvesant High School in Manhattan, Shanker was an excellent student and a hopeless athlete. He reached his adult height of six-foot-three by the age of twelve, a gawky, uncoordinated kid who could barely see without thick glasses. That didn't enhance his popularity, nor did his Jewish faith, in the predominantly Irish Ravenswood, and young Shanker learned early what it meant to be a member of a minority group.

The lesson followed him to the University of Illinois, in Urbana, where he found that the only living quarters open to Jewish students were some six miles from the center of the campus. The consistent pattern of discrimination he was forced to confront, together with his early and persistent contact with trade-union and New Deal philosophies, led to strong social and political commitment by the young Shanker. He was a member of the Young People's Socialist League and chairman of the Socialist Study Club on campus. He organized the few radical activists he could find on the Midwestern campus in the late 1940's to campaign against segregated theaters and restaurants in Urbana. It was his introduction to the picket line and his first commitment to the civil-rights movement, a commitment that, despite Ocean Hill-Brownsville, he has continued to meet (ideologically, at least). These were not popular activities as the nation mired itself in the Cold War. But Shanker has never considered personal popularity a requisite to power.

With honors in philosophy, Shanker was graduated from the University of Illinois and immediately began graduate studies at Columbia. He received a Master's degree in philosophy and mathematics and undertook doctoral studies in philosophy under the personal guidance of Charles Frankel. But he never wrote his doctoral dissertation. In 1952, the aspiring college professor ran out of money and took a job as a substitute teacher in the New York City school system. According to Shanker, he never meant to be a teacher. But the challenge of teaching in the city—his first assignment was a junior high school in Harlem—and the opportunity to play an official adult role in the unionism which was so much a part of his past kept him in the classroom, away from his doctoral studies. He transferred as a permanent teacher to Junior High School 126 in Long Island City in his home borough of Queens. It was not long before he used his union affiliation to become actively embroiled in the politics of the school itself. He formed a close association with a number of prounion teachers, and together they began to rise within the ranks of the Teachers Guild, Local 5 of the A.F.T. (The other teachers included George Altomare and Sol Levine, now both U.F.T. vice-presidents, and Dan Sanders, Shanker's public-relations man.)

Shanker was a member of the Guild's delegate assembly when he met Selden, and the pair were soon close friends. They shared the A.F.L.–C.I.O. commitment to collective bargaining, to the building of a large active union which would control bargaining rights—Selden, primarily because that was his job; Shanker, because that was his gospel. Through the first lean years of Selden's tenure in New York, it was Shanker's job to "build a little union" in every school, to have at least one member in each school so it could be said with only a minimum of dishonesty that a Guild chapter existed in each of the city's schools. (After all, if each school had a chapter chairman, there must be a chapter there—*no?*) He helped get out the literature to the "chapter chairman," to make telephone contact with Guild "potentials," to coordinate meetings, and so on—still maintaining a full-time job teaching. According to both men, the Unitarian Midwesterner and the New York Jew became fast friends, spending long hours in each other's apartment, planning, plotting, counting as-yet-unrecruited members. (Shanker and Selden both lived in Morningside Gardens, a cooperative apartment complex in Upper Manhattan, a "five-minute elevator ride and crosswalk away" from each other.) Selden was the planner, the dreamer, speculating on possibilities, talking for hours about real or imagined intrigues, while Shanker was the listener, then the disciple, familiar with the ways of the Big City, learning eagerly how he could be both an intellectual and a union man. "He was always the senior partner," recalled Shanker. "He came up with most of the notions." It was during these long hours of expounding at Morningside Gardens that Selden would talk of his dream of leading a unified teaching organization, two million strong. Shanker just listened and learned the practical application of dreaming. By the spring of 1959, Shanker was clearly Selden's top assistant, the assistant leader of the Teachers Guild. (Cogen was the "public, the constitutional, but not the functioning head of the union," says Shanker. That he also happened to be the elected head was a technicality.) That spring, back at a small cottage he maintained for a short time in Connecticut, Selden ran over his foot with a lawnmower; while he recuperated, Shanker took over as the full-time leader of the union. Selden frequently attempted to persuade Shanker to join the A.F.T. national staff if Megel, with his Chicago biases, should ever kick in enough money to support the position. Finally, the money was there; Nicholas Zonarich of the Industrial Union Department was convinced that New York teachers were worth the spending of a considerable war chest in order to build white-collar unionism. Would Shanker take the job as an A.F.T. national rep assigned permanently to New York? He said no, and he gave the predominance of non-Jews in the teaching corps as the reason. "Contrary to popular opinion," he says now with vehemence, "neither the city's instructional staff nor the leadership of the union is 98 percent Jewish." Shanker begged off—temporarily. He didn't know why, but he was apprehensive regarding the effect of his being Jewish on the response to his recruiting efforts. Working behind Selden was acceptable, but going out every day to the schools, glad-handing Irish and Italian teachers—maybe that wasn't such a good idea. Maybe it had something to do with what happened in Ravenswood twenty-three years earlier . . .

He knew he had to cross that lot to get back home. Otherwise he'd have to walk around the block and he was late already. But he didn't like it. Those kids always were in the lot, and although he never bothered them, they never left him alone.

"*We're the only Jewish family in the neighborhood,*" his father told him more than once, "*and they don't like us.*

"*Why? Maybe it's their parents. They're poor and they think Jewish people hoard all the money. And they think we're responsible for killing their Christ.*"

One day Albert's father turned the radio on and had him listen to this strange man who always was asking people to form a "Christian Front" and drive out the money-mad bankers who ran Roosevelt's "Jew Deal." It scared the eight-year-old boy; he had heard of terrible things going on in Germany and he wondered if it could happen here.

But no, his father told him, they can't hurt you with words. Just stay away from them. If they don't want you to play with them, you certainly don't need people like that.

But today he had no desire to play with them. He just wanted to get across the lot without being noticed.

"*Jew boy!*" Albert winced, but did not turn to look. He walked faster; he wasn't too far from home.

"*Jew boy! Come here, we want to talk to you.*"

Running now. But without turning around, he knew they were coming closer. He knew he couldn't run very fast, always tripping, looking so silly.

Soon two or three grabbed at his feet and threw him to the ground. He struggled to his feet. He was taller and he flailed his arms wildly, home was a quick run away. Why wouldn't they just let him go home?

But the boys, maybe five or six of them now, they were quicker. And stronger. They formed a circle, pushing him about.

"*You killed Jesus, Jew boy!*" Albert had heard it before and he almost began to cry because of the sheer frustration of trying to deny this undeniable assertion.

A rope! One of the boys had a rope and slipped it around Albert's neck. He fought and scratched, his glasses fell to the ground and were trampled as his tormentors squealed with an excitement that frightened him so much he couldn't scream.

"*You killed Christ, now we're gonna kill you.*"

The boys pushed, kicked and dragged the young Jewish boy to a corner of the lot, by the small clump of trees. The rope burned his neck and he pleaded with them to let him go. Wasn't there anyone around to stop it? Why had his father said this was not like Germany?"

There were hands and arms and elbows all over him, punching, slapping, stabbing, pulling. "*Hey, hold him still while I get this knot tied.*" All the hands pushed as one, scratching his face against the stiff lower branches.

"*Okay . . . Now . . . Leggo!*"

The pathetic little boy reached instinctively up for the rope, he grabbed it. But there was still a jolt. His neck felt afire and he felt nausea as the rope squeezed in on his throat.

He gagged, weakly, desperately, inaudibly crying out for help. The boys laughed. But suddenly panic crossed their faces too. They *were* killing him. The spindly legs which kicked out helplessly, the rush of blood to his face, the dry cackle—they *were* killing him. In fear, they ran, while Albert held on to the rope, aching, his hands burning.

A woman he had never seen before ran to the tree, reached up and cut the wretched lad down. He contemplated her with the same voiceless fear and, holding his throat, he ran home.

"Maybe it would be better if you asked George Altomare," Shanker repeatedly told Selden. But Selden, convinced that if Shanker could do anything, he could provide intellectual justification for the union organization of teachers, pressed his friend. It was a talent badly needed among college-educated professionals, who snobbishly looked down on wage earners, who saw Jimmy Hoffa behind every union label. Selden knew that he himself was painted with the "typical union organizer" brush, a nonteacher transient closely identified with the A.F.L.–C.I.O. But Shanker—here was a quiet, almost retiring young intellectual who by no stretch of the imagination could be mistaken for a teamster or a longshoreman. The local needs you, Al. The A.F.T. needs you. If the A.F.L.–C.I.O. is ever going to make gains among white-collar workers, it needs a strong union of teachers here in New York. Al Shanker accepted and in the fall of 1959 gave up his tenure, his pension rights and his classroom to become an A.F.T. rep.

With an expanded staff—Shanker was soon to become chief of a part-time staff and coordinator of the efforts of other nonteacher union organizers who were lent by the A.F.L.–C.I.O., with an almost limitless well, the I.U.D., from which to draw funds—Selden and Shanker prepared for the organization of the largest union local in the United States. Together, they engineered the merger with the High School Teachers Association, the November 7, 1960, strike, the election in December of 1961, the strike in 1962, the new contract in September, the recruitment effort which took in a thousand new members a month, and a new contract for 1963 and 1964. But Selden grew restless and wanted to play out his long-range plan before Megel wrapped the union up for his followers in the Midwest. Shanker, decidedly confident now, wanted the local presidency. Cogen would go first to claim the union for New York; Selden would follow. Shanker would stay on to ensure that the local union would not reatomize into competing organizations. (To this day, Shanker fears that the U.F.T. would split down previous lines without his strong leadership and that of the J.H.S. 126 group.)

It was not too long after Cogen became president, and Selden his assistant, that Shanker gave notice that he was no longer the junior partner. In a speech to the convention which elected him, Cogen called for federal aid to public and private schools alike. Shanker publicly condemned any private use of public money and settled down to be boss of his own bailiwick. His presidency was the vehicle for beliefs that he had held for most of his conscious life. Now he could make what he believed was a significant contribution to the civil-rights movement: his union supplied teachers to the Freedom Schools in Mississippi and Virginia; it contributed large sums of money to Dr. Martin Luther King's voter-registration drive in Alabama; Shanker himself went to Selma to deliver the keys to station wagons that the union had purchased for the voting campaign. Now he could acquire a leadership position in the labor movement that his father and mother so ardently respected. Teacher-union pickets appeared in support of department-store workers, hospital workers, sanitation men—if Shanker believes in anything, it's union solidarity. (He once tried to get the board to refuse to buy books printed in a factory hit by a strike; he did manage, in 1966, to prevent youngsters from strike-bound St. John's University from serving as student teachers in city schools.) In his relations with the city school board, Shanker started with the premise the members were out to keep the teachers poor. Less than six months after he was elected local president in 1964, he told his membership that the school board had "declared open war" on the U.F.T. and that a strike in September of 1965 was inevitable. He kept up the pressure, predicting a long strike, organizing mass marches, promoting a "no contract, no work" policy which was finally adopted by the local's executive board in June. He already made it quite clear that this union was not interested solely in economic gains for its membership; he threatened to strike immediately if the teachers were transferred or rotated because of a new 4-4-4 school reorganization plan adopted by the board. Just days before the schools reopened in 1965, the union settled. Within months, he began the battle again—this time for the 1967 contract. The net effect of the increased visibility that Shanker brought to the U.F.T. was a strengthening of his power both locally and nationally. By 1966, he was in direct control of roughly half of the A.F.T.'s entire membership. He had formed strong alliances with local labor leaders and politicians. (He himself is a member of the Liberal party.) And he had set the tone for militancy in teachers' unions—and, indirectly, N.E.A. affiliates—throughout the nation.

But the U.F.T. was, after all, still only a union. It had demonstrated its ability to extract money from a financially overburdened city, but the teacher union that he and Selden had talked about on those nights in Upper Manhattan was more than that. It was a power, the power, in the administration of education. If the teaching profession was to be just that, a profession, it was imperative that it have some determining authority as to where nonsalary funds were to go. Educational programs had to be administered by the union; personnel policies, control of the distribution and the content of teaching materials must be vested within the profession and the organization which controlled the profession. The U.F.T. created a "More Effective Schools" (M.E.S.) program, essentially a compensatory education project, which called for a reduction in size of classes and an increase in specialized services, such as social work, guidance, remedial reading and mathematics, and psychiatric assistance. This program was presented to the school board with the demand that it be established in the schools and that it be "jointly administered by the board and the union." In addition, the U.F.T. demanded strict control over students whom its members identified as disruptive and a reduction in the services traditionally performed by teachers—such as escorts for children from buses or through hallways, playground and cafeteria supervision—but now declared "nonprofessional chores." The city school board, as early as December of 1966, rejected the demands as "out of the sphere of collective bargaining."

But Shanker persisted. It was, at the same time, the wrong and the right season to press for union control over policy and personnel matters. The summer of 1967 dispelled any illusions that the teachers might have had about peaceful social change. And ghetto blacks adopted programs which called for control over the schools, which they knew would never be integrated. Demonstration school districts with expanded community control were in operation or were forming, supported strongly by the new mayor, John V. Lindsay, a politician who owed considerably less to the city's unions than did his predecessor, Robert F. Wagner. It was the right time because many teachers felt that they needed a "law and order" kind of organization; because if union power was not asserted now and successfully institutionalized within formal school operations, it might never be; because if the decentralization bill, as supported by Mayor Lindsay, was adopted, the U.F.T. might very well disintegrate back into the scores of competing area- and specialty-based organizations that existed prior to 1961. It was the wrong time because if the nation's cities needed anything, they needed a sensitive, responsive teaching staff which identified with the local communities' horrors and hopes, not a massive, centralized teacher union which saw ghetto explosions a threat to its own power. Within their own union, top leaders like Altomare and Richard Parrish recoiled at Shanker's insistence on forcing the power issue when reason demanded at least a low profile. Shanker apparently read these expressions of dissent as just symptoms of what was in store unless the U.F.T. asserted itself now. And, of course, as Lyndon Johnson was learning, there's nothing like a war to unite dissenters. On September 9, 1967, Shanker announced: "There will be no teachers, no schools." He was right; the following day, there was neither. It was a mass resignation, not a strike, he explained; strikes are considered a "strong-arm technique," while resignations are "acts of desperation." He fooled no one, of course, and the blatancy of the assertion does not even qualify it as an example of the big-lie technique employed by national reps. Perhaps the most telling comment about the strike was made by Shanker himself, who told *The New York Times:* "We have found it necessary to engage from time to time in a kind of civil disobedience. I am not a martyr, but there would be no teachers' union today if we did not defy the law."

The primary issue continued to be the establishment of M.E.S. schools throughout the city,* and Shanker continued the strike even after basic money issues were settled. The board resisted. Not only were key members unconvinced of their effectiveness, particularly when they were costing some five or six hundred additional dollars per student, but they also were adamant about retaining management and policy prerogatives. The compromise which ended the strike after two weeks included the establishment of a ten-million-dollar fund for educational improvements and the impaneling of an advisory committee to determine how the money would be spent. Shanker lost; no new M.E.S. schools were created and his union, far from obtaining administrative power, gained only a share of advisory authority. But he also won; he had

---

* M.E.S. schools had been established in twenty-one of the city's schools since 1964. But they were not "pure" M.E.S. in the sense that the board reserved for itself most of the controlling powers the U.F.T. was demanding in 1967.

forced the board to concede that the U.F.T. could make it adopt at least a program for "educational improvement," no matter how vague. Several key union officials were dissatisfied, particularly Richard Parrish, who publicly charged that Shanker went in only for economic benefits and brought the teachers back without making a significant contribution to education in the city. Parrish also expressed concern about what the strike had done to the experimental demonstration districts, whose nascent efforts in the fall of 1967 were trampled on by the walkout. Members of the community board retaliated in blind anger by handing over to local draft boards the names of striking teachers, informing the Selective Service that the teachers were no longer employed in the deferred teaching occupation and were now susceptible to induction and Vietnam. (Shanker had said they "resigned.") Concerned that unless the M.E.S. program was expanded, the walkout would indeed appear to be a "strike against the community," David Selden himself flew in to New York to plead with Shanker to stick with educational demands, playing down union power and economic issues. At one break during bargaining sessions at the mayor's official residence, Shanker angrily rebuked Selden, ordering him back to national headquarters and out of the business of the United Federation of Teachers. It became quite obvious now who was the "senior partner." The timing of Shanker's jailing for contempt of court arising out of the 1967 strike formally put the U.F.T. in opposition to local community efforts at decentralization; he insisted on going in December, if he had to go at all, so he would be free in January of 1968 to lead lobbying efforts against the decentralization bill in the New York Legislature.

In many ways, Shanker's actions may have constituted a blunder. While it did formalize his and his union's power within the city school system, it created divisions within his own local and the national organization, divisions which prevented him from becoming the national union's president.

Despite Selden's insistence that he would run in 1968, the Progressive Caucus clearly expected Shanker to take formal control of the national. "I could have won it almost by acclamation in 1968," Shanker says now, and although his support was hardly that solid (there was a convention walkout by prodecentralization and antiwar forces), he did have the votes. But the angers he had unleashed in 1967 required the sovereign's presence at home; if he had become A.F.T. president, there is little doubt the U.F.T. would have become splintered and the national would be in the same weak position it was in in 1960. And he hadn't yet completed killing decentralization—another matter which required his presence in New York. So, in 1968, after easily beating two prodecentralization candidates in New York, he settled for picking the next A.F.T. president, Selden, and strengthening his control over the decision-making caucus.

Although details of the disastrous 1968 strike will be discussed in the following chapter, one important point is worth mentioning here. And that is that much of Shanker's behavior for the thirty-six days of the walkout may have been attributable to purely intra-union political considerations. Through his propaganda against the Ford Foundation suggestions for "reconnecting" the schools to the people, he had created the rough equivalent of right-wing hysteria among the bulk of his teachers. Within the union, there was no shortage of leaders of the left wing, union teachers who wished to cooperate in the creation of local community boards. To retain his leadership, he was required to move to the right, at once creating and being captured by fear of massive dislocation and transfer of teachers. He would have been a hollow progressive candidate for president, but a legitimate conservative one. Of the 53,000 eligible union voters, only 20,000 cast their votes in the 1968 U.F.T. election, and 17,000 of these went to Shanker. (One of Shanker's arguments against community school boards is that only a minority participate in local elections.)* Shanker is a sensitive enough politician to know that these 17,000 represented those who felt threatened by Ocean Hill-Brownsville and the other community districts; when the local board there transferred nineteen teachers and supervisors in May of 1968, it unwittingly strengthened his position in the union. A kind of "I told you so" syndrome. It gave him a new constituency to replace the one he lost because of the failures in the 1967 strike. In any event, Shanker exhibited a rare kind of teacher jingoism in the 1968 strike—he simply would not stop until he killed the idea of community participation and successfully punished its advocates. Three years later, in retrospect, Shanker said:

> Regrets? Nope. We'd do every single thing over again. (Like the Pope, Shanker speaks in the first person plural.) Things have worked out fine. That entire Board of Education is gone. That Superintendent of Schools is gone. We got a decentralization law about 80 percent of which is consonant with what we wanted. We were able to get an excellent and unprecedented contract the following June because the city was unwilling to face another shutdown. It would have taken us ten years to get the benefits we got in that one single contract.

Shanker overcame the problem of his inability to leave New York to take over the A.F.T. presidency by neutralizing the power of that position. When Selden came to the 1969 convention determined to prove that he was the teacher-union leader in fact as well as title, Shanker's Progressive Caucus blocked every one of his attempts. Selden wanted the A.F.T. on record against the war; Shanker said no, and the A.F.T. did not take a stand. Selden wanted a statement of support

---

* Keith Baird and Sol Jaffe, Shanker's opponents in the 1968 U.F.T. election, charged that a special issue of the union's paper, *The United Teacher,* which carried their platforms, somehow never got to the membership. The teachers, they said, were never aware they had a choice. That could account for the low turnout.

for student dissidents; Shanker said no, and the A.F.T. took no stand. When Selden quit the Progressive Caucus for its failure to support its president, Shanker was not too concerned. He knew Selden would have to come back in order to retain even a powerless title. Which is precisely what he did. He even managed to neutralize headquarters staff by moving in the executive council to have nearly every one of them fired.

Why? Shanker believes that no one but Shanker, no one in the executive council, no one on national staff, not even Selden himself, takes teacher-unionism seriously enough. Taking it seriously means strict solidarity with the leadership of the A.F.L.–C.I.O.; it means not doing anything which reflects "radicalism" within the union, thereby alienating possible recruits. The A.F.T. must, above all things, be "responsible"; it must accept its institutionalization (his word) and give up acting like a Movement. Only when the A.F.T. realizes its own legitimacy, he believes, will it finally become a truly national organization, putting an end to the National Education Association, which got where it was by not tolerating mavericks. Or, at least, that is what he claims to believe.

Hell, we're not playing games. There's the future of American education involved and a good part of the labor movement, an entire union. We live and breathe this thing day and night, and there's some people who don't understand—so we're supposed to be very sympathetic about this thing?

It's every bit as serious as national and state politics. And the only way to develop any responsibility is that people have to be educated to the fact that what they do will have consequences. I know that whatever I do has consequences. Everything I do makes friends, makes enemies, makes the organization look a little better, a little worse, gives us good p.r. [public relations], bad p.r.

It's all got that—now why is it only Shanker has to understand that?

From this it follows that attacks on Shanker's position within the union are attacks on teacher trade-unionism. And should be dealt with accordingly. Late in 1969, Shanker started his drive to make the staff "more responsible." It began with Len Lewis, the young black who holds the title of A.F.T. civil-rights director. Lewis is simply not a controversial young man who would use his position for the furtherance of anything, much less his own power. Like most of the nonrep staff, he functions like a bureaucrat, willing to take orders, to shuffle papers—but not to make waves. Following what he thought was Shanker's lead in making a presence for the teacher union in the South, Lewis lent A.F.T. support to a voter-registration drive in Georgia. He also ran a series of "civil-rights workshops" but made the mistake of inviting Richard Parrish, Shanker's archrival, who took the occasion to promote union cooperation with decentralization movements. It is unlikely that Lewis consciously meant to embarrass Shanker. Parrish, after all, was then an A.F.T. vice-president and chairman of the executive council's civil-rights committee. Parrish was the obvious choice for speaker. Shanker moved in the executive council for Lewis' dismissal on the grounds that he had gotten the A.F.T. embroiled in local Southern politics and that Lewis himself was participating in union politics.

In February of 1970, the A.F.T. was conducting a hopeless collective-bargaining election in Buffalo, New York. Shanker insisted the drive be successful for two reasons—to make the U.F.T. presence felt upstate and to increase the number of delegates New York would have. One of the A.F.T.'s warriors, part of the eleven-man team sent into the city to wage war against the Association, returned to his home for three days to be with his dangerously ill wife. The Buffalo Federation lost the election. Shanker moved to have the rep fired for insubordination and leaving his job without permission.

That same month, David Elsila, who calls himself the

A.F.T.'s token radical, came out with an extra edition of the union paper he edits—*The American Teacher*—with a headline screaming: "Police-State Tactics Hit N.J. Teachers—Is New Jersey a Fascist State?" One of the stories in the four-page edition said sheriff's deputies were "clubbing scores of [prounion] demonstrators." The political nature of New Jersey's government and the nature of the tactics its police use are matters of opinion; but the sheriff's deputies who broke up the demonstration in question purposely left their clubs in a nearby paddy-wagon to avoid just such a charge. I was there, and not one teacher, not one sympathizer, was hit with club or fist. Shanker was enraged and demanded Elsila's dismissal, complaining that the young former teacher from Michigan "was trying to turn teachers into Weathermen." (Shanker himself is an officer of the League for Industrial Democracy, whose youth group at the University of Michigan became the first chapter of Students for a Democratic Society, the S.D.S., in 1959.) It was not the first time Elsila crossed Shanker. With Patricia Strandt, his loyal associate editor (together, they *are* the staff of *The American Teacher*), he went out on strike against the A.F.T. The two are members of the American Newspaper Guild, A.F.L.–C.I.O. They stayed out only a few days, but their threat to embarrass the union as an antiunion employer helped them to avoid the fate that fell on other A.F.T. employees who have struck—dismissal. Shanker simply doesn't care for such irresponsibility.

Some A.F.T. staffers believe that Selden and Shanker engage in a kind of scenario to neutralize errant staff members. Shanker moves to have one fired, Selden argues against it, and the matter is tabled. But the staff member knows that his job is in jeopardy. In this way, Selden demonstrates his independence, Shanker puts the staffers on notice, but no one is actually fired. Just brought into line. Those who refuse to step back into line are eventually fired outright. Ironically, Shanker calls this belief "McCarthyite paranoia" and says Selden really is blocking his attempts to purge the national staff. The results, however, are the same. The staff member so marked by Shanker usually does behave himself in a manner less likely to irritate the vice-president from New York.

In the political affairs of the union, Shanker's method is less subtle. He is simply out to eliminate the opposition. In 1970, with the entire union split over a score of issues, Shanker refused to allow Parrish to run on the Progressive Caucus slate for vice-president. (That he almost won as an independent is some measure of the unrest among the troops.) Parrish, according to Shanker, "has never done a damn thing to build this union. All he's done is to go around the community talking against the union." After eliminating Parrish as a power, he trained his sights on William Simons, of Washington, D.C. Simons is an exponent of community control in the nation's capital and has lent his union's support to the creation of an experimental, community-run district. Shanker believes that Simons worked with community-control promoters in New York during the strike in a "conspiracy" against the U.F.T. But that is not what really bothered Shanker so much. Shanker had made a deal with Simons, he said, a deal to ensure the election of both men and Selden. It was simple—Shanker would turn over New York votes to Simons in his race for the vice-presidency if Simons agreed to give Shanker and Selden Washington's votes. But Simons never delivered; consequently, Shanker and Selden both nearly lost, while Simons received more votes than any vice-presidential candidate. "A dirty political game," Shanker asserts. Democratic procedure, says Simons, who indicated that it is his practice to release Washington's delegates at national conventions. This time around, he explained, they chose not to vote the Progressive slate.

Strangely enough, what really aggravates Shanker is that Simons was not ashamed of what he had done. The vote for president and vice-president is a secret ballot. But after the 1970 election was held and the results were announced, anti-administration delegates demanded a roll-call vote. Not surprisingly in this case,* the administration leaders did not try very hard to defeat the motion, and the roll was called. Shanker explains what happened:

> When the open vote came, Selden got nearly all the votes in the caucus. In other words, most people were ashamed and/or afraid to do publicly what they had done privately. Not Simons' group. Simons' group *even openly* voted against Selden. It was pretty obvious, the game he was playing.

For this lack of shame and/or fear, Shanker decided that Simons must be punished. When the new executive council met to reorganize, Simons was not given a committee chairmanship and thus was denied a seat on the policy-making executive committee. Why was it necessary to punish Simons? Shanker replies:

> Would you expect Barry Goldwater, if he'd gotten elected, to appoint Nelson Rockefeller to a cabinet position, after what Rocky did to him at the national convention in 1964 —and afterward? Would Hubert Humphrey have named George Wallace to the cabinet? If you can understand that, then you can understand my behavior.

It's not likely that Shanker will stop at stripping Simons of a seat on the executive committee. Simons may someday lead a much stronger insurgent movement against the Progressive Caucus; if he can, Shanker will weaken his adversary's position in the Washington local by interrupting the flow of aid

---

* Not surprisingly, because a roll-call vote in this case was safe enough and it would identify the delegates who voted against the administration or would force them back into line. The latter consideration was probably the more important one for the administration leaders, since they could tell, anyway, because of the arrangement of the voting machines, precisely how each delegation had voted. Those who balked, privately or publicly, were temporarily refused national aid, until some of the locals began to make noises about leaving the A.F.T. for the American Federation of State, County and Municipal Employees or the Teamsters. The possible loss of per capita dues is one sure tonic for angered union politicians.

and services. Without the presidency of the Washington local, Simons can hardly be a threat. Says Shanker:

> I don't know how long the leadership of that local will stand up, internally. You see, Simons cannot continue what he's doing inside the A.F.T. and the labor movement without his own union being hurt. And without his members finding out why.
>
> Simons, more than anyone else, depends upon everybody throughout the rest of the country because he has to deal directly with Congress. He can't afford to play that sort of politics. His members are going to find out fairly soon a large part of their troubles are due to a large number of locals throughout the country not providing the kind of support he needs if he continues to play a dirty kind of politics.

Whether that kind of friendly persuasion will work should be obvious the next time Selden runs for president in 1972. (One should, of course, be eternally grateful to the A.F.T. for finally taking politics out of education.)

But whither Albert Shanker now? Still a young man in the early 1970's, Shanker need not devote all his time to building the U.F.T.; nearly every employee of the New York City school board already is a member. And it's doubtful that he will lose control of the national. Although the U.F.T.'s percentage grows smaller as the A.F.T. grows larger, Shanker, at this writing, is prepared to make his union a statewide organization, thus controlling the delegate votes of nearly 250,000 teachers, paraprofessionals, secretaries, attendance officers, specialists and clerks. Unless the A.F.T. suddenly grows to more than a million members, Shanker's relative power is not likely to diminish. Particularly when Shanker himself has so much to say about how the A.F.T. will grow.

Some suspect that Shanker will move to control the A.F.T. formally just when the Great Merger is imminent. From there, from the leadership of a two-million-member organization of teachers, the kid from the Lower East Side will capture the presidency of the A.F.L.–C.I.O. in the name of white-collar unionism. Shanker himself believes the Great Merger is "too far away" for such speculation. Maybe he would do it, he says, but he believes an aspirant to George Meany's job would have to spend too much time working on the affairs of the A.F.L.–C.I.O., and the problems of the A.F.T. are too great at this time to allow that luxury. For the immediate future, says Shanker, he will spend his energies "getting the state together."*

That will mean, of course, an even greater involvement in state politics than he exhibited during the battle to kill decentralization. He first must persuade the Legislature to permit statewide collective bargaining and a statewide agency shop. Then he must travel the state campaigning for the election of the A.F.T. After that, Shanker, as statewide president, must exert his efforts to strengthen tenure laws, kill antistrike legislation and prevent the spread of performance contracting (which could do to the teaching profession what automation did to other trades), the voucher system and other non-collective-bargaining issues.

Perhaps it was for that statewide perspective that he put the U.F.T. directly into the 1970 Congressional and legislative elections, endorsing and supporting selected candidates. Perhaps, too, that is why he shied away from supporting Arthur Goldberg for governor, even though Goldberg in 1960 argued brilliantly and successfully for the right of teachers to select an exclusive bargaining agent in New York. It is certainly no fun to back losers—at a statewide level. And Shanker himself has moved upstate a bit, to Putnam County, where he lives with his wife and three children. (He organized Edith Shanker in 1960, made her picket captain in the November strike and married her in March of 1961.) Leading a very respectable home life, he reads incessantly, plays

* Late in 1971, all union teachers in the State of New York united under Shanker's leadership. Merger talks with the state's N.E.A. affiliate began almost immediately.

bridge and chess, tinkers with photography and wine making, drinks dry martinis, and lends his name to all good civic movements in Putnam County.

Although a registered Liberal, he's not above helping Democrats. After all, he's a bit of a New Deal Democrat himself, believing in federal control and financing of education, eschewing the "nutty radicals" of the New Left and writing frequently that the labor movement still is the most influential liberal power in the United States. "On Haynsworth, on Carswell, on tax reform, oil depletion allowances, consumer interests—it's obvious the labor movement is not conservative or reactionary." Shanker does, after all, have a good civil-rights record. And a good law-and-order record. And the more people who insist on interpreting the 1968 strike as a Lindsay–Ford Foundation blunder rather than a momentous fit of pique on Shanker's part, the more that stigma will be removed from his career. True, he was jailed twice. But once antistrike regulations are removed—as they already have been in some states—Shanker will be more the visionary leader than the ex-con.

And when one considers the deplorable state of the Democratic party in New York since the death of Robert F. Kennedy . . . Well, someone could at least make the case for Shanker for governor. Someone with the persuasive powers and political acuity of, say, an Albert Shanker.

6

⟫ Anatomy of a Teachers' Strike

IT WAS THE EVENING of Day One of the Newark teachers' strike, February 2, 1970. Nearly 75 percent of the city's 3,800 teachers refused to show up for class. But it had been a peaceful day. Le Roi Jones, a vocal union opponent and the city's contribution to culture and racial understanding (Philip Roth only writes about Newark, he doesn't live there anymore and it's Allen's father, Louis Ginsberg, who teaches poetry at the city's Rutgers University campus), had frightened a few pickets at one of the schools by showing up with a number of *Simbas* ("young lions"), his elite paramilitary guard. But there had been no violence, and a moderate number of black teachers had gone out with the white teachers. Threats of reprisals from a number of "black community leaders" had not materialized.

All in all, it was going well, thought Robert Bates as he circled aimlessly in the massive hallways of the city's school-board offices. He swung his hands out and clapped them together in an effort to show nonchalance, which only betrayed the intensity of his excitement about the strike. As he waited for the school-board's negotiating team, he said he felt grateful that the responsibility of actually running the strike was not his but that of Larry Birchette, a black rep from Philadelphia, called in as outside man to show the city's nearly 300,000 black and Puerto Rican residents that, despite anything they had heard about Albert Shanker, the A.F.T. was not a racist organization.

The large number of teachers who joined the strike and the then relative political impotence of those angry black leaders gave Bates time. He could, for the present, direct the course of negotiation. How long he had was an open question; inevitably, there would be confrontations. And, just as inevitably, there would be some form of court action taken against the teachers. But right now, anyway, it was Bates's ball game.

Off the hallway, the other five members of the union's negotiating committee, all local teachers or officers, reinforced one another's spirits with mention of how well the first day of the strike had gone. A number, new to the game of strikes, insisted the board would capitulate, work for a fast settlement and, in the hasty process, grant major concessions. Others warned that this board was not inexperienced, that it could be, indeed, a long strike.

Suddenly, the creaky door of the building's automatic elevator opened and the board members, on average perhaps twenty years older than the teachers' committee, stepped out, turned and walked toward the meeting room. The union teachers scrambled to their places on one side of a long table, quickly opening up their loose-leaf binders, which contained the union's 320 contract demands. The board members were in an oddly casual mood, smiling a greeting to the teachers. The union representatives, mindful of what they had been told about strict discipline, did not return the greetings. After they had filed into the room, Bates came in, grim-faced, and took his place in the center of the union side.

Bates opened the black binder, carefully paged through a section and with the routine solemnity of a priest ready to read that Sunday's Epistle, began. "Now, gentlemen, if I re-call, we were discussing—"

"Pardon me for interrupting, Mr. Bates." It was Harold Ashby, the school-board president, a tall, light-skinned black man who was, for reasons he would not explain, attempting to grow a Malcolm X goatee. Ashby was a successful lawyer and chairman of the state parole board. "But you seem to have the intention of not mentioning the fact that your teachers are engaged in an illegal strike. Perhaps you are not aware."

"I certainly am aware of that," Bates answered, forcing a sign of impatience. "That's why I am here. I am one of the A.F.T.'s best negotiators. I was sent here to end this strike as quickly as possible through good-faith collective bargaining. Now can we get on?" Ashby said nothing more. Bates returned to his book of demands and began reading the union's position. The board members appeared to pay little attention.

Bates was interrupted again. "I hate to interrupt your beautiful reading of that very fine document," said a leathery but cheerful-looking old man. It was Jacob Fox, a lawyer who had retired from service as the school-board's attorney shortly after successfully prosecuting contempt charges against teachers involved in a 1966 strike.

"Yes, I'm afraid to interrupt but I think something dreadful has happened," Fox said, squinting at the union member across from him. The teacher sat rigid, eyes caged, expressionless. "I believe this man is dead." The board members laughed; Bates scowled.

"Mr. Fox, can we please continue?"

"Sure, sure, Mr. Bates, but you know, I've never seen a more serious bunch of young people." He stared again, at each member of the union local. "You know, Harold," he elbowed Ashby, "I do not believe they *are* breathing." Ashby emitted an awkward, brief laugh. "Come on, boys and girls, it's not the end of the world. Let's have a little life. Right,

Harold? After all, we should all keep our sense of humor."
Harold said nothing.

Bates rapped at the table with his fingers, whistling faintly through his teeth. Fox drolled on:

"Look there's humor in everything—even this." He picked up his copy of the union demands and dropped it on the table. "For example, let's see . . . oh, this one. 'Every teacher shall receive a two-week leave of absence with pay for the purposes of a honeymoon.' Fox leered with mock lechery at the union's only female negotiator, Mrs. Carole Graves, the local union president. "Hey, honey, you want we should buy you the hot-water bottle, too?"

Bates sprang to his feet. The union negotiators held at first, but then one broke up and chuckled, a severe breach of discipline.

"A-ha!" Fox pounced on him. "You *are* alive!"

Bates ignored the breakdown in decorum by the union teacher. Only the chief negotiator, the A.F.T. man, was permitted to smile at an adversary's joke. Casualness breeds chumminess; chumminess makes for breaks in the union's lines. It is dangerous. A sign of weakness.

"Gentlemen, let me refresh your memory. This city is on the brink of catastrophe. Nearly eighty thousand innocent children have been taken away from their teachers because of the stupidity of this board . . ." And on and on went Bates in a variation of the standard A.F.T. crisis speech. His short stature undermined his attempt to tower over the proceedings, but he made up for it with often bitter sarcasm. Each A.F.T. warrior finds his best style and lives it. Bates cannot be imposing. With his boyish moon face and freckles, he really cannot intimidate school boards. He has decided to irritate them. Bates is snotty. "So," he concluded, "I am wasting my valuable time here trying to prevent a major crisis in this city. That's the only reason I agreed to be sent to this cesspool of a city."

"This *what?*" It was apparent from the tone of anger that

Bates had drawn blood. It came from Dr. E. Wyman Garrett, one of the city's wealthiest physicians, a gynecologist, a young black man from the city who made good by working his way through college on a basketball scholarship. He is fiercely egoistic, fashionably militant.

"You, Mr. Bates, are talking about my city, my home." Bates thrust his hands into his pants pocket and stared at the ceiling like a petulant child listening to a lecture from an irrelevant grandparent. That drew more blood.

"Mr. Bates," Garrett's words were distinctive, each punctuated with an increasing sense of anger, "Mr. Bates, I'm going to kick your butt."

Bates did not act alarmed. He closed his binder, tied up his loosened necktie and announced that the union was leaving. "I expected amateurs. But I did not expect threats of violence." He led his team out of the room. Fox smiled broadly at Garrett's failure to see his opposite number's irritating arrogance as a bargaining technique. Garrett called after the teachers: "Know where you're staying, Mr. Bates, gonna get you." The door slammed behind the last teacher. Fox laughed huskily. Garrett pounded his fists in anger. Ashby said, "Better call Victor and tell him to go ahead."

Victor De Filippo is the school-board's attorney, a small slight man with an incongruous pomp of a hairdo. He wears metal taps on the bottom of his pointed black shoes which click purposefully as he walks on the stone floors of the board building's hallways. De Filippo is an effective legal technician who is almost proud of his distaste for the purely theoretical implications of educational law. He is a believer in legal overkill, whether it is in negotiating construction contracts or attempting to "kill" a strike. Weeks before the strike, Victor De Filippo assiduously worked on a legal counterattack. It was a battle plan which, he was confident, would make him the Curtis Le May among school-board attorneys. "I told the board if they let me go, I'm going to do the job the right way, my way," De Filippo said with the deadened nasality of a Newark (Noo-wuk) accent, "and if I do it my way, it's going to be almost impossible to stop. That's the only way."

When the initial attempts to end the walkout through negotiation degenerated into what amounted to playing the dirty dozens, Victor De Filippo's attack was unleashed. That decision provided the country with an excellent example of what happens when a school board decides to "let the courts handle it." The Newark school board's legal attack against the A.F.T. surpassed anything the Loeb board in Chicago could have contemplated in 1916. More than two hundred teachers were arrested, including David Selden, the A.F.T. president. The city was treated to a spectacle of county sheriffs, in their cowboylike uniforms, chasing teachers through downtown Newark traffic, arresting them, dragging them back through the traffic and loading them into paddy-wagons. Passers-by were arrested. Guerrilla warfare between the sheriff's deputies (controlled by Republican Ralph D'Ambola) and the city police (controlled by Democrat Hugh J. Addonizio) broke out after De Filippo's attack could not be stopped when the mayor demanded it. Even the local chapter of the American Civil Liberties Union, which regularly expressed concern about the lack of participation granted to community groups because of the teachers' union, denounced the school board, charging it with using "the worst forms of antilabor repression since the 1930's."

Not that the leaders of the strike, local or national, acted with reason or were motivated by a genuine concern for the educational welfare of the residents of one of the nation's most neglected cities. No, this was a wartime condition. The A.F.T. needed Newark badly in order to complete its list of unionized major American cities. The A.F.T. needed Newark in order to strengthen its hand in the continuing merger negotiations with the National Education Association. The state Federation needed Newark because, of nearly six hundred school districts in the state, only four contained A.F.T.

locals with bargaining-agent rights. The A.F.T. warriors needed a big victory in Newark to show that they meant to work hard for teachers in a way which might not be possible if Selden were allowed to go through with the merger some of the warriors so vehemently detested. No antistrike court actions would stop them; Newark was too important a pawn in the game.

The "militant corps," an A.F.T. warrior's dream, had prepared the area for battle. These young, fiercely loyal local union teachers played diligently on the fears of the city's white teachers that their job security was endangered unless a strong contract could be obtained. Representatives from the union local developed quiet "understandings" with Anthony Imperiale, the law-and-order vigilante who managed to become a councilman at large, and Imperiale's followers, the young toughs who patrolled the streets of the city's black section at night, wearing green uniforms with black helmets, sniggering at the name they gave their nightly forays—"jungle patrols." The local leaders were even cynical enough to arrange the election of a black woman, Mrs. Carole Graves, as union president. But she was not allowed to talk informally with the press and all her presentations in public were carefully written by other union members. "Carole is a very bright and sincere girl," said a vice-president of the local who, through the strike, dressed in black and wore almost opaque sunglasses, "but she can get us into a lot of trouble by not knowing when to keep her mouth shut." Other local leaders were given the task of convincing "Tony's boys," the white teachers who lived and worked in Newark's predominantly Italian North Ward, that "the blacks wouldn't get everything" because of the election of Mrs. Graves. The national A.F.T. leadership did not condone the cynical and, possibly, dangerous behavior of its local people; but then it did not condemn it, either. The national warriors simply do not care.

Reason and compassion had long been scarce in Newark.

As the city entered the last third of the century, it was a mad social scientist's dream of how miserable life can be in urban America. It had the highest venereal-disease rate, the highest tuberculosis rate, the highest infant-mortality rate of any city its size. The crime rate was so bad that even junkies were nervous about facing the streets at night. Very few white people alive today have ever seen any but a few of those streets after dark. The city, and particularly the school system, were victims of the most incredible insensitivity. During a twenty-five-year period which ended in the mid-1960's, not one new school was constructed in the city. Local school-board officials had to return federal school funds because of serious questions of management. Many schools were nearly a century old, some older. Children had been bitten by rats in the schools, which provided not even temporary escape from the impossibility of being a child in Newark. Reading failure was almost 100 percent; the dropout rate, nearly 50 percent. Books, classroom space and teaching materials were scarce and often nonexistent. The editor of a prestigious educational magazine called the Newark school system "the anus of the educational universe," and he meant it.

The local government hardly recognized that there was a school system at all, unless it could be abused in some way or unless the city tax rate could be lowered by cutting back the educational budget. In 1967, Mayor Addonizio attempted to place an old political friend in the position of school-board secretary. (Both were subsequently indicted on a variety of charges.) A number of responsible black groups put forward the name of Wilbur Parker, a brilliant man and the state's first black C.P.A. Addonizio persisted; so did the blacks. The school board's hearings into the appointment became nightmarish marathons of threats and recrimination. "If the Mayor gets his way," one young black shouted at a school-board meeting, "blood will flow in the streets of Newark within six weeks." The mayor relented; the incumbent school-board secretary canceled his retirement and agreed to continue. But it was too late. Within six weeks, blood, along with armored personnel carriers, did run in the streets of Newark. And the riot began on the night that Mayor Addonizio told a nation-wide television news show that "we have no racial problem in Newark."

By the end of the decade, the conditions of the Newark schools were worse, not better. The lessons offered by the July, 1967, uprising had been ignored or forgotten. The desperation of parents who knew that schooling in Newark was virtually a cruel waste of time was translated into the creation of small but virulent parents' groups which demanded more and more some redress from the failing school system. The school board itself, when it was aware of smoldering problems, was extremely reluctant to intervene. Schools Superintendent Franklyn Titus was either never told by his subordinates about serious local problems (his secretary handles much of the schools' business by telephone) or too exhausted physically to do much about them. But local black parents understood little about the traditional reluctance of school boards to become actively involved in the problems of an individual school and could easily be excused for their lack of sympathy for the personal problems of the school superintendent. Frustration and rage often led to a sit-in or other form of demonstration, aimed against a local teacher or principal, usually white. The board would then finally act in a most indelicate way, by either firing or ordering the involuntary transfer of the teacher or principal.

This haphazard personnel policy was bound to cause trouble with the teachers, the parents, or both. The teachers, then represented by a local affiliate of the National Education Association, remained curiously quiet as a score or more of their number lost their positions. Intimidation became the accepted mode of problem solving. Finally, in the spring of 1968, a minor fight in one of the city's two integrated high schools (of the other six, one is all-white and five are all-black) erupted into a citywide confrontation between black and white youngsters. Le Roi Jones stepped forward for the blacks, organizing the more militant young people into shock forces; Imperiale championed the white youngsters, promising to back them with his armed might. Education in the high schools ground to a halt. Renewed violence erupted in a city which had passed through several bad nights after the murder of Martin Luther King, Jr. And everyone in the city began to think about July of 1967. Even the school board.

It was drastic-solution time again for the schools. That meant calling in Victor De Filippo. Within a few weeks, De Filippo came up with a plan for saving the schools in September. It was simple. "A big complaint then was that, in a city with nearly 75 percent black and Puerto Rican, there was not one black principal. That was a big problem, right?" True. The testing procedures employed to select principals militated against the selection of minority-group members. More black faces in the school offices was a demand of the Black Student Council, which had formed under Jones's guidance; it was one of the few demands which met with sympathy from black parents. "So the solution is, appoint black principals, right?" True. But there was one problem. The promotion procedures had been worked out through negotiation with the local teachers' association. Changing them would necessitate a reopening of negotiation; no solution, if one was ever found, could be developed by September. De Filippo, as expected, urged overkill. In August, the school board announced a unilateral cancellation of its contract with the teachers' association, scrapped the selection procedure and arbitrarily appointed eleven black principals and vice-principals. "It was a courageous act," declared De Filippo, who already had prepared for the expected lawsuits, all of which were, by 1971, won by the school board.

The decision put the teachers' association in an untenable position. It could not tolerate an arbitrary rupture of its contractual position with the school board, yet it could hardly come out against black principals. For years, it had blamed the school board for its failure to be racially sensitive. Michael Limongello, the N.T.A. president, acted out the teachers' schizophrenic feelings by condemning and applauding the board action in two separate statements in the same week. Finally, Limongello convinced the N.T.A. leadership, despite strong membership objections, to do nothing about the violation of contract. Local union leaders, careful not to condemn the effort to integrate the supervisory staff, talked about how the union could have obtained for the teachers a contract which provided for the orderly promotion of teachers of all colors. Eventually, twelve teachers, all of them due for promotion under the contractual arrangement, appealed the decision. State Education Commissioner Dr. Carl Marburger, refusing to touch it, sent it back to the school board. The state school board intervened and, in a rare display of conflict at the top, ordered Dr. Marburger to make a decision. The educator, the former Detroit schools superintendent, winced and found for the school board. "It was a hairline decision," he confessed. The teachers took it to court and lost. "The board has the authority to take such steps as it deemed necessary and proper to promote the educational welfare of the Newark school community," the judge said. In other words, when faced with the possibility of a riot, punt.

The Association was a shambles. It could not ensure the integrity of its own contract and, furthermore, its halfhearted resistance to the step angered both blacks and whites. The following year, the Association, once the strongest teacher group in the state and a model N.E.A. affiliate, seemed totally ineffective when it failed, after eleven months of negotiation, to come up with a contract for the 1969–70 school year. Newark's 3,800 teachers, frustrated by working under almost impossible conditions, frightened about the rise of black militancy in the schools, apprehensive about their future advancement, now faced life with the lowest salaries in the county.

The union leadership was giddy with expectation. A few days after school opened in September, Local 481 petitioned for a collective-bargaining election. For years, the group had been the repository for malcontents within the system. In the early 1950's, with a little help from the Newark newspapers, the Newark Teachers Union was discredited as a "commie" organization. Now, however, it had grown with the national union movement. A little of the glamour of Albert Shanker had rubbed off on the Newark group, primarily because Shanker was the main speaker at nearly every formal union function. The election was set for November 18.

Meanwhile, field representatives from the New Jersey Education Association, the state N.E.A. affiliate, were sent into Newark to find out how its local group could have behaved so miserably. The N.J.E.A., sensing that a loss of Newark meant problems throughout the state, suggested that Limongello would be happier maybe, as the N.T.A.'s recording secretary. The group's Senate failed to come up with enough votes to impeach the president, but did manage to pass a strike recommendation. Limongello refused to call a strike meeting. The Senate invited him to resign within twenty-four hours. He declined. Finally, the Senate gathered enough signatures to call an emergency strike meeting. Limongello contacted as many teachers as possible, told them he would refuse to recognize that the Senate had ever really asked for a strike meeting and, in any event, he would never lead a strike. On October 30, less than three weeks before its contest with the union, the Association held a strike meeting. About 250 teachers showed up. Seventeen voted to strike. The rest walked out. "Please don't go," pleaded the Association's vice-president who conducted the meeting.

Meanwhile, the A.F.T. brought in two veteran warriors, Joseph Cascella and Charles "Chuck" Richards to organize the campaign for the union. They had just engineered the Baltimore campaign, and Newark provided a brief opportunity for the men, both Jersey natives, to visit relatives. The local union, with the A.F.T.'s help, became everything to every teacher. To the older teachers, the union promised security and a chance for the long-sought promotion. To the young black teachers, the union leaders provided the promise—without mentioning the disadvantages—of M.E.S. To the young white teachers went the assurance that even if the student population was 110 percent black, they would not be fired every time a "community leader" cried for their skins. If the union obtained anything, it would be a contract with a grievance procedure that included binding arbitration. If the board tried to break that one, a labor arbitrator, not some education commissioner or do-good judge, would decide. That's for sure.

When the balloting was over, the union beat the Association by a four-to-one majority. It also defeated a challenge from an all-black organization, the Organization of Negro Educators (O.N.E.), which had campaigned on a no-strike pledge. Mrs. Graves showed up at the State Office Building, where the votes were being counted, and passed out a written statement saying the victory was a mandate from the teachers to the union "to do everything in its power to improve education in Newark." "Does that mean strike?" she was asked. She appeared puzzled. She didn't notice one of the other union leaders frantically signaling her to stop talking. "Yeah, I guess so." There was a groan. "She didn't mean we were out to strike," said the teacher. "I didn't?" asked Mrs. Graves innocently. (By 1971, however, Mrs. Graves had assumed full control of her union.)

Within a week, Bates arrived in Newark for the compilation of the package of demands. The city prepared for a strike when what was left of the N.T.A. contract expired February 1. (It already had "expired," but teachers like to stand on ceremony.) Victor De Filippo sat down and made preparations. Imperiale was given indirect assurances by the union that North Ward schools would not be affected and an indirect request for protection for the pretty white teachers who would have to serve picket duty in the black Central Ward. Le Roi Jones made preparations for the operation of the schools with a combination of Simbas, Young Lords, parents and black students from area colleges. Little thought was given to finding ways of averting the strike.

In late December, the Newark Teachers Union presented its package to the board. It was virtually a copy of the gift that Lindsay had handed Shanker earlier in the year, capped with a $10,000 starting salary—beginners' pay was then $6,700— and that all-important grievance procedure that ended in binding arbitration. Other important elements included a demand for the creation of twenty M.E.S. schools and a return to the old way of promoting principals. Rep Larry Birchette came in to handle the teachers and the press. David Mann, another black rep, Robert Strauber, the A.F.T.'s "tough guy," John Converse, the A.F.T.'s public-relations man, and Cascella, a native Newarker, made stops to help out with the strike organization. Telephone networks were set up. Picket signs were printed, complete with a blank space left for the words "On Strike" to be printed later. Bates kept the negotiations focused on important things, such as whether or not the union had the right to put up a bulletin board in each school. As a sign of good faith, he dropped the paid-two-week-honeymoon demand.

An A.F.T. local rarely goes into a strike without a firm assurance that it will be a strong one. That assurance usually can be obtained by some form of demonstration prior to the calling of a strike vote. Most school-board members view such demonstrations as a show of strength, an attempt to intimidate them. That's not true. It is a test of strength; if it fails, the outside man is given more time to develop prostrike sympathy. Four days before a scheduled mass meeting, the strike leadership brought out 1,800 Newark teachers for an afternoon of picketing in front of the school-board offices. It was bitter cold; Birchette monotonously reminded the teachers: "This is a solemn occasion. Do not talk." That was a test of discipline. The teachers passed the test; they refused to answer reporters' questions about the demonstration. The union leadership was pleased; they could call for a strike with little fear of breaks in the ranks. For now, anyway.

Strike and picket instructions were distributed over the telephone network two days before the scheduled meeting. That was a test of the network's efficiency. It also worked. Teachers left school on Friday, January 30, carrying the contents of their desks. That same day, local black leaders rented a sound truck and drove through Newark, warning as they passed by each school: "This is a warning to the Newark teachers. If you strike Monday, you better never show your ass around here again!" Le Roi Jones sent word to Superintendent Titus that his supporters would keep the schools open; he also sent word to the union, asking for a meeting.

That Sunday, the teachers voted to strike. The following morning, 848 of Newark's 3,773 teachers appeared for classes. It was Day One.

During the first days of the strike, there were a number of attempts to resume negotiation, but they all evaporated in name calling and Bates's planned petulance. There was no reason now to push for a hasty conclusion. Birchette was telling the teachers of how the board members refused to talk (not true) and how their man Bates was desperately trying to get good-faith negotiation started (also not true) and how the black community (whatever that is) backed the teachers 100 percent (decidedly not true). To prove his point, Birchette usually came up with a black woman who identified herself simply as a "parent" or a "member of the community" and, to the self-deluding cheers of the teachers, told them how only strong union action would save the schools. She usually neglected to mention, however, that she, too, was a member of the union, a teacher aide, who had a vested interest in the continuance and successful completion of the strike.

By the middle of the first week of the strike, an important agreement had been reached. Theodore Kheel would be accepted by both parties as a mediator. Kheel, who never accepts payment for his mediation services in public-employee walkouts, had been in Newark and other parts of New Jersey on teacher problems before and had gained deserved respect for the integrity of his actions. Birchette lauded Kheel as being a labor partisan (not true) and said that his arrival in Newark showed the board was beginning to weaken (also not true).

Despite the agreement on Kheel, however, Victor De Filippo was busily executing the board's plan against the teachers. The day before Kheel was scheduled to arrive in Newark, De Filippo spent four hours in the offices of Superior Court Judge Ward J. Herbert, who had issued the routine injunction against the strike several days earlier. But De Filippo felt the board was no longer interested in the routine prosecution of contempt charges.

That afternoon, a number of the board members remained in the offices of the schools superintendent, curious about exactly what De Filippo could do. None of them knew exactly. Suddenly, there was a sound of metal cleats clicking nervously against a stone floor.

"It's Victor," announced Dr. Michael Petti, the chairman of the board's negotiating committee. The other board members, who had been sitting at desks in the large office, listened for the cleats and wondered aloud about "what Victor's accomplished."

Victor burst through the door and, with a flourish, tossed a stack of papers on a huge counter. "Gentlemen, there it is." He stepped away from the counter and peered at the papers as if he were an artist attempting to gain perspective on a completed canvas. Petti stared at the papers but confessed he couldn't understand the language. "Victor, what have you done? What does it all mean?" The lawyer explained:

"With these orders, gentlemen, we can obtain the immediate arrest of the leaders of the strike. No need to return to court and ask for a contempt citation. These *are* contempt citations and orders for immediate arrest." He paused, looking for a reaction. "And—yes, there's more—and, I'm happy to say these orders require the Essex County prosecutor to handle the entire case. They'll have all the problems and we won't be forced into a position of agreeing to drop the case. We can't. We're not holding it."

De Filippo allowed the board members to look over the arrest orders briefly and then gathered them and put them carefully into a briefcase. He turned to leave. "Just a moment, Victor," Petti said. The lawyer turned, almost shocked that one of the laymen had a question. "Victor, there were only three names on those orders—Graves, Nicholas and Fiorito. What about the rest?" De Filippo was tolerant. "Mike," he said, "these things take time. The judge didn't want to sign any of them. There will be more. Just have patience."

He reached the door. "Victor, another question. When will these three be arrested?" Now the attorney was impatient. "I've already taken care of that," he replied curtly. "The sheriff's deputies are out right now, rounding them up. Good night." He left, obviously pleased with what he believed would be the effect of that parting statement. He had reason. The board members nodded their heads at each other in agreement and admiration of their attorney's clean efficiency. "He works fast," one said.

That evening, a score of county deputies fanned out through Essex County, searching for Mrs. Graves, Frank Fiorito, the local union's executive vice-president, and Donald Nicholas, a former state Federation president and now a member of the local's executive committee. They failed to find all three, even though one officer of the law came to the union's headquarters and asked Fiorito if he knew where Fiorito was. "No," said Fiorito, and the officer left. Nicholas' case was a particularly sad one, reflective of the A.F.T.'s absolute insistence on discipline. He was designated as a member of the local union's negotiating committee but made the mistake of chatting freely with a reporter about the union's strategy in the strike. The reporter used the material, although he was careful not to mention Nicholas' name. The A.F.T. organizers were infuriated about the use of the material and fired Nicholas from his position as a negotiator, thereby making him vulnerable to antistrike prosecution. It is an unwritten, though often violated, rule of teacher-strike negotiations that members of the bargaining committee are free from prosecution so they may continue to negotiate during the strike. Nicholas was later sentenced to sixty days in jail and fined $500. He accepted the consequences of his friendship with a reporter philosophically. "That's union discipline," he said.

On Thursday, the fourth day of the strike, Kheel kept an appointment with the union and board negotiators at a downtown Newark motor inn. While Kheel is a scrupulously fair mediator, the A.F.T. always is pleased to have him enter talks, for two reasons: Kheel treats such disputes as labor problems, not as acts of contempt against a political subdivision of the state, as a school board and the local press might believe; and, with so prominent a name, the local membership finds it easier to legitimize the union as a strong, viable organization. After all, would Kheel come in if the A.F.T. was not a powerful force? That Kheel takes no money for his services during a public-employee walkout is reasonable. Lately, Kheel provides very little service in these "small" strikes. It is usually his bright young assistant, Lewis B. Kaden, who does all the work.

Kheel met briefly with both sides and declared them ready for negotiations. Then he left. Kaden, a former aide to Robert F. Kennedy, managed to calm the union's anger at the immediate arrest orders and set an evening meeting. Two hours before the meeting was to take place, Victor De Filippo left the county courthouse with arrest orders for three more union leaders. The union negotiators refused to talk when they learned of the action. Kaden went back to New York.

Bates and Birchette then established the "dual reality" syndrome common to teachers' strikes. It is an approach based on the assumption that teachers, in a strike situation, are probably more paranoid than other workers in similar crises. This comes from the easy rhetoric employed—supervision is often repression, antilabor maneuvers are oppression, criticism is a threat to academic freedom, and so on. In such an atmosphere, it is relatively easy to convince teachers of almost anything, no matter what the contrary evidence. Both A.F.T. warriors knew that teachers, on an average, are uneasy about the prospects of arrest. They would object to the union negotiating with the board so long as De Filippo continued his battle plan. So Birchette simply told the membership that negotiations would not be resumed until the union received a pledge from the board that the arrests would stop. Bates, meanwhile, realizing that the union's excellent position of just a few days before was in jeopardy because of the arrests, continued to support any attempt to keep talking. When the city's two newspapers reported a resumption of negotiations, Birchette would deny it, reminding the teachers how the two "antilabor" papers were working with the board to split the union ranks. The A.F.T. reps received considerable help in promulgating the Big Lie from certain New York radio and television stations, which relied solely on Birchette for information about the strike. The teachers reassured themselves that he was telling the truth because, as one teacher said, "CBS wouldn't let Birchette get away with lying." It is something of a commentary on the education of teachers that they are so easily swayed and so reluctant to investigate the truth; the knowledge of that tendency always has been a powerful weapon in the A.F.T. arsenal.

Some comfort, perhaps, could be found in the realization by A.F.T. reps that such massive deception has a short life span. Bates knew that he could no longer afford to be the snotty, arrogant, big-time organizer; substantive negotiation had to begin. The first weekend of the strike there was a minor breakthrough: a number of the board members began to talk seriously about granting a grievance procedure with some form of arbitration as a last step. While Kaden pushed both sides to reach some form of accommodation that Sunday, the strike organizers prepared the first mass meeting since the walkout began. The speaker was Bayard Rustin, a black man who is

apparently sincere in his belief that the American labor movement, despite all the evidence to the contrary, is the hope and
salvation of the American black. His appearance was part of
the plan to make the A.F.T. look as racially progressive as
possible.

As Rustin approached the speaker's podium, a sharply
dressed man walked up to him and handed him a copy of the
antistrike order. It was all Rustin needed; the strike organizers
couldn't have been happier. Rustin stood before the 2,500
angry and apprehensive teachers, waved the order contemp-
tuously and said, "I now urge you to strike, to picket, to con-
gregate about for the purposes of striking . . ." Rustin took
the language from the order, deliberately defying the section
of the injunction which forbade even verbal support of the
strike. Any of the fears the teachers might have felt about
strong legal action were dissipated in their explosive cheers for
Rustin. Phase one of the board's attack on the teachers fell by
its own weight.

Back at his office two days later, De Filippo refused to
admit the failure of the "Rustin move." The purpose had been
to show that no one, not even a person as prominent as
Rustin, was immune from the wrath of the law. Instead, it had
put thousands of anonymous teachers shoulder to shoulder
with one of the big lights in the civil-rights movement. It also
had provided justification for those black teachers who opted
for the strike. But every good general learns to accept failures
and to pull together for the next battle; and the board attorney
was no exception.

"This will do it," he told a reporter at his office. "But I
can't tell you exactly what it is. But our efforts must now be
directed at opening up the schools. One of the major obstacles
to that is what? The pickets." He sat down, pulled his chair
closer to his desk, pounded a fist lightly on the table. "The
pickets. We will remove the pickets and allow for the free
entry and egress of the schools." *Mass arrests?* "I wouldn't like
to call them 'mass arrests.' " Even he was repulsed by the op-

pressive sound of the phrase. "We are *freeing* the schools."

The following day, nearly a hundred deputies, with their cowboy hats and their fearfully imposing (to white, middle-class teachers) black leather jackets, spread out through the city and arrested sixteen teachers as they picketed in front of the schools. Not a big haul, but big enough. Several hours later, De Filippo announced that he had obtained a court order requiring the union to turn over their books to the county prosecutor. And any money the union might have collected for use as bail. Money, as De Filippo was quick to realize, is the soft underbelly of the teacher-union movement.

It was time, Bates realized, for the "private deal" scenario. It is risky, of course, because it can lead to membership cries of "Sellout." But it often can be effective if, as in the case of Newark, open covenants openly arrived at were made impossible because of the constant legal pressure being applied by De Filippo and Birchette's persistent assurances to the teachers that the union would not deal with "a repressive board."

A few hours after the first mass arrest, a top state union leader arranged a secret meeting, between Fox and Bates. Mrs. Graves, whose arrest had made her a much more forceful leader, insisted on coming along. There was another participant, Robert Strauber, an A.F.T. warrior who was the staff's "tough guy." He is a taciturn Floridian who joined the A.F.T. after the National Education Association withdrew its support for the statewide Association strike in Florida. Although he was one of the more philosophical A.F.T. reps (he objects to the Big Lie approach and A.F.T. manipulation of minority groups), he also was one of the more fearless. He doesn't say much and when he does speak, he is usually profane.

Fox appeared punctually for the meeting and settled down for what he believed would be a long session. He dropped his folksy chatter and humor, his personal style as a negotiator. The subject was binding arbitration. Fox was convinced that allowing an outside arbitrator to settle questions of, say, promotion and transfer would tie the board's hands if it ever was faced with a crisis like the one in 1968. Bates knew that was precisely the reason why the union had to have it. The local Association had been destroyed by such a move and he could not afford that mistake. Several black community leaders warned the board against granting arbitration, knowing that it tied their hands if they wanted the removal of an unpopular teacher or principal. Le Roi Jones said the acceptance of binding arbitration would put the power of personnel decision making into the hands of the union. He was close to the truth; that is precisely what the union wanted.

Fox faced his union adversaries, his hands folded before him. "I'm prepared to recommend arbitration in some form. I believe we can allow it if a teacher feels he has been treated arbitrarily. I believe we can write the language in such a way as to provide the maximum protection for the teachers and still retain the board's statutory power over personnel decisions." He paused, waiting for an answer. Mrs. Graves looked at Bates. She was willing to go for it. Maybe. Bates wanted no part of it, but an outright rejection might cause a split with the local leadership. He said nothing. Strauber walked over from a corner of the hotel room, leaned over the table and peered into the old man's eyes. "Mr. Fox," Strauber said coldly, "you know what that means. That means the teachers still get fucked." Fox, genuinely shaken by what he felt to be a severe breach of respect for his position, silently gathered his papers together and left.

Strauber had performed a service for Bates. He put an end to any possibility that the strike might be settled through such a secret meeting, thereby limiting the chances that the local Newark leadership would, as the local New Orleans people had done, settle "under the A.F.T.," without the national's permission. Confrontations would now be frontal attacks, over the table, with a mediator. There would be no cry of sellout. It was Strauber's way, and now it would have to be the Newark local's way.

The move put the A.F.T. actions in Newark on a different level. Bates realized that he needed more help; he needed a national focus on the strike in order to embarrass public officials in the state, most importantly the newly elected Governor William T. Cahill, who had refused to intervene in any way. Within hours, the entire national A.F.T. staff set up temporary quarters in Newark. Joseph Cascella, the A.F.T.'s most imaginative gimmick man and a skilled across-the-table negotiator, was sent in to shore up Birchette's faltering public-relations efforts. Len Lewis, the A.F.T.'s civil-rights coordinator, flew in, along with George Brickhouse, national director of federations; John Schmid, national state federations director; David Elsila and Pat Strandt, the A.F.T.'s editorial specialists (who also reflect far-left opinion in the A.F.T., and are used to garnering supporters among local radical groups); national reps David Mann and Vinnie Russell; and the chieftain among A.F.T. warriors, national organization coordinator James Mundy. This movement of A.F.T. artillery served several purposes beyond providing support for Bates. The top officials were there to advise President Selden. They also were there to prevent any break in rank-and-file support for the strike. That was a real danger; now more than a third of the teachers were returning to school. And it was necessary to bring in almost the entire staff because, at that time, members of the national staff were busily engaged in planning the Los Angeles strike and they had to remain together. A.F.T. strategy in that ill-fated walkout was worked out at the bar at Newark's Holiday Inn.

The need for the big guns became ever more apparent that evening when Seymour Cohen, the Newark local's dapper and sardonic attorney, greeted the A.F.T. staff members at dinner. "Gentlemen," he quipped, "I'd say you needed a lawyer." Cohen had spent the day trying to quash the order for the Newark local to surrender its records and its cash. He also investigated rumors that the county prosecutor was about to convene a grand jury to build a case for criminal conspiracy against Birchette and the local strike leaders; the rumors were true.

Cohen was particularly sour that night and lapsed into orations, comparing the De Filippo attack with the nationwide police conspiracy against the Black Panther Party. Bates, essentially apolitical as any good soldier should be, demanded to know what had happened. It seemed, Cohen explained, that Joseph Weintraub, Chief Justice of the New Jersey Supreme Court, was taking the defiance of the antistrike injunction very seriously. "He thinks it's an attack upon the state," Cohen lamented. "You know, you guys are just like the S.D.S. or something." The lawyer leaned back, placing a firm grip on a drink. "If I were you, I'd prepare a lot of your people for jail."

That night, the A.F.T. machinery began to roll. Cascella, aware that the board was getting all the press because of its hard antilabor line, stressed the need for "something dramatic, something big." He contacted state A.F.L.–C.I.O. leaders and arranged a massive march through downtown Newark for Friday, February 13. He needed political support. The local union's indirect links to Imperiale, then an announced candidate for mayor, were activated. The North Ward schools would be allowed to open; what could be obtained in return? The answer came back: Imperiale, the champion of law and order, would publicly support the teachers. Good. Now what about Le Roi Jones? Cascella knew he couldn't gain Jones's support—he didn't really want it. But he arranged a meeting with the black playwright anyway, "just to investigate the possibilities." Finally, Cascella knew, as most A.F.T. reps realize, that in a mayor-appointed school board, the power rests not with the board but with the mayor. State labor leaders close to the power in the Democratic party were enlisted to help pressure Addonizio into intervening. Meanwhile, there was no sense negotiating now.

Within hours, things began to click. Imperiale came through, and pickets were removed from North Ward schools.

State labor leaders told Addonizio, then under indictment for extortion, bribery and tax evasion, that Republican Governor Cahill was planning a dramatic entry into the Newark crisis. If the governor settled the strike, Addonizio was reminded, the city's chief executive would look even more like a loser in the May election. In fact, Cahill wanted no part of the strike. But the tactic worked; the mayor pledged to enter the negotiations on the weekend. Meanwhile, he would use whatever influence he had with the Republican sheriff to stop the arrests.

The following evening, Cascella sent black union members and A.F.T. staffers to "community meetings." He himself arranged a secret meeting with Jones. Jones wanted an entente with the union, a solid front against a school board that the black artist had fought for years. What was in it for the union? Cascella asked. Community support, Jones replied. Let's talk about it, Cascella answered. Jones, as Cascella found out that night, is one of the most widely misunderstood black activists in the nation. While much of his artistic work reflects almost uncontrolled rage against and hatred for the white man—"smash their jelly-white faces" is a favorite phrase—Jones himself is a pragmatic politician. In the past, he had made an alliance with a supposed archenemy, Tony Imperiale, to keep the white man's "jungle patrols" and Jones's Simbas from killing each other, and many innocent residents along with them. During the strike, he activated a well-oiled organization—the New Ark Community Coalition —to provide substitute teachers for the schools. The school board needed the schools opened in order to prove an actual strike in court, and Jones obliged. At the same time, Jones was working on developing an organization which would ensure the election of black city engineer Kenneth Gibson to the mayoralty; he made alliances with the most unlikely powers in the city—business, the press, the university administrators. Now he felt a need for an alliance with the union. He told Cascella that the presence of Jones's allies in the schools proved that neighborhood residents could, in fact, provide community control. The problem now was not how the community and the union would struggle for power, but how that power could be torn from the board.

What price this community support? Cascella asked. The union would have to provide for popular (read "black") participation in personnel policies. It would have to recognize the community as an equal partner in operating the schools. No deal, Cascella answered. The A.F.T. rep knew, again from the New Orleans experience, how unreliable was community support. The people would rise up against the teachers, Jones warned; Cascella scoffed and challenged the black man to provide evidence. Jones, who knew about Friday's demonstration, declared "thousands" of black parents and young people would be mobilized to counter the labor rally. Cascella expressed doubt, but promised he would wait and see. The meeting ended. The following day, there were fewer than one hundred counterpickets at the City Hall rally—and more than one thousand strike supporters. One major union fear, that of Jones's sway over the city's black parents, was temporarily put to rest.

The rally began peacefully enough, with a march down Broad Street, the city's central avenue. Traffic was badly snarled, but traffic in Newark always is badly snarled. The marchers approached City Hall. On the building's steps, sixty uniformed sheriff's deputies waited. It had been organized very much like an antiwar rally. There would be a march. Those satisfied that they had expressed their dissent would be allowed to leave; those who felt "they must show their concern by individual acts of conscience" would remain. The New Left leanings of some of the A.F.T. staffers were evident in the composition of the march. Representatives from local peace groups and radical organizations were in the ranks.

A crowd of only about two hundred gathered at City Hall after the march. Birchette, who had led the walk, ducked into the doorway of a nearby restaurant. Bates and a number of other A.F.T. staffers waited there. They watched and waited for the "militant corps" to do its collective thing. A few of the younger teachers shouted "Off the Pigs" to the deputies. The crowd chanted "Good-bye, Huey" in monotonous sing-song. Hugh P. Francis, a young assistant county prosecutor and the son of a state supreme court judge, ordered a copy of the antistrike injunction read to the crowd over a megaphone. The deputy had difficulty reading the legal language. The crowd laughed in derision. Meanwhile, the city police were not cooperating. Traffic had not been rerouted, and the noise of the crowd was combined with the blaring of horns; it was deafening. Francis paced nervously on the lawn of the gray Classical Revival Municipal Building. The crowd would not disperse.

"Give them five minutes and then go in after them. Arrest everybody with a sign," he told Sheriff D'Ambola. Moments later, waves of deputies spread out into the crowd, arresting everyone they could find, sign or no sign. They were called back; maybe a dozen persons had been arrested.

The crowd was smaller now, but more militant. "Pigs! Pigs! Pigs!" shouted a number of the younger male teachers. The deputies became enraged. A few broke ranks and began chasing individual teachers down the broad avenue, ducking in and around buses, past trucks, into alleyways, emerging moments later, dragging a teacher to a paddy-wagon. The deputies used no clubs. But they didn't use much discretion either. An accountant for a federal agency was making his way back to his office after lunch. To his surprise, he met his teacher-wife in the crowd. He was about to say, "What are you doing here?" when a large deputy grabbed the collar of his overcoat and dragged him into a paddy-wagon. Panic does strange things to a man. As he was being loaded into the wagon, he cried out: "It's not me, it's my wife you want. I'm not a teacher." The deputies didn't listen; but later, they arrested his wife too.

It was over within a half hour. Francis, apparently appalled by the sloppy handling of the arrests, ordered the deputies back to the sheriff's office. A small crowd still remained. Nearly fifty persons had been arrested, including two vice-presidents of the state A.F.L.–C.I.O. and an unknown number of innocent passers-by. Addonizio was furious; the labor people blamed him. No labor support, come this May. The mayor ordered his police to ticket every illegally parked car owned by a deputy sheriff. Within a week, scores of tickets were handed out.

But the leadership of the A.F.T. was pleased. The union now had the offensive in terms of exposure. The major networks carried just enough film to show young, conservatively dressed female teachers being less than politely carried off into paddy-wagons. And finally, much to the relief of the local organizers, a young black woman had been arrested. Previously, the deputies arrested only white teachers, even though loyal black women union members asked to be arrested. Within two days, the A.F.T. put out an extra edition of *The American Teacher,* carrying a huge picture of the young woman being arrested and the headline, "Is New Jersey a Fascist State?" The story was incredible: it related how club-swinging deputies, heavily armed, brutally arrested young, innocent teachers. (The deputies were clumsy and undisciplined, but hardly brutal.) But the article was believed. Contributions from locals throughout the country poured in. The Newark strike was now a national teachers' cause. Governor Cahill, vacationing in the Virgin Islands, was picketed by teachers there. Meanwhile, Bates and Mundy planned their approach to resumed negotiation. This time the mayor would be there and the A.F.T. warriors would go in for a quick attempt at settlement. But the union people made a serious mistake in judgment; they assumed that Addonizio wanted a quick settlement. He did. But they also assumed that the mayor was the power behind the board, that he could pressure his appointees into settling. This was a mistake. Bates and Mundy badly underestimated how complete was the erosion of Addonizio's power base. The mayor once had been one of the most powerful Democrats in the state. He was a strong and liberal Congressman in the 1950's. His sweep to the mayoralty in 1962 marked him as a man who might very well succeed Richard J. Hughes as governor. But he badly botched the 1967 disorders, turning the city over to state military control practically within hours of a statement he had made on television assuring the people of the nation that the city had no racial problems. Despite his liberal distribution of patronage positions to prominent city Negroes, he angered many in the black community by attempts at blocking the appointment of a bright black accountant to the position of school-board secretary. His insistence on the construction of a medical school in the heart of the city's black district brought angry charges that he was eliminating the growing black voter registration. His support among working-class Italian-Americans disappeared in the support given to vigilante Imperiale. His support among the few remaining middle- and upper-class whites in the city evaporated when, in late December of 1969, he was indicted by a Federal grand jury for bribery, extortion and tax evasion. Now it was February of 1970. The thought that he could influence anyone was tragically laughable. Within months, he would lose his position to Kenneth Gibson; everyone—everyone except the A.F.T. people—knew it.

Negotiation was to begin Monday, February 16. The mayor was delayed reaching the negotiating sessions because of a Board of School Estimate meeting gathered to determine the schools' 1970–71 budget. The board consisted of the mayor, two school-board members—Dr. Garrett and Mrs. Gladys Churchman (both Negro)—and two councilmen—Imperiale and Louis Turco, a strong Addonizio supporter. Addonizio sought to put the burden of paying for the eventual settlement on the state by refusing to fund fully the school system. (It also was a good way to keep from voting for a certain tax increase in an election year.) But Dr. Garrett and Mrs.

Churchman voted against it, and Imperiale refused to show up. The beefy white-power advocate knew he could not vote against a budget cut because he too was running for mayor; he also could not vote for a budget cut, because he had pledged his unlikely allies, the city's teachers, to support full funding for salaries. The board was deadlocked; the two board members refused to vote an adjournment. Dr. Garrett ordered enough "good Southern-fried chicken" to distribute among the audience at the meeting-turned-circus, and Addonizio announced he had asked "the state police, the Newark police and Mr. Imperiale's personal police force" to find the missing councilman, whom he referred to as "that jerk." Garrett wandered about the City Council chambers, passing out the chicken, telling how he would really like to kick "Mr. Bates's butt." "I don't hate white folks," he would say in mock jive, "but I sure do hate that Mr. Bates." After six hours, Imperiale showed up but refused to vote. "I won't do anything," he said with admirable candor, "that's going to destroy me." Addonizio, once powerful enough to direct the fate of the New Jersey Democratic organization, could not control a Board of Estimate meeting. The meeting adjourned, without action, and Addonizio left for the negotiation meeting.

Bates and Mundy were waiting. When the mayor arrived, they asked for a private meeting. Addonizio agreed. Bates opened the encounter with an assurance that the problems were not severe, that "the board just needed a little talking to." He outlined the areas of disagreement and asked the mayor for a commitment on a board majority for the union's position. It would be simple.

"But I can't do that," the mayor replied, with an incredulous grin.

Bates brushed off the objections and repeated his request. Surely, he said, the mayor had some influence on the board, enough to ensure passage of items such as binding arbitration and—

"I'm being quite sincere, gentlemen, I can't promise you anything."

Mundy looked angrily at Bates, bewildered at the failure of his warrior to understand the local political scene. Bates shot a scornful look at one of the local union members, obviously annoyed that he hadn't been told of the mayor's impotence.

"I can't believe that," Bates said, somehow looking for a graceful way out. Addonizio threw up his hands and got up to walk out. One of his aides pulled Bates over to the side. "It's true," was all he said. Bates and Mundy put together their entire negotiating team and walked out. The next day, Birchette told the radio and television reporters that the mayor had reneged on a deal which might have brought a quick end to the strike. Open season on a fallen politico means precisely that.

Meanwhile, the A.F.T.'s public-relations campaign continued. The following morning, David Selden showed up outside a Newark school, carrying a picket sign. (Earlier in the strike, this particular school had been made safe for union picketing when Imperiale and his toughs managed to clear it of some Young Lords who were providing volunteer instruction.) Local union leaders had given twenty-four hours' notice of Selden's intent to defy the injunction. The officers arrived, but Selden was late. "Please, wait," asked one of the local's militant corps. "I know he'll be here." The officers stayed, chatting the while with some of the more attractive pickets. Finally Selden arrived, and within minutes he was arrested. He had not arranged it, he told reporters.

Back at the A.F.T.'s temporary headquarters, Bates was grim. He picked at his lunch and ordered another drink while he complained about the local leadership and its failure to inform him about Addonizio's position. George Brickhouse, a bear-like black union veteran, joined the table. He was grinning broadly; he had just left Selden at the county jail.

"What news from our fearless leader?" asked Bates.

"You might be happy to hear Selden's refused bail," Brickhouse said, chuckling. "He's in for the duration. He won't come out until we settle."

Bates laughed grimly. "Goodbye, David."

Cascella flashed a broad grin. "Here's something to think about," he said. "What if every member of the local insists on going to jail with Selden—wouldn't it be great . . ." Not for nothing is the A.F.T.'s Cascella considered the organization's best gimmick man.

Meanwhile, the board had something like that in mind. After the union's walkout on negotiation, the legal attack had been resumed. Now more than two hundred teachers were arrested. In a few days, Frank Fiorito, one of the first to be picked up, would be sentenced. The time was right for the *coup de grâce,* a move which its members believed would bring all the teachers back to work by Monday, break the back of the strike and discredit the A.F.T. in the eyes of the teachers. The next step, simply and unbelievably, was the arrest of teachers who did not show up at work, the arrest of teachers in their homes. The county prosecutor was then compiling the names and addresses of the striking teachers.

But the county prosecutor never got to use that ultimate weapon. A majority of board members, apparently sickened by the seemingly endless procession of arrests, faced with a possible rebellion by high-school students who, as each day passed by, saw already slim opportunities of making it to college fade, and warned by state education authorities that, despite the efforts of Jones and company, the schools might be considered formally closed and therefore ineligible for continued state aid, suddenly reversed themselves and sued for peace. Through mediator Kaden, who was in New York awaiting the most advantageous time to return, the board asked the union what were its conditions for a resumption of intensive bargaining. The answer: no more arrests. The board replied that it could not stop the arrests of pickets, but indicated its willingness to try to stop the legal onslaught. Bates, now for the first time in two weeks in some kind of tenable bargaining position, said the union would return to the table if it could receive a commitment on binding arbitration and the removal of Fox, still strong in his opposition to outside arbitration, from the board's negotiating committee.

Early on the morning of Friday, February 20, a badly divided school board voted to accept the conditions. Fox, the state's foremost expert on school law and a long-respected public servant in Newark, was fired. De Filippo was ordered away from the nearly month-long war of attrition against the city's teaching staff and told to attend the planned negotiation as the board's legal adviser. For the Newark local, the board decision came just in time. A small group of local leaders was privately urging a graceful but unmistakable surrender. Later that day, Frank Fiorito, the second-highest local official, was sentenced to ninety days in jail. Bates knew that, had it not been for the renewed hopes of settlement through negotiation, the local might have settled under him.

The burden now fell on twenty-seven-year-old Lewis B. Kaden to settle. Beyond his standing as a labor mediator, Kaden felt a considerable motivation to bring the strike to a speedy conclusion. Within a matter of weeks, he would begin a Congressional campaign in New Jersey's 15th Congressional District. Although it was his home territory, he was relatively unknown. The settlement of the state's longest and most bitter strike could not help but project him into statewide prominence as a competent and gifted attorney.

Kaden returned to the Newark debacle on his terms. He was to be in charge, arranging the selection of hotel rooms for both sides, and even finding a suite for a group of angry black parents and ministers who wanted to be close enough to the negotiation to prevent a feared sellout by the board. He provided a room for the news media and arranged for regular briefing both for the reporters and for the community representatives. Like an experienced handler of men inflamed

by controversy, he glided in and out of board and union caucus rooms, lecturing men much his senior in age and experience about the necessity to keep order both in their utterances
and in their positions. Kaden tolerated the overprotectiveness
of the police guard that Addonizio slapped around the hotel
and in the hallway outside his room, the passionate rudeness
of the blacks, the petulance and arrogance of the union negotiators, the outright ignorance of labor practices of the board.
Lewis B. Kaden, the son of a Perth Amboy trucker, provided
the first bit of class the Newark school system had seen in a
month. And longer.

Kaden was graduated from Harvard Law School in 1967,
served as an aide to United States Senator Harrison A. Williams and as an adviser on manpower matters to Senator
Robert F. Kennedy. At the age of twenty, Kaden worked for
the State Department, traveling throughout the campuses of
Britain, lecturing fellow students on the intricacies of American politics. After Kennedy was assassinated, Kaden wrote a
manual for civil-rights lawyers, participated in a city-planning
project in Washington, D.C., and coauthored a book with his
future partner, Theodore Kheel. Kheel asked Kaden to stay
with him as a fellow mediator in November of 1968. With
only two or three weeks of instruction from his famed senior
associate, Kaden settled the Jersey City teachers' strike of
1969 in two days. From there, he became immersed in labor
and social problems ranging from a Teamsters' pay dispute
to a confrontation between the Young Lords and a conservative Puerto Rican church. A number of Newark's board members scoffed at the young man's lack of experience. But Kaden
made up for it with a host of experiences.

None of the three sides in the dispute intended to make the
mediation effort an easy one. Bates and Cascella took over
the negotiations for the strikers; local union representatives
were delegated to little more than clerical chores. The two
A.F.T. reps casually jettisoned the union demands which had
made the local's claim of concern for educational reform

credible—smaller classes, more academic specialists, increased social and psychiatric services, a rational procedure for the distribution of supplies. They concentrated on those items which enhanced the union's struggle for control over operations—personnel policies, grievance procedure, arbitration. If this was to be the crucial battle of the war, then the soldiers wanted a concentrated frontal assault. The board, acting like an inept victim of a sharp home-improvement specialist, searched for ways to get out of its commitment to binding arbitration by insisting that only the language of the contract could be arbitrated and then trying to keep the language minimal and general. The score of self-appointed community representatives openly vowed to slow down the procedures, fearing that a hasty solution would lock out any future hopes for community control of school operations.

Kaden soon discovered the conventional rules of collective bargaining simply did not work in such a volatile and confused situation. He was faced constantly with sheer stupidity and unashamed arrogance. Some board members, fearful of future retaliation, often took their orders from the caucus of community representatives lodged several floors below their suite. In at least one instance, such behavior almost broke the delicate balance that kept the two sides together.

The two sides could not agree on what constituted the factors that would be used to determine appointments and transfers of personnel. The union insisted on qualifications, seniority and preference of the teacher; the board, remembering what it felt it had to do in 1968, insisted on integration of the staff, educational sensitivity and community interests. Both parties left the language up to Kaden, who wrote that personnel decisions will be based on "qualifications, seniority, preference of the applicant, integration of staff and the welfare of the children in the community." The language was accepted. But then Ashby told the third party to the confusion of the new wording; they would not accept it. Ashby pledged to change it, but never spoke of the pledge to Kaden, the union or his colleagues. When board secretaries transcribed the clause, the word "in" in the phrase "the welfare of the children in the community" was changed to "and." The new wording read: "the welfare of the children and the community." No one could account for the mysterious change, but the board refused to put "in" back.

Bates and Cascella were enraged. Cascella grabbed for a telephone, called the city's two newspapers, the major wire services and metropolitan radio and television stations to announce that the board had broken off the talks after it had been caught toying with already agreed-upon language. Kaden counseled moderation, but the A.F.T. reps would have none of it. Unless. Bates suggested a compromise—the union would accept the language if the board agreed to create one M.E.S. school in Newark by September. If not, the union would walk out. The board agreed. For the simple word "and," the city of Newark took on the $300,000 tab required to staff an M.E.S. school. More importantly, by allowing the M.E.S. school, it set the precedent for the union to control most of the administrative functions of that school.

Later in the five-day session, Kaden set up a precariously delicate mediation procedure that was aimed at arriving at the settlement of salary differences. The procedure forced both sides to make quick and irrevocable decisions. In the middle of crucial deliberations, a number of community representatives burst into Kaden's room and demanded an accounting. The young man, determined not to be driven to passion, straightened his tie, put on his jacket and spent an hour explaining the present status of negotiations. The chances for progress in the talks dissolved.

Just as Kaden, later the same morning, thought he had reached a middle ground in the salary dispute, he was again torpedoed. This time by the board. He was in the caucus room of the union, wearing Bates down, persuading him to accept a salary package that had been offered by the school board.

Suddenly, a local union member came to the door. "Addonizio is announcing a settlement."

Bates looked at Kaden angrily. "Lew, I'm tired of this bullshit. Get the hell out of here and tell the board they can keep their offer." He blamed Kaden for double-crossing him and the union side. But the mediator had not known of any settlement.

In the hallway of the floor above the union caucus room, reporters, photographers, board members, mayor's aides, police detectives and assorted community leaders awaited the announcement of the end of the strike. Addonizio, appearing exhausted but confident, waited for silence in order to make a statement announcing settlement. He began: "I've called you together to—"

"Hey, wait a minute, for Chris'sake." The voice was pained, impatient, angry. It was Bates. "Somebody told us something about a settlement." The rep was slurring. "Well, that's a lot of bullshit. The union is walking out and you people can talk all night to the reporters." Bates wheeled and disappeared down the hotel corridor. Several minutes later, the union checked out of the hotel and negotiations. It was 3 A.M., Tuesday, February 24.

Later, in his room, Kaden spoke of the absurdity of the evening and wondered whether he shouldn't quit. "Ted [Kheel] told me days ago to let the lot of them go to hell. And it's a strong temptation." Twenty-four hours later, he managed to reach a settlement. With a two-hour speech, he had convinced a majority of the board members to let him determine a final money figure for the settlement. Then he asked Bates to come up with an absolute rock-bottom figure for a settlement. The A.F.T. rep, more exhausted now than at any time in his career, forgot the figure that he and Cascella had determined. Kaden set it at $560,000. The two sides agreed; a settlement had been reached, twenty-three days after Day One.

Even the questionable honor of formally announcing an end to the strike was denied to Kaden. The two sides agreed to hold a joint press conference at 1 P.M., February 25, to make the announcement. But Selden, having languished in jail now for seven days, couldn't wait. He finally agreed to accept bond, traveled across town to the hotel and told the waiting reporters that the strike was over. Did he think his self-imposed imprisonment helped pressure a settlement? Well, he would have to be modest, but it must be a terrible thing for a city to have to lock up a president of an international union.

Kaden, circulating unnoticed through the crowd, didn't mind Selden's show-stealing. Something else was bothering him. It was after 1 P.M., and there was no sign of the mayor or any of the board members.

He found them crowded into the suite reserved for Hugh Addonizio. They stared silently into open space; no one appeared ready to go downstairs to make the settlement announcement. Kaden asked what the problem was.

"Lew, we can't go down there. Someone's made a mistake." Kaden was puzzled. "Mike"—the mayor addressed Dr. Michael Petti, a board member—"you tell him. I can't."

"Mr. Kaden. It seems we've underestimated the cost of this settlement. Now there's not enough votes to approve the settlement." Petti appeared intolerably embarrassed.

"Underestimate? By how much?"

No one wanted to answer. The grown men appeared like children who had just broken the cookie jar and couldn't find a place to hide the pieces. Finally, Petti spoke out. "Three quarters of a million dollars." Kaden admitted later he had had difficulty suppressing a laugh at this final statement of the board's ineptitude. He pulled himself together.

"Gentlemen," he said with a cool ease, "at this moment, I'm going downstairs to announce that we've reached a final settlement. With or without you." He walked out the door. Waiting for the elevator, he heard the door reopen. Addonizio and Petti would come down and make the joint announcement.

That night the teachers ratified the settlement, and they went back to school the following day. There were no reprisals, as expected. The board, after listening to hours of denunciation for allowing binding arbitration, ratified the contract the following evening—by one vote. Kaden returned home to begin gathering a staff for his McCarthy-like peace campaign. (He lost.) Bates, Cascella and most of the other top A.F.T. officers transferred operations to Los Angeles for the next strike. The Newark strike was over.

For the A.F.T., it was a victory. The reps had sustained a long and brutal strike. Newark was now firmly in the camp; some one thousand teachers had joined during the walkout. The contract was a solid one, and the board would have serious doubts about trying to break it in order to provide for more black principals. Or to do anything else, for that matter. Most importantly, however, the Newark experience showed that the union could withstand the most concentrated legal attack ever attempted by a school board. Although Birchette had managed to alienate the press, he had been able to maintain the tricky "dual reality" needed to sustain mass paranoia, an essential ingredient of a long teachers' strike. Teachers in Newark still believe that Birchette always told the truth and that the press lied.

A.F.T. reps like Bates, Cascella and Strauber believed the ordeal was worth it—worth the two hundred arrests, the nearly $100,000 in fines and legal fees, definitely worth the sixty-day imprisonment of Selden on charges of unlawful support of a strike.* They adopted the attitude that someday, somewhere, such a legal attack would have to be unleashed. Someday, somewhere, school boards had to learn that the

---

* The U.S. Supreme Court, in November of 1971, refused to consider the teachers' appeal. Within weeks they began serving their prison sentences, terms ranging from ten days to three months.

strict enforcement of laws would not work. Just as well in Newark as any place else.

Oh, yes—and the children. Nothing much was new with them. A number of high-school seniors lost scholarships and the chance to go to college. All of them were expected to lose at least a month in their already poor reading averages. But that's war.

One year later, the Newark teachers struck again. This time, for three months.

7

Tragedy in Ocean Hill-Brownsville

THE SACRED CALENDAR of the American Federation of Teachers does not mark the days May 20 through May 25 as high holy days of teacher-unionism and this, I submit, is an unforgivable omission. For the union, these should be days of triumph, of hope, days set aside for every A.F.T. member—and especially every actual or aspiring A.F.T. leader—to ponder what greatness could be theirs. A kind of Bird Day, Arbor Day and Millard Fillmore's Birthday tossed together into one unforgettable week of festivities. These were the days in 1968, after all, when an A.F.T. local president bravely seized the time and successfully killed a major educational reform, threw an entire state legislature into something not unlike confusion, hampered the campaign of a Presidential contender, made black anti-Semitism a real fear and destroyed years of work by countless lexicographers who no doubt believed the verb "to transfer" was substantially dissimilar in meaning to the verb "to fire." This A.F.T. leader, Albert Shanker, also assumed control—momentarily but definitely—of policy making in the New York City school system by ordering teachers to do precisely what their schools superintendent ordered them not to do. Never before had a teacher trade-union exercised so much authority.

As that week marked the zenith of power for New York City's United Federation of Teachers in the decentralization controversy, it also marked the nadir of hopes for the essentially conservative experiments in community control (those in small towns read "public control") of educational policy making and administration. It was the week the U.F.T. leadership proved that it could control enough New York lawmakers to kill decentralization, the week it began to dabble dangerously and cynically in the awesome game of racial and religious fear, the week the first shovel of dirt was thrown onto the grave of the experiment in local educational control that came to be known by the names of the two Brooklyn communities in which it was tried—Ocean Hill and Brownsville.

On Monday, May 20, Shanker arrived in Albany with five hundred teachers and U.F.T. supporters to unleash a massive lobbying campaign, which would, within the week, kill a strong decentralization bill.

Less than two weeks earlier, the governing board of the Ocean Hill-Brownsville experimental school district had transferred out of the local system thirteen teachers and six supervisors. But transferred teachers have few rights under the school board's bylaws or the board-U.F.T. contract, certainly no right of a hearing or arbitration through grievance procedure. Teachers who are "fired," however, are entitled to full hearings, to full "due process." Since the thirteen teachers were not given hearings, to which they were not entitled, Shanker chooses to call them "these illegally fired teachers." In the weeks to come, lazy journalists and people who should know better began to refer to the transferred teachers as "fired" teachers.* Semantic flimflam, no doubt, but Shanker's most

---

* A letter by the local board sent to the nineteen reads as follows:

The governing board of the Ocean Hill-Brownsville demonstration district has voted to end your employment in the schools of this dis-

powerful weapon in the Legislature, in the press and among misguided civil libertarians.

Shanker's arrival statement in Albany was a masterpiece of double-think, calmly referring to a situation which simply did not exist. It continued: "If charges are to be brought against these teachers, they should follow the normal procedure." Since under the school board's bylaws no charges are necessary in even involuntary transfers, there were no "normal procedures" which required anything at all in the way of administrative or board hearings.

In that statement, Shanker ordered the thirteen teachers in the group of nineteen back to the schools, in contravention of the wishes of both the demonstration district and the central administration. Schools Superintendent Bernard Donovan, who didn't appear to mind that too much, compounded the confusion by announcing, that same day, hearings for the transferred teachers. (He later reinstated the teachers to the local district, because the local board had not filed the charges which were *not* necessary so that the hearing which did *not* have to be held could be.)

On Tuesday, May 21, the U.F.T. lobbyists began distributing in the legislative chambers literature which warned that decentralized school districts would be operated "on the basis of local prejudices based on color, race or religion." For those lawmakers who would not be frightened by that, the union

---

trict. The action was taken on the recommendation of the Personnel Committee. This termination of employment is to take effect immediately.

In the event you wish to question this action, the governing board will receive you, Friday, May 10, 1968, at 6 P.M. at Intermediate School 55, 2021 Bergen Street, Brooklyn.

You will report Friday morning to Personnel, 110 Livingston Street, Brooklyn, for reassignment.

Fired teachers in New York simply are not reassigned. Ironically, the local board, in offering a hearing, gave the teachers more rights than they would have under the central board, which does not offer hearings on transfers.

flaks, with all the subtlety of a Mack truck, warned of massive retaliation at the polls if they voted for decentralization.

By Wednesday, May 22, despite the pressure, prodecentralization legislators had forged an apparently winning coalition. Time again for verbal transubstantiation: in Ocean Hill-Brownsville, some 350 teachers who had boycotted the district for more than a week in support of their transferred colleagues were ordered to a meeting with the local superintendent, Rhody McCoy. There was nothing illegal or unusual about the order. But they refused and Shanker screamed "Lockout." The precarious prodecentralization coalition collapsed. The bill was dead.

On Thursday, May 23, from the roof of a sound truck, Shanker addressed two thousand supporters at a City Hall rally. He scraped at the unhealed wound of black anti-Semitism, a kind of intangible but real ghetto tension for years, by referring to unnamed people in Ocean Hill-Brownsville as "Nazis" and threatened to use the U.F.T.'s ample treasury to defeat legislators who still might be thinking of voting for a strong decentralization bill.

On Friday night and Saturday morning, May 24–25, with Shanker sitting in the galleries and Nelson Rockefeller stumbling home from the Presidential hustings, the state Senate voted to adopt a measure which delayed consideration of decentralization for a year. Hours later, the Assembly repeated the action.

The U.F.T. president had used fear, threats of retaliation and media control masterfully well. And he had exhibited a knowledge of politics that very few critics appreciate—even now. He had supported the successful delaying measure sponsored by State Senator John Marchi of Staten Island. New York Mayor John V. Lindsay, the most active proponent—then—of strong decentralization, could not afford to cross the Staten Island lawmaker, because Marchi was chairman of the Senate Committee on New York City and an important keeper of the keys for Lindsay's perennial begging for more state aid for the city. The Lindsay forces could not, and did not, lobby against the "Marchi Bill."

In addition, Shanker had made a name for the Conservative Marchi, who went on to defeat John Lindsay in the 1969 Republican Mayoralty primary and rolled up 550,000 votes against Lindsay's 990,000 in the general election. Shanker, remember, was an old-time Socialist, a registered member of the Liberal party. Union interests knew neither party label nor ideological commitment. Marchi would get the endorsement of New York's Conservative party. (There were some who might have suggested there were no ideological differences between teacher-unionism and conservatism.)

Technically, the Marchi Bill delayed for just one year the formulation of a decentralization plan. It allowed Lindsay to increase the number of board members, thereby ultimately giving him a prodecentralization majority. In addition, it permitted the new school board to delegate some of its powers to local school districts—if it wished. Those powers which by law accrue to the school superintendent remained unchanged —and these included power over personnel. It was assumed that during the year the three experiments in decentralization in the city would offer possible approaches. Unless, of course, they failed miserably or were prevented from bearing results.

To kill decentralization, then, or to manage it so that it benefited whatever special interest wielded the most power, it was essential—to its opponents—that one or more of the districts should fail. While the primary opponents of the community-control idea—the U.F.T., the school board and the Council of Supervisory Associations (which represented principals and other supervisors)—were busy delaying the implementation of the hypothesis in Albany, the culture of decentralization was rapidly growing strong in the medium dish of the city's ghetto areas. If the experiment could not be proven a failure, the culture dish had to be dropped and smashed to preclude the obvious results. Shanker and the U.F.T. leadership, the most powerful group in the city at the time, willingly volunteered for the task.

The school years during which the decentralization tragedy was portrayed certainly were not the best of times for the flagrant abuse of organizational power—particularly in such a sensitive, volatile area as public education in the cities. The era contained too many tragedies, too many funerals for hope, too many shocks to the nation's central nervous system. From the fall of 1966, when the I.S. 201 crisis produced the first articulation of demands for community control, to the spring of 1969, when the Legislature passed a hopelessly confused and painfully weakened decentralization bill, the city and the nation remained in an almost constant state of recovery from one disaster or another. The smoke from Watts and Hough still burned the nation's eyes and the slaughter in Vietnam numbed its conscience. War, terrible and swift, engulfed the Middle East, and who knew if it would not devour the world. Flames engulfed substantial areas of the cities of the nation. The generals asked for hundreds of thousands more young men to die while the rationalization of sure victory crumbled during a holiday known as Tet. The people began to rise up against their leader and forced him into retirement, many of them wistfully falling behind an incongruous poet-politician named Eugene McCarthy, or the gritty compassion of Robert F. Kennedy. Wasn't liberation near? No, America appeared bent on murdering its future—first King on a motel balcony, Kennedy on a hotel kitchen floor. James Earl Ray, Sirhan Bishara Sirhan, flames from the burning Washington ghetto send smoke over the Capitol and people rush to the gun stores. Were we really going mad? Revolution at Columbia, a great university brought to a halt. Revolution in France. In Czechoslovakia, revolution, and another Hungary. On the streets of Chicago, good guys and the bad guys clash between commercials, and America cannot identify which is which. Is the world going mad?

No, these were not the times for any powerful group to claw at the scabs of a city, to risk conflagration by pitting Jew against black, to smother hope for reform—even if that reform had not been a proven success. Yet a group which relies on power, is structured for the most effective use of power, can't help but use it. Particularly when there are no inner mechanisms for accountability to the public for its actions. A teacher union is compactly constructed to act quickly and with force to achieve what its leaders perceive to be its ends—the protection of its members and the easing of their workloads. It is not in its nature to worry about tragedies. And Albert Shanker knows enough of the workings of the press, of the reactions of lawmakers, of the general direction of public opinion in times of fright, to use tragedies for the U.F.T.'s aims. Some may call this cynicism. But it is the political way, and teacher-unionism in New York and in many areas of the nation is essentially political. (With a hitch—the public cannot go to the polls and *un*elect a Shanker.)

Within such a context of swirling tragedies and monumental events, it is relatively simple to take actions without fear of close analysis by the press or the people. It is simple to convince lawmakers that certain educational reforms might only increase racial tensions. And simple to make people fear, fear enough to forget old weathered ideals in the retreat to safer havens of indifference. Within such a context, the U.F.T. prepared its battle against the idea of local community control, brought it to a conclusion successfully and then managed to lay the blame before people and organizations whose major efforts were to reduce the fears and improve the system. No better proof of the U.F.T.'s victory over the forces of reform exists than the widely held belief that the decentralization story, the story of Ocean Hill-Brownsville, is so confusing that it defies understanding. Even now, when teachers and parents question the aims of the A.F.T. in the light of the New York experience, the official answer goes something like this: "You don't really know the whole story. It was essentially a political battle, and the teachers found themselves caught in the middle. But it's so confusing it would take weeks to explain. Believe me, Shanker's for decentralization. He knew what he was doing."

To some extent the events lent themselves to confusion. Or, more accurately, they lent themselves to exploitation in order to confuse. The meanings of words were consistently changed, and innocuous phrases such as "decentralization" and "community control" and "due process" were sloganized and became, like Pavlov's bell, signals for reflex action, yea or nay. There were scores of decentralization plans, any one of which could confuse the interested observer, numb the casual one. The number of teachers who were transferred out of the district constantly changed and these were merged with the number who were suspended for violations of the state's Taylor Law forbidding strikes by public employees. Depending on the day, the U.F.T. would insist on the return of 19, 13, 7, 350, 100, 89, 83 or 6 teachers to all or one of the eight schools in the Ocean Hill-Brownsville district. There were really four strikes in New York in 1968, not one—and just as many settlements, panels of mediators, fact-finders, arbitrators and concerned citizens. The parties in the dispute were wont to hide either their opposition to or advocacy of varying positions in the controversy by taking public postures contrary to that opposition or advocacy. Shanker was in favor of decentralization, he said, but of course he wasn't. Lindsay was appalled by the brute power of the union yet chose on one occasion to offer a plan to Shanker by which the U.F.T. could close any school it felt might be the scene of violence. The school board promulgated administrative changes it called decentralization while denying legitimacy to the actions taken by actually decentralized school districts. Add to this the various side issues—Lindsay's insistence on increased executive control of school financing, black racism, white racism, anti-Semitism practiced and imagined and exploited, splits between writers of the New Left (Nat Hentoff) and the old (Michael Harrington)—and it is quite simple to understand why there is a strong temptation to believe that the story of Ocean Hill-Brownsville is inexplicable. It is somewhat like trying to appreciate a painting while viewing it only through a microscope, stroke by minute stroke.

In fact, the controversy and its attendant strikes by the U.F.T. can be understood. And must be understood if the public schools of the nation are ever to be returned to the people who pay for them and send their children to them. The pretended confusion surrounding the community-control tragedy, despite the admittedly chaotic nature of details, is still just another example of the "dual reality" ploy used to justify actions of the union leadership both to the public and to the membership.

To summarize: From a wide-ranging variety of sources, the concept of decentralizing the administration of the New York City school system and the concomitant control over personnel, curriculum and budget in a small geographic area was offered as a possible solution to the city's apparently impossible educational problems. The idea received support from a variety of organized community groups, such as anti-poverty agencies, which had had some experience in local program and budget control. It also was endorsed by Mayor Lindsay, who saw it not only as a means of improving education but also as a means of reducing the power of the city's educational bureaucracy and of wringing more money from Albany. The New York State Board of Regents, by law the technical overseer of all public education in the state, also supported the idea as a means of improving the notoriously poor quality of instruction in the state's largest city. The Ford Foundation, which provided planning funds and technical assistance to the experimental districts created to test the idea, endorsed it, viewing it as a method of renewing the interest of local residents in the successes or failures of public schools

—and thereby providing a catalyst for improvement. Several members of the state Legislature, some for fiscal reasons, others for political or educational, lent their support.

Arrayed against the concept were those institutions, organizations and people likely to lose the most from the implementation of a radical restructuring of the educational bureaucracy —the school board which controlled it, the educational administration which ran it, and the two major trade-union organizations which derived their power from it, the Council of Supervisory Associations and the United Federation of Teachers. They represented the educational status quo. Of these the U.F.T. was by far the most powerful, the least susceptible to public accounting and ideologically the most prepared to fight against the concept. Once the school board had had its collective mind changed for it through the addition by Mayor Lindsay of prodecentralization members, the U.F.T. stood virtually alone as the major opponent of reform.

Through a series of actions which included a general refusal to accept the legitimacy of the decentralization idea and its experiments, four strikes, intensive lobbying efforts and the use of a public-relations campaign, the U.F.T. was able to produce a decentralization bill which absorbed, and therefore destroyed, the apparently successful experiments. It was also able to make the terms "decentralization" and "community control" synonymous for many people with black racism, turmoil in the schools and potential civil disorder, thus making it almost certain that such reforms would not be tried again in New York or in any other major urban center in which the A.F.T. holds bargaining rights. (And the A.F.T. holds bargaining rights in nearly every urban center.)

"Things have worked out fine," Shanker was to muse months after his victory. "That entire board of education is gone. That superintendent of schools is gone. We got a decentralization law about 80 percent of which is consonant with what we wanted. We exhibited enough strength so that the black and Puerto Rican paraprofessionals voted for us rather than a rival group, because they wanted a strong organization. We were able to get an excellent and unprecedented contract the following June because the city was unwilling to face another shutdown. I think it would have taken us ten years to get the benefits that we got in that one single contract."

Too simple a summary? Perhaps—but not in terms of *what* happened. The *why* of it all, the reasons for such strong opposition to decentralization by the U.F.T., merits further exploration.

A teacher trade-union, like many other trade-unions, grows according to a pattern set by the employer with which it must deal, a mirror-image bureaucracy, a symbiotic relationship if one is prepared to think of an educational bureaucracy and a teacher union in terms of parasites. Any change in the system's administration has reverberations within the union bureaucracy. The more radical the alteration in administration, the greater the impact on the union. Decentralization, if it had been implemented as originally planned, would probably have led to a drastic restructuring of the union itself. It is unlikely that the U.F.T. would have survived the transformation.

Why? The answer lies in the second major reason why a strong teacher union in an urban center must oppose decentralization. The power of the organization lies in its own strict centralization with authority concentrated at the highest levels. Only within such a structure can the union mobilize quickly and effectively to exercise its not-so-ultimate weapon, the strike. Such decisions cannot be left to local, semiautonomous subdivisions. Only within a structure which provides for an upward flow of support, a downward flow of power, can the union direct with potency such activities as lobbying or campaigning for favored candidates. Its negotiating committee can act with strength only if its members can direct responses by the entire union. The credibility of its leadership would be weakened without centralization. It is no mistake that "rank-and-file discipline" is one of the major concerns of local leadership as well as the national representatives. The teachers' union always has pictured itself a combatant, and war, or its educational equivalent, cannot be fought without a high command which expects every teacher to do his duty.

There was a time when teachers thought of themselves as intellectually independent souls, nonconformists who made a virtue of arguing why they felt they should not join any organization, much less a union. Teacher-unionism has, to a considerable degree, extinguished the trait, but its memory still brings pain to national and local leadership. A union decentralized to cope with a decentralized school administration would tend to encourage refragmentation, an identification with the local community rather than with the central leadership. Writing in a special tenth-anniversary supplement to *The United Teacher,* Shanker warned of the consequences:

> We have shown that a strong, united organization is best for everybody, but this is a battle which must be fought over and over again. In every set of negotiations, with every disappointment, *there is a constant tendency to split back into . . . parts.* It is a tendency we must continue to resist. [Italics mine—R.J.B.]

Local autonomy in big-city teacher-unionism also increases the danger of "raiding" by other organizations or unions. Even now, the U.F.T. in New York and the A.F.T. nationally are engaged in intense competition for the loyalties of public employees with the American Federation of State, County, and Municipal Employees—to say nothing of the nonunion N.E.A.

A third reason why teacher-unionism must oppose true decentralization and community control is that such reform would ultimately weaken the power, actually and symbolically, of the union's contract with the school system. Ultimately, a decentralized system would require local negotiation and local contracting tailored to fit local, not central, requirements. Not only would this require the formidable task of negotiating a score or more of different settlements, but it would weaken the symbolic effect of the contract. In modern teacher-union-ism, such documents are not merely laundry lists of wages and working conditions; they are the instruments by which teacher unions, technically private associations with no standing under the law as policy-making bodies, are recognized as equal partners with the school boards in the operation of public schools. Contracts to teacher unions provide a status denied most other unions, the status of top-level decision maker, a status shared only with school boards, which may or may not reflect the sentiments of the residents or parents of a school district. (In large cities such as New York, the chances are they do not.) The contract can and does dictate expenditures for personnel, textbooks and instructional materials, determine transfer and assignment policy, establish criteria for hiring and promotion and dismissal, and create the general objectives of a school system. The powers and responsibilities negotiated away by theoretically public school boards to unquestionably private and inherently unresponsive teacher unions—as well as associations—increase each year. And attempts to dilute the union's authority are viewed as unconscionable threats to the very existence of the organization and can produce a New York in 1968 or a Newark in 1971. One simply does not mess with the A.F.T.'s sacred ark of the covenant.

But most important, perhaps, is the increased accountability resulting from a transfer of public educational power from one large bureaucracy to several smaller school districts. Teachers are, technically, the intermediaries between the people and the public power structure, the most accessible of all public servants. But the frenzied, frustrating growth of a bureaucracy, big enough and impersonal enough to be blind, deaf and dumb to the complaints of parents and children, combined with the shelter provided the teacher by a stronger, and more impersonal, union contract, removes the learning process further and further from the student and his mother and father. It is tempting, it is easy and, sadly, it is all too frequent that mistakes which radically alter the lives of young people can be hidden, their perpetrators shielded from the anger—or even the desire to help—on the part of the people. Decentralization and community control were designed, in the words of one of the many plans, to "reconnect" the educational system with the people of a reasonably small school district. In a sense, the union would have to pay for its power by spiritually locating itself near a constituency—as would a local school board. But a union—especially one with the size and the power of the U.F.T.—is not structured to be responsive to the public; it is hardly structured to be responsive to its own membership. To accept decentralization and community control would be to accept ultimately a sharing of its power through a new responsibility to the children, the parents and the taxpayers. The A.F.T. has yet to learn how to accomplish this.

These, of course, are *my* reasons why the U.F.T.—or the A.F.T.—opposes local control of urban schools. Not Albert Shanker's. In fact, the U.F.T. leader still insists that a decentralized school system would enhance the union's power:

> I think the fragmentation of local school boards together with the centralization of the union, from a pure power point of view, is the best way of doing it. From a pure power point of view what Bundy and the community control people wanted to do in New York City was the ideal thing for the union. If they could have had 250 community districts,* each of them very small, with a central union that has a multi-million-dollar strike fund, with expert legal advice and negotiating and other services . . . we could run rings around little districts. We could strike them one at a time . . . two at a time, whipsaw back and forth.

Ironically, this is precisely what the U.F.T. attempted in the early stages of the Ocean Hill-Brownsville crisis—to strike

---

* The maximum number of districts suggested by the "Bundy Panel" was 60, hardly 250. With 60 districts, the average enrollment would be some 20,000 students, hardly a small school system.

only the district that it considered errant. And the attempt failed because, while the single district was temporarily disrupted, it could not be pressured into obedience. No, the only way the union could beat the demonstration district was to strike the entire system, forcing the political powers of the city and the state first to suspend the governing board and ultimately to disband the entire district. Meanwhile, during the citywide strike, the Ocean Hill-Brownsville district operated quite successfully, while the rest of the schools in the city were closed, despite the multimillion-dollar strike fund and the expert legal advice and negotiating and other services. With 250 truly decentralized and locally controlled school systems in New York, the individual districts might very well run rings around the clumsily centralized U.F.T. giant, locking out one chapter at a time, two at a time, proving the inflexibility of a centrally controlled, top-heavy union.

But now to the "real" reasons why the U.F.T.—and the A.F.T.—opposes community control of schools. They stem from the best motivations and tend to find sympathy among the "liberal"—and generally middle-class—communities. The decentralization proposals would, according to U.F.T. literature distributed during and after 1968, end all possibility of school integration, leading to "the establishment of racially and ethnically separate educational enclaves throughout the city [which] would have given official sanction and credence to segregated schools." These enclaves would ultimately develop into isolated, provincial capitals of reaction and bigotry—"like small Alabama towns," Shanker is fond of saying. There would be opposition, he warned, to the teaching of controversial subjects like the United Nations and the history of the civil-rights movement. Local school districts would tend too easily to be racist in nature, to hire or fire or judge the effectiveness of a teacher on the basis of color. Finally, the U.F.T. has charged that the real powers in the city and the nation—the moneyed interests—have used, or will use, community control as an opiate to hide their neglect of public education, a smoke screen to keep teacher and community divided, while the schools are starved of funds and other resources. "The most important step toward improving our schools would be the doubling and tripling of funds. Massively increased resources have never been tried in our schools. . . ." A poor decentralized school district, according to Shanker, will fail as miserably as a poor centralized, non-community-controlled school district. Another "great danger," the fear of which was exploited during the 1968 school year by the union, is that decentralization can "easily lead to the takeover of a district by small, highly organized extremist groups— black or white." This would frighten parents into less participation, says Shanker, "particularly when they have to fight militants who define every issue in terms of loyalty to race or ethnic base."

The arguments are effective, if not totally honest with regard to the condition of the public schools, particularly in the cities of the nation. Surely, no good men amongst us want to see an educational system based on apartheid or provincialism or neglect or the paranoid militancy of a few well-organized demagogues. It is a worn union gambit to declare for the good—so that the critics of the union appear to be declaring for the bad. Witness the title of the A.F.T.'s ultimate solution to the urban education problem, "More Effective Schools." The M.E.S. program is riddled with half-solutions and dangers to continued public control of education; yet how does one say, "I am against More Effective Schools." (Capital letters do not show up in speech. It's an almost corny stratagem, but clever.) This same academic—and semantic—hucksterism is applied to the proponents of decentralization. They, the union might have us believe, are against integration, against funding of the schools, in favor of militant control of school districts and racist behavior. Shanker accused Mayor Lindsay of these social crimes on more than one occasion during the 1968 school crisis.

The first point to make about these arguments, of course,

is that the U.F.T. never allowed New York to determine whether Shanker was correct. The behavior of the governing boards in the experimental school districts was very often based on self-defense; no one can know just how the districts might have performed had they been left alone. The community-control experiment was, in a sense, contaminated by the introduction of outside matter. It was not permitted to bear its results. Secondly, the question of local control is essentially irrelevant to either the goal of integrated schools or the remote possibility of adequate funding of public education. Someone who supports community control is certainly not against either—or not necessarily so. If, because of recent United States Supreme Court decisions, massive busing is undertaken to achieve integration, parental and taxpayer control over the directions of the public schools is still a viable possibility. Money, to be sure, can be spent by anyone. The rub comes when an organization of the size and power of the teachers' union insists on delaying an educational reform so pervasive as decentralization and community control while waiting for integration and funding. A report by the New York State Education Commissioner's Advisory Committee on Human Relations and Community Tensions in 1964 said:

> Nothing undertaken by the New York City Board of Education since 1954 [the date of the Supreme Court integration decision] and nothing proposed since 1963 has contributed or will contribute in any meaningful degree to desegregating the public schools of the city.

And little has changed since then; in fact, segregation is likely more entrenched now. And the idea that the public schools ever will be granted the funds they need is at once a self-contradiction—the schools always could use more money—and a flight of unreality which, sadly, reflects on the ability of the beholder to reason properly. But, for the U.F.T., waiting for these Godots is a safe bet; embarking on new approaches requires the kind of effort that educational bureaucracies—whether labor or management—simply cannot accept.

Predicting that locally controlled school districts will be transformed into "little Alabama towns" in which the content of curriculum, the selection of textbooks and the hiring of personnel is based on reaction and racism smacks of the sordid appeals to fear and hysteria that do no credit to the teaching profession. New York simply is not Alabama. There exist in most urban communities, including New York, a whole raft of laws, court decisions and civil-service procedures that militate against such a possibility—to say nothing of the entrance requirements of institutions of higher education and job requirements which impose their directions upon the curriculum of schools at both the secondary and elementary levels. But even these assurances are not the important guarantees. The greatest defense against both reaction in the schools and a takeover by a handful of militants is the assurance, provided by the very essence of popular community control, that the public can change whatever it is that stands between a community and a good education for its children.* This salutary influence does not exist in a system which precludes involvement by the public. Even if there were a momentary flirtation with extremism or a curriculum steeped in eighteenth-century ideas, the parents of such a district would have the ability to change it once its disastrous effects became clear. That right would not exist in a school system controlled and operated by the "professionals"; only union members can vote in U.F.T. elections. All of which brings us again to accountability, the fear of which motivates most, if not nearly all, of the A.F.T.'s opposition to real public control of public education.

Without such a context, the series of strikes which paralyzed New York's schools for nearly two months in 1968 are a jumble of disconnected events, a jumble that could serve only to

---

* One might also point out that, under a decentralized system, an ideological militant group might take over a few schools in one district. In a centralized system, a better-organized group—such as the U.F.T. —could take over the entire system.

confuse and ultimately to bore those who attempt to find meaning or wisdom from such disasters. The U.F.T. action, first against the Ocean Hill-Brownsville experimental district and then against the entire school system, was very much the inevitable consequence of unbending opposition to placing real control in the hands of those outside the teaching profession. And that opposition stems directly from a conservative bias built into any organization which grows up around conditions that ultimately must change. It is the first rule of bureaucracy—to resist dysfunctional change. The pity is in the resisting.

It was, then, only a matter of time, only a matter of which of the three experimental districts would provide the real or imagined provocation, only a matter of circumstance. The transfer of thirteen teachers and six supervisors, had the U.F.T. been a partisan of local control, would have led to some angry words and frantic negotiation and compromise settlements. Or it likely would not have occurred at all. The maneuverings of educational diplomacy are a daily occurrence. It is only when one party deliberately makes an issue of the commonplace that a crisis develops. And that is what happened at Ocean Hill-Brownsville in 1968.

For a variety of reasons, the union and its leadership needed the confrontation at that time and of that magnitude. Throughout the early months of 1968, the U.F.T. had been lobbying intensively against the so-called "strong" decentralization bills that had been supported by Mayor Lindsay, the Ford Foundation, the state's Board of Regents and an odd coalition of reform and conservative upstate lawmakers. Shanker had even chosen to go to jail early—during the Christmas break—in order to be free later to direct the efforts. But as the legislators hurried toward the summer recess—pressed on by a Nelson Rockefeller who wanted to get on with the business of becoming President—the U.F.T.'s efforts were failing. In order to upset the balance, whatever it was that happened in Ocean Hill-Brownsville had to be treated by the union as a major

development. Settling it peacefully would have assured passage
of a meaningful decentralization bill. "We have today a very
tragic situation existing in one district," Shanker told a rally
shortly after the local board transferred the thirteen teachers,
"and it will exist in many more if we don't win here."

The timing was important for yet another reason. For the
first time since David Selden and Charles Cogen went on to
their greater reward in Washington, Shanker faced a serious
challenge to his leadership. His obsessive opposition to community control had produced serious cleavages among top
leadership. In June of 1968, he knew he would be challenged
by a "New Coalition." It is, of course, impossible to know
whether he would have been defeated; but if he had been, his
control over not only the local but also the national leadership
would have slipped. These were high stakes, and Shanker
needed a crisis at that time to reduce the odds of losing. Union
members, with their traditional penchant for security, often
will believe that they are faced with the ugly threats of racist
and religious bias if they are told long enough and convinc-
ingly enough. And a time of insecurity certainly is no time to
flirt with reform-minded candidates.

Little mentioned but highly important was the U.F.T.'s demand, then, for a grievance procedure which ended in binding arbitration—a contract item it failed to obtain in the
settlement that ended the New York strike of 1967. Many
smaller unions and, more significantly, local affiliates of the
National Education Association, had managed to win impartial arbitration of grievances arising from the interpretation
of the contract. The omission in New York hardly enhanced
Shanker's leadership. As early as February of 1968, with no
apparent provocation from any of the experimental districts,
Shanker was threatening to close down local districts if arbitrary actions were taken against teachers. The incident which
provoked the threats, the suspension of a teacher for striking
a child, had nothing to do with the experimental districts.
But the U.F.T. leader called a press conference, accused the

central board of "playing into the hands of extremist groups," and demanded the impartial-arbitration clause as a condition for the U.F.T.'s agreement to live with decentralization. But there was no provision in the 1967–69 contract for reopening negotiation. Only a crisis that required renegotiation could bring that item—a crisis like a strike.

These developments provided the time. But why was the victim Ocean Hill-Brownsville, not I.S. 201 or the Two Bridges district in Lower Manhattan? One of the primary reasons was the success of that particular district. It was working and, had it been left alone, might have provided a persuasive case for the most advanced community-control bills. The elections for the local governing board had drawn more than twice as many voters as had voted in a local State Assembly election. The board had hired as its district superintendent a respected supervisor, Rhody McCoy, an educator who knew something about the use of media in instruction and was willing to try a variety of innovative approaches to schooling: team teaching, bilingual learning, a Montessori class, courses in Afro-American history and others. Attendance within the schools of the district had risen substantially and the local district acted as a kind of informal referral service for residents with health and housing problems in order to generate a true feeling of "community," a community with its schools as the centerpiece.

Not only did the district appear to be successful but it had made progress without the U.F.T.'s "More Effective Schools" program, a considerably more expensive approach to urban education. The local board had specifically rejected M.E.S., a move that angered the U.F.T. There is a whole series of offices at the U.F.T.'s Park Avenue South headquarters devoted to proving that M.E.S. works; the union didn't need the local experimental district to prove that M.E.S. wasn't necessary.

Most significantly, however, the Ocean Hill-Brownsville governing board was willing to fight, to do something not

even the central school board or John Lindsay was willing
to try—challenge the U.F.T. hegemony over public education
in New York City. Rhody McCoy could have, as most administrators in the system had done, informally "worked out" the
transfer of unwanted teachers with U.F.T. representatives.
But at the time, the U.F.T. had no contractual authority over
transfers; it would have been a violation of administrative
prerogatives of the local and the central board as well as
silent and forced tribute to the union, a power without real
standing. McCoy and the governing board would not budge;
the administrative power over transfer was not for sale. When
the suspended teachers and administrators defied McCoy's
order of reassignment, he formally charged them with insubordination—something Bernard Donovan was unwilling to do
after the teachers in Ocean Hill-Brownsville began taking
orders solely from Shanker. When 350 teachers struck the
experimental district in support of the original nineteen, Mc-
Coy charged them with excessive absences and asked for the
invocation of the state's Taylor Law against strikes by public
employees—again something Donovan refused to do, although even he could not swallow the U.F.T. statement that
the 350 had been "locked out."* Throughout the crisis, it was
McCoy and the local governing board who "played it
straight," not Shanker and the U.F.T. The union through
"informal negotiation" with the central board had won the
right of unlimited transfer *out* of the experimental districts,
a violation of its own contract with the central board and
an initially devastating blow to the nascent and vulnerable
experiment. This certainly was not playing it straight. Inevitably, McCoy and the local board lost; they had, perhaps
foolishly, perhaps bravely, perhaps both, challenged the
U.F.T. and the union had to destroy them, both to preserve
the union's own credibility as the strongest organization in
town—a bit like the United States "keeping its commitments"

---

* The 350 even managed to be paid for their holiday.

by nearly annihilating a client country—as well as to paint true community control the most awful shade of failure.

The U.F.T., of course, would have been readily content not to engage in such clumsy and obvious slaughter, had either the school board or the political structure done an adequate job in behalf of the union. For the first few acts of the tragedy, Shanker said and did little, viewing the drama warily but passively from the union's Park Avenue perch. That appeared to be the correct approach; after all, any good bureaucrat—and Shanker is that—would know that the central board would do its utmost to prevent amateurs from proving its expendability. Only when it became apparent that the central administration lacked the muscle to kill decentralization did the union become an active belligerent—and only when the demonstration districts expressed their pointed intention of ridding themselves of all past vestiges of failure, union and board alike.

As a result, the U.F.T. was little heard from during the prologue that was the I.S. 201 crisis of the fall of 1966. The episode was a classic example of centralized insensitivity to popular, neighborhood wishes. Intermediate School 201 was to have been a fully integrated school—only the central board built it square in the center of an all-black-and-Puerto-Rican neighborhood, and its designated "feeder" elementary schools, search as one might, could not find a white student. It was not so much that the parents, many of whom joined the East Harlem Triangle Association, wanted to be friendly to whites or were particularly upset about the city school board violating the spirit of the 1954 Supreme Court decision, but there was a conviction that the city could not possibly get away with treating white children as poorly as it treated black. A good percentage of white students, with angry white parents ready to have their complaints registered, would have assured, the black parents thought, some possibility of improved education. But the school, an inspiring example of modern American riot architecture—perched on fourteen-foot

pillars and with no windows—was built at 127th Street and
Madison Avenue, a location not known to attract many white
people, built opposite a bar, a liquor store and the Penn
Central railroad tracks. First the school-board people told the
parents that their premise was, sadly, mistaken—we never
said it would be integrated, we said it "had the potential for
integration," because it was so modern, so beautiful and
would, honest, contain many new and daring approaches to
education. But no whites. (It was such a "magnet" that when
the school board sent out ten thousand invitations to parents
in white sections of town, ten returned cards expressed an
"interest" but no white children were registered.)

Left without the shields of more respected white children's
minds to protect them against the ravages of a poor education, the black parents came to the conclusion that if they
oversaw the operations of the new school, *their* complaints
would certainly be heard. The Triangle Association became a
focal point for the parents, who vowed not to let the school
open unless it was integrated, or unless the parents themselves
had the power to determine curriculum, budget allocations and
personnel policies. The school-board officials answered that
talking about either was "a waste of time."

So the parents closed the school. And kept it closed until
the board promised to enter into negotiation about the "possibility" of delegating some authority to local parents to run
the school. For a while, the U.F.T. said little, just complaining now and then that its members had to work in the obso-
lete schools that I.S. 201 was supposed to replace. Throughout
the remainder of the fall, then the winter, and then the early
spring, the talks continued, punctuated by tantalizing little
statements from the school board that it was considering "decentralizing" the administration of the schools. Mayor Lindsay had entered the talks and with him he brought
representatives of the Ford Foundation. Shanker was there,
too.

Ironically, the union pressed for inclusion of Ocean Hill-

Brownsville into any plan for decentralization experiments. It saw that the ghetto, treated differently than the rest of the school system, might serve as a show place for its More Effective Schools program. Several community and antipoverty groups had expressed an interest in M.E.S. as a possible way out of the grim educational trap the schools provided. (On the theory that anything might help.)

As expected, the school board was not rushing things—not until Lindsay made it clear that the city's executive branch would control more of the educational finance and administration. The new mayor also had come to the conclusion that the state would be able to provide more money for the city schools—therefore less would have to come from local taxation—if the system could be subdivided into a number of smaller units. (It has to do with a complicated tax formula and has nothing, really, to do with education.) With subtle jibes at the Lindsay administration for attempting to put the virgin school system under local political control, the school board on April 19, 1967, finally released a statement indicating that it was willing to decentralize and to attempt a number of experiments at reform. Ten days later, after the Legislature gave Lindsay until the following December (Lindsay now, not the school board) to produce a plan for local control, the mayor appointed a "blue-ribbon" panel to devise a scheme to decentralize the schools and ensure public involvement in their operation. If parents are to receive more power, then teachers must receive more power, said Shanker—who then proceeded to plan the strike that was to take place the following September when the latest contract expired. No contract, no work, decentralization or not.

Although the school board waited until July 5 to announce the three districts, local antipoverty agencies and other groups in the areas knew of their imminent designation and began to plan for implementation of models for community control. The day after the board announcement, key residents of the three districts gathered at the Overseas Press Club in New

York to announce that they had received $135,000 from the Ford Foundation to begin the decentralization program. Ominously, no Ford representatives appeared, but a statement by F. Champion Ward, the Foundation's vice-president for education and research, pleaded for understanding for what were, after all, simply experiments, tests of an idea.

> As in any genuine experiment, there are risks and uncertain factors. What is certain, however, is that a start has been made toward programs of educational reform that arise directly from the communities concerned, are designed to improve the climate for education and have the *official cooperation of the school system and the teachers.* [Italics mine. —R.J.B.]

Governing boards, which would establish plans for operating the schools, were to be created. I.S. 201 and four Harlem "feeder" grade schools would constitute one experimental district; one junior high school and four elementary schools in the area of Lower Manhattan near the Brooklyn and Manhattan bridges ("Two Bridges") would be the second; and two junior high schools and six elementary schools in the Ocean Hill and Brownsville sections of Brooklyn would be the third. If there was any question as to what the local groups intended to do with the powers over curriculum and personnel outlined at the press conference, David Spencer, chairman of the I.S. 201 negotiating committee (later chairman of the governing board), should have eliminated it when he noted with enthusiasm that "the Board of Education will call it decentralization. We would like to carry it further. We call it community control." The school board said nothing; for the union, things were getting out of hand.

The first outward evidence of conflict between the union and Ocean Hill-Brownsville erupted shortly thereafter as union teachers began to complain that the local planning board—the precursor of the governing board—was intent on implementing a plan during the summer when the teachers were not available. Why teachers could not make themselves available if they were really interested—not all of them go to Europe or take graduate study—was a major unanswered question. A second question was why U.F.T. officials were on hand to help plan the strike for the following fall and not the new operation of the local district. Relations were all but broken when planning-board members refused to insist on making every grade school an M.E.S. school. Superintendent Donovan had promised "beefed-up" programs but no M.E.S.—and the local planning board was not about to spend time and energy fighting a union cause. The board members had a much more pervasive dream. Eugenia Kemble, the U.F.T.'s official historian of the decentralization tragedy, wrote in *The United Teacher:*

> It was precisely this deleted part of the plan [the M.E.S. schools] which teachers felt was particularly valuable, and it was with these features in mind that the U.F.T. had urged teachers to cooperate in the initial phases of the planning.

With the local district shunning the role of a ready-made M.E.S.-interest group, the union had no further use for decentralization or local control. While the planning board set up and then conducted the governing-board elections, while it selected a unit administrator, while it planned for a school year filled with new hope, the U.F.T. ignored it, refused to cooperate. The local residents considered the plans one last effort at cooperation, a development of incredible importance; the U.F.T. yawned condescendingly and planned for its biggest strike ever. At about that time, in the summer of 1967, with nearly all of the nation's once great cities burning or smoldering, New York's junior Senator, Robert F. Kennedy, was telling a United States Senate committee that "we pass bills and appropriate money and assuage our consciences, and local school systems keep right on doing things the way they've done them for decades."

The union, too, was insisting on doing things the tradi-

tional union way. For more money, for more M.E.S. schools
—which meant ultimately more free time for teachers, more
control for the union and more money—the U.F.T. struck
the city school system. In two weeks it had its money—and
little else. Not only had the union spat at the faltering begin-
nings of the community-control idea by first refusing to
cooperate and then striking against it as if it didn't matter,
but it had the presumption to offer the experimental district
a promise of future cooperation if it, in return, supported the
strike by closing the schools. In other words, the U.F.T. was
not recognizing the district governing board as a legitimate
employer and responsible authority for the conduct of the
schools; in typical union terms, it was simply another interest
group, either for it or against it.

From that point, there was no hope for a reconciliation
between the local districts and the U.F.T. Shanker stepped
up his attacks on the various decentralization bills, warning
of "chaos" and "destruction," and making little effort to understand the urge to control one's own destiny. (That is not
part of the trade-union ideological infrastructure any more,
apparently.) The U.F.T. joined with the Council of Supervisory Associations (C.S.A.) in a court attempt to blunt
some of the local districts' authority and, in the absence of
any forthright stand by the central school board against decentralization, made it clear that it would not accept "rule by
extremists," the people of Brooklyn.

The school board did nothing. The local community boards
floundered without direction, demanding clear-cut guidelines
for operation. McCoy threatened to close the schools unless
he had some idea of how they were supposed to be run; John
Bremer, unit administrator at Two Bridges, quit in disgust,
unable to obtain even some idea of what these experiments
were supposed to be testing. Bremer stated:

> My conclusion is that to continue the demonstration proj-
> ect under these circumstances would be a betrayal of our

mission and that I would be doing a disservice to decentralization and educational improvement by continuing to work within a framework provided by the Board of Education.

In a few words, one down, two to go. But McCoy and Charles Wilson, unit administrator at I.S. 201, were determined to make the dream a reality, at least to test the idea of community control, and to run the schools as if they were, in fact, controlled by the community governing board. In March, the Ocean Hill-Brownsville governing board, convinced that it probably never would hear from the central board, adopted its own formal agenda for running the schools and submitted it to the central administration for anything—approval, rejection, negotiation, anything. Until it heard otherwise, it would take at face value that it was, in fact, an experiment in local control.

It logically followed that, given this context, the board had the power of transfer over personnel. It also followed that, since local U.F.T. people were not cooperating with the board and the U.F.T. itself was lobbying in Albany for the board's dissolution, the governing board had reason to suspect how well U.F.T. loyalists fit into the experimental district. And, no doubt, the local board was desperately trying to determine, through one test or another, exactly what powers it had and whether, as it had been led to believe by Ford, Lindsay and, to a certain extent, the central board, it truly operated the schools in Ocean Hill and Brownsville. So, on May 8, 1968, the governing board voted to transfer out of its district to reassignment by the central board thirteen teachers, including the U.F.T. chapter chairman, and six supervisors. The "Year of the Dragon," as McCoy was to call it, began.

The U.F.T. struck four times that year—once in May, against just the one demonstration district, and when that didn't work, three more times against the city during the months of September, October and November. Reading a detailed account of the strikes, the heroes and the villains and the settlements, is almost as exciting as reading the Manhattan telephone book, but less enlightening. Several salient points are, however, important to the understanding of the union and how it works. The first is that a strike against a single district, a move that Shanker said later would enhance the union's power, was a failure. The central board, which never cared much for the experimental district anyway, hardly lost sleep because there were no teachers there; the local board, like a child grateful that his alcoholic father is out somewhere getting drunk and not beating him or his mother, managed to do middling well without union teachers. It was not until the union struck the entire city that it was able to obtain an acceptable settlement. That's the second point: it did win—the reinstatement of teachers, the suspension of the local board and three of the more supportive principals, makeup time so the membership would not have to lose too much money, and an arbitration procedure, which it had failed to obtain in the 1967 contract. By the following April, it had won everything. The Legislature adopted a weak decentralization bill which dissolved the three experimental districts, a bill which was all but written by the union. The U.F.T. had made the experiments a failure; the experiments themselves were inconclusive because they were destroyed before they bore fruit.

The U.F.T. also proved itself a totally pragmatic organization that would stop at nothing in its effort to win. It widely distributed anti-Semitic hate literature which, even if one concedes it was not written by the union leadership itself, would never have received the wide circulation it did had not the union lent a hand. It insisted on police—sometimes as many as one thousand in a radius of a few blocks—in and about the schools, a sure way of disrupting education and aggravating racial tensions. While preying on the law-and-order paranoia of legislators and others, the U.F.T. very nearly escaped breaking the laws against public-employee strikes. The fines and the fifteen-day sentence for Shanker were really mild punishment for an organization that had closed down the schools for virtually three months.

Most important in terms of future implications for other cities across the nation, the U.F.T. exhibited the power of bestowing upon whatever political or governmental agency *it* chose the ultimate responsibility for operating the schools. It never dealt directly with the governing board; it simply refused to recognize it as an interested party and thereby stripped it of its power. The U.F.T. finally dealt with the city administration and the state Education Department to end the strike—forcing the two agencies to create those conditions which were best for the union and to take responsibility for them. In a sense, labor chose its management, a through-the-looking-glass reversal of the despised company union. The union thus becomes the ultimate in unresponsive bureaucracies—it is not itself responsible for the damage it may inflict, but has the power to choose which political subdivision will be responsible. An incredible power. And one that could conceivably not only take the public out of the public schools but also replace it with a private organization so untouchable —and therefore free to take whatever action it chooses according to the divine right of its enlightened leadership—that it will be able to assume quasi-dictatorial powers over the system which it is supposed to be serving.

In a very real sense, the future of public education in New York rests with the U.F.T. And the leadership of the U.F.T. is the leadership of the national teachers' union. It's an awesome thought.

8

All in the Name of the Children

AFTER ITS IRRESISTIBLE display of political clout in the New York strike of 1968, the American Federation of Teachers succumbed to the temptation of believing its own campaign literature. Into the 1970's it remained a trade-union whose staff and resources were devoted primarily to recruitment and getting the membership into and out of strikes with the best possible contracts. Yet its leadership showed distinct and ominous symptoms of believing that the A.F.T. not only had the capability and integrity to assume the role of savior of our schools, but also had the right, a kind of divine right, derived from clout, to do so. Contract proposals—and successes—saw the union's locals becoming more and more shadow school boards, wielding increasing authority in matters of policy without the bother of political accountability.

All of which would be very tidy—for the A.F.T., at least —except for some rather glaring defects in this kind of arrangement. The union hardly has displayed a depth of understanding of either the political or the educational process which would motivate a community willingly to turn over its schools to its kindly command. And there is little in its history, its present operations or its leadership to indicate that the A.F.T. would know what to do with the public schools of the nation should it manage to assume control through contract—beyond, of course, increasing salaries, decreasing workloads, picking up more members and strengthening leadership control at the top. Its research facilities manage to rediscover innovations in education discarded or improved years ago. Then, of course, there are the annoying problems created by people and groups who cling to the belief that the schools are the instruments of the people as well as the financial burden of the people and, as such, should not be controlled by a private interest group. These groups, variously described by union leaders as collections of radicals or reactionaries, along with student groups and a mélange of other special interests, are becoming more persistent in their demands to control all, or a piece of, the educational activity.

Such competition breeds conflict—war—in the public schools. The A.F.T., with its skilled corps of warriors, its war chest and its battlefield experience, is, temporarily at least, the odds-on favorite to win, likely to surpass in the near future the National Education Association as the most powerful interest group in public education. (Its collective-bargaining units now represent more teachers than the N.E.A.—although the Association still has a better than two-to-one lead in dues-paying membership.) Each new battle becomes increasingly draining—both on the A.F.T.'s resources and on its ability to convince local residents that it is striking *for* the children, not against them. More and more school boards are allowing the teachers to stay out as long as they can, until financial pressure—or political intrigue within the local—forces a return to work. Significantly, this kind of retreat-to-the-steppes-beyond-Moscow approach to collective bargaining, hardly more reasonable than the union's posture, is gaining support from the more vocal residents of big cities, who themselves volunteer to take over the abandoned classrooms—community control through the back door.

The A.F.T., however, is not likely to concede victory to school boards that are as unconcerned about children as the A.F.T. itself. In the years following New York, whenever a school board has put up stiff resistance to the contract onslaught, A.F.T. strikes have been accompanied by harassment, intimidation, and even violence, to help along the old collective-bargaining process. In order to force the political governing board to lean on what are theoretically autonomous educational agencies to produce settlements, the A.F.T. has resorted to the kind of community organization that is nice if you don't mind a riot now and then. In New Orleans in 1969 and in Newark in 1971—simply the most dramatic, certainly not the only illustrations—the Federation brought tense cities to the brink of disaster, perhaps beyond, in order to prove its point.

This distinct lack of civic-mindedness is not at all surprising. It is characteristic of an organization that has taken a kind of adolescent glee in being the bad boy of American education. Each local president sees himself as a radical social reformer; his leadership of a union—rather than the more accepted Association—marks him, he may believe, as a nonconforming seeker of truth and justice, just this side of Joan of Arc or Samuel Adams. The national reps often act as if they believe they were Bondian double agents, hardworking, hard-living, thoroughly romantic masters of intrigue. It makes the pervasively dull life of a union organizer more tolerable. Making deals in closets or in lavatories or on airplanes is, after all, rather silly; but it makes for something to talk about in those long nights in depressingly similar hotel bars. There is, in short, something politically immature about the A.F.T., an immaturity which pervades the organization.

It is reflected in how the present leadership assumed power —and there is little chance for major change. The A.F.T.'s caucus system, dominated by Shanker and Selden, militates against change because winning an election depends almost entirely on selection by the caucus. The caucus has hardly gone beyond the big-city political boss system. In fact, it *is* the political boss system, with power weighted in favor of the cities. Since a small leadership clique can control the delegate votes of a big-city local—through appointment and patronage and special favors—the political leadership of the union rests in the hands of the few. Shanker becomes, in effect, the king maker, as well as the dissident-breaker. "Of course this is power politics," Shanker once remarked. "What other kind of politics is there?" The system has simply marvelous devices of persuasion for those who buck the trend. The most obvious is removal of dissenters from decision-making positions in the union. Another is depriving a disloyal local of financial assistance from the A.F.T.'s "militancy fund," sometimes with the result that the local will be unable to mount an adequate defense in court or on the picket lines.

Almost all organizations consisting of more than two persons are, of course, political. But the severely centralized structure of the national union and the vesting of national power in so few hands very often result in policies derived from personal whim or ambition. Or paranoia. The imaginary intrigue which so often marks the actions of the national representative also pervades the national office. A knowledgeable visitor to the offices on 14th Street in Washington, D.C., becomes immediately aware of the undercurrents of court plotting so seemingly out of place in an organization out to capture the loyalties of more than two million teachers. Part of the national staff devotes its energies to preparing for the day when the Selden-Shanker hegemony is defeated; another part watches very carefully for signs of disloyalty in the others. Still another group carefully cultivates contacts in various factions, hoping to keep their jobs no matter how the political winds blow.

One of Selden's tasks while assistant to Charles Cogen was to be aware of possible political activity among staff members. John Schmid, a former national rep and director of state Federations, now watches on behalf of Selden. Since Selden's close call in the 1970 election, he admits he keeps a particularly watchful eye on the reps and has regionalized their activity, or simply kept them away from important assignments, to prevent empire building among the rank and file. Mundy, probably the most effective organizer and strike strategist the A.F.T. ever employed, still is considered "The Leader" by a number of the reps, despite his dismissal. A number of the staffers slip in and out of his Washington town house. Especially mistrusted reps have been given assignments far from major urban action. Early in 1971, Cascella was assigned to recruitment drives in New Mexico. Bates had been, until recently, kept away from locals which requested his presence.

At the local level, Federation presidents attempt to derive more financial and organizational help by openly flirting with competing organizations—the N.E.A. and the fast-growing American Federation of State, County and Municipal Employees, A.F.L.–C.I.O., a rival public-employee union. (The two groups recently formed an "alliance" to protect public workers and never bothered to invite the A.F.T. to the press conference announcing the plan.) State and local presidents feel that developing a "relationship" with rival organizations is the only lever they have to keep the money, the service and the patronage coming.

At times the intramural conflicts are too obvious to be hidden. The editor of *The American Teacher,* David Elsila, simply does not get along with Shanker; and Shanker makes no attempt to moderate his insistence that Elsila be fired. Shortly after the Ocean Hill-Brownsville debacle, the young, self-proclaimed radical editor ran a full-page reproduction of a poster which lauded attempts at community control, an obvious embarrassment to Shanker. Most of the time, however, the conflicts lie just below the surface, waiting for the next convention to be resurrected. The inevitable purge of dissenters—or loyalists—follows the convention.

Despite the intrigues—or perhaps because of them—the

A.F.T. leadership is driven by the desire to appear respectable. And to be solvent. The original nature of the organization—a symbol of protest among timid teachers—was lost shortly after its membership numbered more than a few thousand. Now the union avoids controversy; faced with a necessity to choose sides it will almost always opt for the more established, even if that means betraying first principles or retracting previous public statements. It happened in the 1930's when the A.F.T. remained with William Green's A.F.L. instead of following John L. Lewis into the C.I.O., despite repeated endorsements within the A.F.T. of the C.I.O. policy of organizing the less skilled and the unskilled. In the 1940's and 1950's, despite its decades-long public embracing of academic freedom, the union turned its back on those identified by others as Communists and ended up refusing them membership within the national. There has been little change in the knee-jerk reaction to stick with the moneyed, with the obvious winner. The latest act of betrayal came in the late 1960's, when the A.F.T. refused to follow the U.A.W. and the Teamsters out of George Meany's A.F.L.–C.I.O.—despite Walter Reuther's essential role in creating and financing the teachers' union and policy statements by Selden which sounded as if they had been written by Reuther himself. The convenient excuse was, of course, "labor unity," a hollow phrase when one considers the internecine war the A.F.T. is beginning to mount against A.F.S.C.M.E.

Not that the A.F.T. does not adopt causes. It does—but respectable ones. It is for integration, for Cesar Chavez, against pollution and for the right of public employees to strike. But present it with a choice that would demand an independence of thought and action, and the A.F.T. will invariably hold to the Meany line. Vietnam, perhaps, is the best example. Selden—though not Shanker—insists he has been against United States policy in Southeast Asia "before it was respectable" to be antiwar. Yet when Meany declared the entire labor movement in support of the invasion of Cambodia in May of 1970, Selden said nothing. Publicly. Privately, he insisted that he believed it was a mistake; but he refused to join with Jacob Potofsky, a long-time friend of the A.F.T. and the only member of the A.F.L.–C.I.O. executive committee to dissent openly from Meany's statement on behalf of workers everywhere in the nation.

The betrayal became even more heartless when the more concerned teachers within the union forced the Vietnam question in a nationwide referendum. Shanker campaigned vigorously for defeat of a resolution condemning the war and demanding an immediate withdrawal from Vietnam; he opposed it primarily on the grounds that it had little to do with teachers and that passage of the resolution would "lose friends" in the labor movement. Selden remained silent. And when the resolution passed—just barely—he declared that it meant little because so few teachers had voted.

Sadly for an organization which has the muscle and the skill to join with students, parents and others concerned with significant reform of education, the A.F.T. has all but betrayed its founding principles, including those articulated by its most prized member, John Dewey. Where Dewey had urged unionization of teachers in order to bring them closer to the concerns of the poor working community, Shanker has urged more and more exclusivist contracts, which put a shield of legalism and bureaucracy between teachers and the poorest of urban communities. The object now is not so much to challenge things as they are, but to take advantage of them, to drive toward the least common denominator in order to build membership, to win collective-bargaining elections, to earn respectability no matter what the cost to conscience or community. Shanker himself points out:

> Part of our major problem within the A.F.T. is not the major locals with bargaining rights. For instance, Detroit, Chicago and the major part of Boston was with us [the Progressive Caucus at the 1970 convention]. The basic problem

. . . is between locals which have exclusive representation and have made it and those locals that are sort of permanent minorities, shut out, representing say five per cent of the faculty . . . essentially a group of people who are not so interested in unionism or collective bargaining as those who have made it.

The locals which haven't made it are more interested in international or other issues—which is exactly the reason why they have not won over the majority of teachers.

Now as states (rather than local districts) get the agency shop, either these locals will either shape up and appeal to 51 per cent of the teachers in their districts or they'll get shut out by the local association which will get the agency shop and they'll be finished.

There's a process of institutionalizing the A.F.T. that's going on. The A.F.T. has been a movement and, as a movement, all movements are more radical than the institutions which they later become.

And as it certainly grows to be an institution—perhaps one day *the* educational institution in America—the A.F.T. loses much of the intellectual, educational and social integrity which, after all, was its *raison d'être*. Not since Dewey has the union been able to produce an advocate of brilliance or of true foresight and sensitivity. In the most generously broad definition, Shanker may qualify as an intellectual, but his efforts have been devoted primarily to pure-grit unionism, devising new strategies and public-relations games that are devoted exclusively to economic welfare and job security. Bayard Rustin is invariably pulled out to justify the A.F.T.'s position, but his slavish and often chauvinistic espousal of union platitudes, though delivered articulately, hardly represents new or insightful thinking. "Ghetto kids are going to get jobs and earn good money by learning how to read, not by going to some phony African art exhibit," he told a union rally in 1971, apparently part of his answer to the searing, complex problem of pluralism within the public schools.

Educationally, the A.F.T. has produced little beyond the M.E.S.—a collection of the most generally agreed-upon and, until lately, unchallengeable educational improvements: small classes, extensive psychological care, team teaching and so on. It is no coincidence that adoption of this More Effective Schools program relieves teachers of a great deal of work; it is no coincidence that contractual commitment to M.E.S. by a school board would mean direct union control over every aspect of public education, because the entire school system would be committed to contract language. But what is new in all of this? What fundamental questions have been asked by the union about how children learn, how the traditional approaches to education can be changed to accommodate an overpopulated, increasingly urbanized and polarized and polluted world? None, really. Educational institution as it may aspire to be, the A.F.T. does not have the resources or the imagination to offer any real alternatives. If it were to assume full control of all aspects of public education the day after you read this book, nothing much would change—except perhaps that you would have even less, perhaps nothing, to say about the direction of the school to which you send your children and your tax dollar.

Politically, intellectually, socially and educationally, the A.F.T. is bankrupt. Not because its teacher-members want it to be so, but because it is a traditional labor union grafted on-to an educational system which, too, is all but bankrupt. Because it is a union first and foremost, its organization is geared to war, to servicing strikes, to collecting new members, to protecting teachers—whether or not they deserve protection—never considering the possibility that teachers, as surrogate parents, should really derive their true protection from the pure love they provide for their children and the respect they earn in a community, a neighborhood or a town. A.F.T. leadership behaves like the leadership of any other established union—that is, with an eye to staying in power as long as possible. (A former union president is simply a teacher without a regular job, far away from the benefits of power and prestige.) Although it pays considerable lip service to local autonomy and union democracy, the national trains its reps to mold opinion, to exploit fears, if necessary, to promote paranoia and hysteria and even racism among its teachers, for the war must be won.

As a protest organization, and not the educational establishment it aspires to be, the teachers' union might have become the central organizing force for all the diverse elements which, within the public schools, are demanding change. Oriented to local concerns, allied with what should be their natural allies—parents and students—organized teachers might have been able to provoke reform, even through mass action like strikes, while still maintaining a sound enough base among the local gentry to ensure competitive salaries and tolerable working conditions, something that every teacher and public employee, something that every worker, deserves. But the creation of a union with national ambitions, with designs on controlling the direction and the shape of public education everywhere in the nation, requires an upward flow of power and concern from the local to the national and a substantial surrendering of local initiative to national plans. Strikes often are called to meet national objectives; they may be called off for the same reasons. The flow of services and funds are determined by the national. Contract proposals, negotiating techniques and general policy are dictated at the national level, and acceptance is a matter of union discipline and union loyalty—a virtue promoted within locals, particularly large, bargaining locals, to the detriment of loyalty to the local community or, if that it is too difficult for a teacher to accept, to the ethics and ideals of the profession.

The union leadership—the political leadership, not top staff—denies that the union is determined to control education exclusively, to deliver the final death blow to the possibility of schools *for* the people operated *by* the people. Selden insists that he believes in lay control of public education, but is quick to concede that only a strong union presence prevents the schools from falling into the hands of special interests or business or government shackles. He apparently cannot see the union itself as a special interest. Shanker believes that laymen must decide "what kind of society they want" and leave the creation of the society up to the "experts," the teachers. This is more than simply an artificial and unworkable separation of ends and means in public education.* Learning, the education of a society, cannot be compartmentalized into such neat categories. Teaching a child how to learn is both an end and a means. The process is, or should be, a continuum which extends far beyond the high school or the graduate school. The distinction between layman and expert in learning also reinforces the fabricated aura of mystery around learning, as if it were something that parents had nothing to do with—even as a child's first, and perhaps best, teachers. Such a distinction may support the bid of a special interest to base its power upon the public schools, but it denies the very real process of learning which is drawn from the vast world outside the classroom: the home, the streets, the family, the job, the church and daily relationships with other people. Many competent urban educators have found that the key to learning for disadvantaged youngsters lies in relating the classroom work to the ghetto experience. So-called "schools without walls" (such as the Parkway School in Philadelphia), which draw upon man's achievements and follies as they exist in the community, are gaining more and more popularity among successful and innovative educators. The horrendous "methods" courses in teacher-training institutions are among the logical and absurd consequences of treating teaching as a pure science, understood only by the "expert." These courses, this approach, are fast being disgraced. Put into disgrace not so much by the "expert educator" whose special interests demand their survival as by the concerned laymen who will no longer tol-

---

* Significantly, an attempt to create this kind of model in Ocean Hill-Brownsville was destroyed by union activity.

erate the failures of methodology to help their children. A definition of education as an organic process precludes control by one elite or the other; that sort of thinking cannot be tolerated by an exclusivist organization like the A.F.T.

Even if the public, thoroughly political statements of the present A.F.T. leadership leave some doubt about intentions, the actions and the goals of the staff cannot. To the union's reps, the union someday will control education. Trained to treat school boards as the enemy, to ignore popular movements unless they show the political clout that can aid in the procurement of a "good" contract, and to use the needs and the aspirations and the futures of children and parents as levers with which to gain bargaining strength or public sympathy, the union's warriors are, almost to a man, devoted to union hegemony over the public schools. There are only a few of these warriors—but these few control the direction of every major local's action, and it is at these times of conflict that the precedents are set and the future course is determined. The staff has an impact far beyond their numbers. To some, the time cannot come fast enough when they will not be controlling policy *against* a local school system, but *for* it. One or two others see the dangers in replacing one stultifying organization—the N.E.A. or the school board—with another, the A.F.T. The "new tyranny," one rep calls it. But that is why that rep was removed from major assignments and sent to missionary work in the decidedly antiunion Southwest; that is why he is all but ostracized by his fellow reps. To say that staff does not set policy is a myth; the reps set it where it most affects the daily workaday citizen, at the most local of levels.

National policy comes to surface most dramatically in union contract proposals "recommended" by national staffers— men like John Converse, who became a teacher to join the union. And it is a policy of control gained through the contractual establishment of a shadow school board and administration controlled by the local union according to national guidelines, and the reduction of the minutest detail of daily school operations to contract language so that any change must have union blessing. It would be of no use to the union to eliminate the administration or even the school board; these agencies serve the useful purpose of taking flak from the public, which has little, if any, input and is granted no real authority in the negotiation process. Angry demands by parent groups are shunted conveniently over to the conventional board or administration; control can be exercised without an accounting.

A typical contract calls for a special union-selected committee to meet regularly with the superintendent for "general policy discussions." The number of union committee members and the frequency with which the superintendent is required to meet with them matches exactly the number of school-board members and the frequency of scheduled school-board meetings. The superintendent must first consult with this "shadow" board before making any changes in practice or policy. The union president, or his representative, is granted authority similar to that of the superintendent—the right to visit schools at will, to be included in personnel matters, to speak during private sessions of the school board. The school board itself is required to meet regularly with the "shadow" board to discuss a formal agenda of items determined jointly by the two parties. This arrangement implies that the school board may not act without prior consultation—prior approval, really—of the Federation's own "board of education."

Few people would argue against increased teacher participation in policy-making decisions. But it must be made clear that this is not an arrangement between teachers and representatives of the public, but one between the union and the centralized school board. In other words, it is an exclusive sharing of power between an unresponsive private interest and a chronically unresponsive public one. Under union contracts, teachers do not necessarily find themselves in policy-making positions, but union representatives do; they are not necessarily and often not likely the same. In the standard preamble to any "good" union contract, there is a statement to the effect that the union and the school board—not teachers and parents—declare their "mutual intent to work cooperatively toward achieving common aims." This represents an institutionalization of the union's role, often resisted by school-board members, resisted not because such resistance will enhance public control, but simply their own prerogatives.

But aren't "union rights" sections simply designed to create advisory committees? No. Since the remainder of the contract delineates quite specifically terms and conditions of employment, as well as the routine operations of the school, there is little need for "union advice." It is more the creation of a joint administration of the contract that dictates the administration of the school itself. A building representative takes on the role of a shadow principal not so that he can "advise" the appointed, but in order to "help" him administer the school according to contract provisions.

Once the union's right to co-administer the contract is established, the model contract proposals move on to actual working conditions. Hours and wages are, of course, established. But so are priorities in facilities and classroom sizes. And, in incredibly simplistic definitions, exactly what a teacher is. So, a faculty lounge must be established in every school, complete with refrigerator, stove (or hot plate), soft-drink and snack vending machines, and comfortable furniture. Professional journals must be provided, along with an adequate number of cabinets and cupboards. Parking spaces must be provided for teachers' cars—or the teachers must be held harmless from parking violations. Class sizes are limited, as are the number of students with which a teacher must come into contact each day. Teachers are to be freed from "nonprofessional chores" which include not only clerical and attendance work but also correcting standardized tests and homework. Teachers are to come into contact with their students only in the classroom, not in the hallways, the playgrounds or cafeterias; they are to come into contact with their principals only upon five days' written notice, a notice stating the reason for the meeting and informing the teachers of their right of representation by the union representative.

Arguing against smaller class sizes, of course, makes one sound like the educational equivalent of Ivan the Terrible. I certainly have no objection, but it should be pointed out that locking such a provision in a contract reduces the kind of flexibility necessary to introduce such innovations as the "learning center" or "open classroom." Small classes are not best under all conditions; but if they are stipulated in a contract, not only do they commit the school board to potentially monstrous capital construction projects, but they must be applied universally so that innovation as to class size suffers. Teachers, of course, should not be required to perform any tasks which demean their status as professionals. But the "nonprofessional" chores clause in a typical union contract has had the effect of further separating the teacher from the child, dehumanizing, in a sense, an all-important relationship. What can make this standard clause particularly odious is that it is aimed, from a union point of view, not at making teachers more professional, but at forcing the school board to hire paraprofessionals and others to supervise the children at play, in the lunchrooms, at crosswalks and in the hallways, thereby creating more members for the union, more per capita dues. There have been instances in which teachers refuse to do such chores—and the board, displaying an unconscionable, though typical, indifference, refuses to hire teacher or school aides, thereby leaving children unsupervised while at play or in the hallways. Teachers who voluntarily perform such tasks are first reminded by the building representative that they are violating their contracts and are then made subjects of a grievance through the standard grievance procedure.

Model proposals also base assignment of teachers to regular classroom activities and also to extracurricular activities purely on seniority—and with rotation, so all might get a share of the well-paid extra work. While no one would deny seniority's claim on privilege, this does produce sticky problems. Should someone who doesn't particularly care about journalism be assigned as moderator of the school newspaper? Should a winning coach be "bumped" by rotation? Should unpopular or disinterested teachers be assigned to particularly sensitive or specialized activities, such as art and drama clubs, or political clubs? And doesn't all this insistence on seniority ensure that the oldest teachers—those furthest from the children, at least in age—will be forced into the greatest contact with the students? All of the knottier questions can be worked out, of course, through "consultation" between the union and the administration, thereby again pointing up joint administration of activities—without public participation.

While model contracts display an almost paranoid concern for what is called "academic freedom"—teacher grade books may not be shown to anyone, the teacher is "to be considered the expert," and so on—they also include a potential dose of intimidation for errant principals. The supervisors must undergo regular evaluation by the staff and the "evaluations are to be considered binding." Union-selected committees must be established to screen potential principals and superintendents. The school board may choose its appointments only from committee recommendations. The union—not the teachers—must be represented on all boards of examiners or in any other selection process.

Meanwhile, the school system must rush to the defense of any teacher in a civil or criminal jam, including paying for "lawyers of the teacher's own choosing" and holding harmless any teacher who might accidentally burn down a building as long as it is in the course of the school day. Theoretically, if a teacher was brought up on charges for striking a child, he could ask for F. Lee Bailey, Melvin Belli, Louis Nizer, Arthur Goldberg, or any lawyer, and the schools must pay the freight.

And that is just the beginning of the personal services that the union's model contracts demand for the teachers. The list of benefits include publicly supported day-care centers for the exclusive use of teachers, paid two-week honeymoons, free dental and eye care—including contact lenses—for the teacher and his family, all medical expenses, including drugs and routine physicals, tuition for all courses at any college, retirement after twenty years or at age forty-five, and paid sabbatical leaves for any reason—including creative loafing—every five years. (While a number of these are generally considered "silly" items by A.F.T. negotiators, they are beginning to creep into a number of contracts.)

As experts, of course, the teachers, through union-selected committees, are given the exclusive and final say on the selection of textbooks and other instructional materials. (Publishers with union troubles have had difficulty peddling their books to some union-dominated systems.) The union committees also have veto power over any curriculum revision proposed by the administration, the board, or anyone else. The number and duties of specialists such as psychologists, social workers, nurses, and so on, in the school is, naturally, determined by the union.

To summarize the model pact: the union operates the schools without genuine responsibility to anyone, certainly not to the public. Not that all of the items and all of the benefits have been included in all union contracts; but they are goals, and contracts won by local unions in New York, Chicago, San Francisco and Newark reflect the spirit, if not the letter, of the policies. With every new contract expiration and renegotiation—particularly with every new strike—the union approaches the ideals set forth by the national. And the national ideals are ever escalating. A most recent addition is the so-called 20-20 plan, which stipulates that no teacher works with more than 20 students for more than 20 hours a week.

As might be expected, local school boards and parent and community groups have not hailed the promise of control by contract as the great salvation of education that the A.F.T. pretends it is—school boards, because they see little sense in giving away authority; parent and community (and student) groups, because comprehensive written agreements between the boards and the union freeze out the possibility of participation in the public schools. The most ever granted to parent, taxpayer and youngster is the permission to view the often senseless haggling between labor and theoretically public management, to suffer the consequences of a strike and to pay for whatever covenant, invariably secretly arranged, emerges out of the fumes of war. In the vast majority of cases, the school board capitulates, surrendering just a little more of the public prerogative each time. But resistance is becoming more common throughout the land, particularly since Ocean Hill-Brownsville in 1968. A board of education may decide to draw the line, usually arbitrarily and at the wrong place, and with very little thought to what damage a protracted confrontation might do to the children. Parent or community groups, representative or otherwise, may attempt to organize antiunion sentiment with which to pressure the board, or the union members directly, into defying the local Federation. The result of resistance is almost always war. A town's or city's children—in whose name, of course, all the battles are fought—may lose one, two, or even three months of schooling. Shanker and other union lights have denied the tragic impact of an extended strike— "What has not been learned today can be learned tomorrow," he is fond of saying. But the attitude cynically ignores the hundreds of high-school students who never return after a strike ends, or the missed electric moment when a teacher inspires a youngster to regard education as important, or the slight retardation in learning which might be compounded again and again as students move through the grades.

Since the New York strike of 1968, lines have been dramatically drawn in Los Angeles, San Francisco, New Orleans, Minot, Pittsburgh, East St. Louis and Newark. Generally speaking, the A.F.T. has won some and lost some. The children always lost. In terms of the horror of their implications relative to the continued survival of a peaceful public-school system, and what they demonstrate about the union's willingness to sink to the lowest in order to "win," New Orleans and Newark-1971 bear the most ominous of messages.

It is Wednesday evening, April 2, 1969, and it is New Orleans. Jim Mundy, the A.F.T.'s chief organizer, is fast coming to the realization that the Bastille is obviously still impregnable. Ken Miesen, the A.F.T. national rep who has been working the Gulf port for nearly six months, now makes no effort to resist the temptation to tell Mundy, "I told you so." There is supposed to be a strike here the following day, but as Mundy, Miesen and a number of other local and national Federation officers concentrate on the supply of Scotch and bourbon, it becomes increasingly apparent that the strike will fizzle—despite months of preparation. The A.F.T. wants New Orleans so badly that it has been willing to spend thousands on invariably unsuccessful recruitment efforts and strike attempts. Selden has managed to schedule the national's 1969 convention in the city, and he and Shanker and the others in the Progressive Caucus expect the A.F.T. to have collective-bargaining rights before they get there in August. The A.F.T. has created a "paper" state Federation to counter the enormous strength of the Louisiana Education Association—but the paper is too thin and teachers can see through it. The national believes that if the South and the Southwest are ever to be taken from the Association, a major city must fall to the A.F.T. New Orleans, considered the "friendliest" to labor in the South—as Southern cities go, anyway—is the obvious choice. There has been an almost totally black local in the city as far back as anyone can remember, but it has failed to develop a wider base. No question—there must be an election, a secret-ballot election to show A.F.T. strength.

Mundy has called it the A.F.T.'s Bastille, both because of its symbolic importance in opening up the South and because of its stubborn disinclination to fall. But Mundy believes its resistance will crumble. "We organized a perfect strike in every way," he recalled several months later. "We laid the groundwork perfectly." The only problem was, of course, that the teachers gave no indication they would follow the union into war. They didn't when one rep attempted a strike in 1966, only to call a "temporary pause" when the bodies appeared in classrooms, not on the picket lines. And they didn't when another never even got as far as a strike vote in 1968. As the level of the liquor sank, so did the hopes. All that money for nothing.

Late in the evening, another Federation member, with a reputation for accepting the extreme with little difficulty, enters the motel room with the proud announcement that no schools will open in the morning. Mundy says he really doesn't want to hear the plan. While the reps were contemplating another New Orleans fiasco, a locally staffed anarchy committee has been busy plugging the locks on schoolhouse gates and doors with liquid lead. It is the beginning of the end of non-destructive tactics for the A.F.T. When the custodians report to work early on Holy Thursday morning, April 3, they find the locks inoperable; but they immediately receive orders to cut the gates open, to smash in the doors if necessary. Dr. Carl Dolce, the parish schools superintendent, insists that he will keep his schools open. On the first day of the strike, called before a three-day weekend to take advantage of traditional high absentee rates and the prospect for negotiation without the pressure of maintaining a walkout, only 29 of 120 schools are closed, nearly all of them in the black sections of the city.

Throughout the weekend Miesen tries to find someone with whom to negotiate. For the last eight months, he has met with virtually every political, business, civic, religious and community leader in the city to ask for support for a bargaining election. But even unionized truck drivers refuse to support the A.F.T. Now with an obviously faltering strike on his hands, he needs a way out. The school board, led by businessman Lloyd J. Rittiner, refuses to talk. "I had nothing to say to him," Rittiner remembers. Meanwhile, Dolce orders extraordinary precautions to protect the schools; the next time the "anarchy committee" goes out, Sunday night, they are chased by free-roaming German Shepherds on the school grounds. By the middle of the next week, all the schools in the city are open, all but a few hundred teachers are back in school. Miesen wants to call it off, Mundy agrees and tries to think of the least humiliating way; but Washington says no. The Bastille must fall.

By the second week of the strike, the A.F.T.'s political position is fast becoming untenable. The union had marched on New Orleans promising equal educational opportunity for black youngsters in a Southern city, but the only place the strike was effective was in the black section of the city. It is clearly a strike against black children now, because the school board is completely ignoring the union and the white schools are operating without any sign of a problem. Since a majority of the local is black, the white-run national staff in the city begins to feel uncomfortable, even unwanted. Joe Cascella is brought in, as is every other rep except Robert Crosier, who is losing in Minot, North Dakota. Cascella organizes a number of marches to City Hall and the school-board offices. There is even a "debate" between union teachers and an empty chair to represent Dolce, who refuses to talk with the local's representatives. Teachers are sent to picket Rittiner's home; but in an infuriating gesture of Southern hospitality, Mrs. Rittiner provides the pickets with lawn chairs and ice-cold lemonade. The A.F.T. is more than ignored—it is being ridiculed.

This is no accident. While Miesen was planning his strategy, Dolce was not idle. He sent a team of staff members all over the country, to cities which had been struck by the A.F.T.; his men were to gather information, to talk about alternatives. He learned from Pittsburgh's Sidney P. Marland—at this writing United States Commissioner of Education—not to panic when struck, but to marshal resources to keep the schools open no matter what. In the past, many school superintendents had shut all their doors as soon as a strike began and had thus made a potentially disastrous, for the union, walkout 100 percent successful. He also learned from Marland that the

A.F.T. feeds off news coverage; the more it is ignored, the sooner it will go away. While this is true, the price will be high. Especially for the black children, who have a habit of being ignored in New Orleans anyway, by school board or union.

Slowly, the number of striking teachers decreases; the activities of the "anarchy committee" increase. A number of high-school students engage in riots in the all-black schools. When the police are called in to restore peace with billies, no union reps are hurt, but many youngsters are. "Someone" buys and distributes among the children large firecrackers—cherry bombs—and one junior high school in the George Washington Carver complex begins to look and to sound like a free-fire zone in Vietnam. Again the police come in, and again children are hurt. Meanwhile, nonstriking teachers throughout the city are finding their car tires slashed, windshields smashed. The madness is capped by the firebombing of a junior-high-school gymnasium. Mundy again unsuccessfully appeals for an end.

Finally, the local black leadership of the union declares it has had enough with the A.F.T.'s goals for Southern expansion. Of the 33,000 children in the 29 schools most severely affected by the walkout and the violence, only 12 youngsters are white. The children who have been hurt in intramural riots have all been black; most of the teachers arrested while sitting-in at City Hall are black. It is beginning to dawn on the local leadership that the Orleans Parish School Board and the union don't mind fighting it out on the backs of black children. On the night of April 16, Mrs. Veronica Hill, Local 520's president, meets privately with Rittiner. ("They said they wanted to come back, and I said that's fine with me.") Without the knowledge of the national staff, the strike is called off; Bates, Miesen and the others read about it in the morning newspapers. They are gone with the next plane north. Mrs. Hill eventually presses charges against nearly every national rep for using the strike as a political weapon within the Federation, but the executive board dismisses the complaint. Several weeks later, the "Biloxi" idea—using violence as a last resort in particularly brutal strikes—is discussed. The A.F.T. may have crossed the line; goon squads, apparently, can be made of teachers. And Rittiner believes it was right to hold the line, to prevent a union from determining board policy. "It worked, didn't it? I notice other school boards are adopting the same strategies. And I'd do it again if the A.F.T. ever tried to come back." The A.F.T., no doubt, will try to come back, and the board likely will resist again.

New Orleans did indeed set an oft-repeated pattern throughout the nation. The parish school board had discovered, probably more by accident than intention, the union's most vulnerable spot—its pretensions. The local was not able to close down most of the parish schools as it had warned; it failed to draw much more than 10 percent of the city's 4,500 teachers. By virtually ignoring the union the board reaffirmed the A.F.T.'s distinct minority status and deprived the organizers of angry controversies around which it could rally believers. The bluff was called, leaving the union with a pair of threes and, eventually, a racial-political mess with which to hang itself. A year later, the Los Angeles School Board let a delicately fashioned merger between the Federation and an Association affiliate hang itself by ignoring it. Other school districts, in small and large cities alike, repeated the process with variations. Despite its initial successes, the strategy is as morally and educationally bankrupt as the jingoism of the A.F.T. Now the children and the parents of a district can be sure that no agency—neither the union nor the board—has dedicated itself to the protection of learning, but only to the protection of its own power. Holding the line institutionalizes and justifies war in the public schools and guarantees future hostilities of greater and greater intensity.

Ultimately, a school board would have to adopt the policy of striking first, of going on the offensive against a union. Once war is accepted as a justifiable means of resolving labor disputes, the role of aggressor is interchangeable. And that is what happened in Newark in 1971, producing a strike that kept 40,000 children, including nearly all the high-school youngsters, away from the classroom for three months. Not that the union was blameless; it wasn't. But the school board's flirtation with Neanderthal union-busting techniques reflected a stupidity which, no doubt, will spread to other urban areas. The Newark experience, a conflict that brought the city uncomfortably close to civil disorders, may have set a precedent justifying the use of irrationality in disputes too complex to resolve with a meat cleaver.

This was radically unlike the Newark strike of just a year earlier, when a well-oiled, nationally directed A.F.T. steamroller struck the schools for four weeks and extorted probably the union's best "first contract" in the nation (see Chapter 6). Within the union, Mrs. Carole Graves, little more than a figurehead and handy sacrificial lamb—and show-black union leader—had evolved into a clever and powerful and undisputed union boss. The crucible of the three months she would have to serve in prison worked to remind her that she was paying the price without reaping the enjoyment of running her own show. When Selden was released from jail for his part in the 1970 strike he took her on a nationwide tour of "bread-and-water" receptions, ostensibly to promote right-to-strike legislation. Halfway through the tour, she said she realized that she was being used, made some sort of excuse and returned home to build her own local as a focal point for anti-Selden, anti-Shanker action. At the 1970 convention, she joined with William Simons, Richard Parrish and a number of staff in the effort to sink Selden. Mrs. Graves espoused community control and denounced, when the opportunity permitted, Shanker's extermination of Ocean Hill-Brownsville. Her local grew—it had numbered only a few hundred during the 1970 strike—and her power and prestige among black union members and medium-size Federations increased dramatically. Needless to say, her attitudes went unappreciated by the A.F.T. leadership, which now looked upon her as a substantial threat to things as they were. If Mrs. Graves was to lead another walkout in 1971, she would have to do it on her own and the national would not be averse to a solid defeat.

Which was exactly what the school board was planning. It was a new school board, really, with four of its nine members appointed by the city's new mayor, Kenneth A. Gibson. The other five members were still smarting from the heavy-handed pressure that former Mayor Hugh J. Addonizio had exerted in the previous strike. When the board made its decision to draw the line, not only to prevent new gains, but also to remove a number of contract provisions favorable to the union, the vote was unanimous. The attitudes of the school board reflected the obsessive desire on the part of the many new people in civil and educational administration in the city to act differently, to try to be as radically responsive as possible, now that the old order, disgraced by negligence and corruption, had been swept away at the polls. Although the poverty, the filth, the deplorable housing and medical conditions, the too-often nonoperative schools of the old Newark remained, those appointed to positions of power by Gibson felt that the new Newark demanded the destruction and reconstruction of as many reminders of the old order as possible—like, for example, the Newark Teachers Union, whether or not that would improve the schools.

Gibson, no doubt, had this in mind when he appointed Jesse Jacob to the school board and the rest of the board quickly elected him its president. The primary qualifications of the young public-housing manager were his rabid distaste for the teachers' union and his proclaimed spiritual proximity to the people on the street. He was a man energized by hate, by frustration, by a black chauvinism which bordered on separatism. During the trials that followed the 1970 teachers' strike, Jacob voluntarily testified against the many teachers he personally served with copies of the antistrike injunction— again as a volunteer. He was an important witness against Selden. Jacob invariably appeared at the unending series of highly charged school-board meetings during the walkout, denouncing the union, calling Shanker "that idiot" and urging the arrest of every teacher who "struck against the children." When he was made school-board president, the union concluded that the new city administration was trying to tell it something. It was right.

What Jacob was to tell the union was that it would have to surrender its very general nonprofessional clause and its grievance procedure if it wanted another contract come February 1, 1971. Since a cardinal tenet in A.F.T.—or any union—doctrine is thou shalt not give up what thou hast received but simply get more, the local union leadership simply could not believe the man was serious. But he was quite serious—for some good, and a number of bad, reasons. The nonprofessional-chores clause won by the Newark union was unlike any other in the nation; it simply stated that teachers shall be relieved of all nonprofessional chores—all of them—without specifically mentioning what was and what was not considered nonprofessional. In effect, it left to the union the interpretation of what its teachers should do beyond simply being in a classroom. The Federation leadership put together the simple equation: the less teachers do, the more teacher aides will be necessary; the more aides hired, the more union members, the more per capita dues, the more power for the now officially "maverick" local within the A.F.T. As far as the leadership was concerned, everything beyond pure teaching was a nonprofessional chore. The union's interpretation was upheld by an arbitrator's decision, which inspired Jacob's determination to get rid of the standard and relatively harmless grievance procedure.

Now, what is wrong with union interpretation of the role of a teacher is that it displays an unwillingness to consult with the parents and the children about what they want from a teacher. In the fall of 1970, when the arbitrator's decision was handed down, a group of parents at Newark's largest elementary school—the South 8th Street School—wanted their teachers to escort their children from the school bus to the classroom, they wanted teacher supervision in the playgrounds and the hallways. The union, of course, opposed it and filed grievances against any teacher who voluntarily stayed with his children at proscribed times. Contracts must not be violated— even if it means basing a grievance on the actions of a fellow teacher. Schools Superintendent Franklyn Titus finally ordered all teachers everywhere in the eighty-four-school district not to perform these nonprofessional chores. The union cared little about local residents' vocal concern for the health and safety of their children—to say nothing of how parents might feel about teachers who did not wish to be with their children outside of the classroom. A contract has no emotions. But parents do, and the impersonality of the contract provisions as well as the indifference of the union representatives at the school and the actions of the school board led to a parental boycott, a popular movement soon co-opted by professional community spokesmen, men like Dr. E. Wyman Garrett, an antiunion board member whom Gibson had refused to reappoint. Again, the failure of a theoretically *public* school system to provide direct parental involvement produced the only means people then have of correcting what they believe to be inequities—extralegal, invariably self-destructive action always vulnerable to exploitation by the professionals in the community-organization racket, the kinds of people Shanker consistently pointed to in Ocean Hill-Brownsville, despite the stabilizing presence of a legally elected and responsible local governing board. The boycott ended with the transfer of three prounion teachers, including the building representative—a clear violation of the contract. But Mrs. Graves quieted the demands for a strike. Then. It would have been too much in the Shanker tradition. Superficially, events were under control.

But the school-board members were not willing to allow the question to remain unanswered. The fear of minor disturbances escalated and exploited into urban implosion has been a persistent and gnawing presence in the city of Newark since the nightmare summer of 1967, and it made them determined to change the contract. No effort was made, tragically, by either the board or the union to settle the matter quietly. It probably could have been done. That might have removed the exhilarating prospects for war and therefore eliminated the absurd test of whether it was the union or the board that dictated contract items. In their frantic search for "community" support and legitimacy for the momentous struggle they were about to confront, the school-board members cultivated alliances with some of the most reactionary and antiunion forces within the city, forgetting for a moment, perhaps, the chestnut about people who ride tigers. The deal was neat; since the school board had to prove the union was anticommunity, it had to create and project a community with which no compromise was possible, one which would be vocal and threatening enough to show to the world that school-board capitulation to the union might provoke more bloodshed in the streets. They found no shortage of professional and self-appointed community representatives.

Since 1967, in Newark and in other cities, the old traditional community leaders appointed by the local government, the sad parade of tired and tiresome ministers and others, has given way to a new kind of community spokesman; and many of that kind are self-appointed, without constituency, but recognized and cultivated by established powers not on the basis of sensitivity so much, or superior understanding, but purely on the basis of how loud they can lash out at the power structure. They are often recognized as black leadership not through some masochism on the part of those who control government, but because they can siphon off the true and angry discontent of a true community. Various levels of government are often happy to provide substantial funds and well-paying jobs on the theory that if the loudest are well paid, they will keep the truly disfranchised quiet. Certainly not a new idea; simply an extension of colonial governance. It was no coincidence that the most virulent opposition to the union came from leaders and members of the city's antipoverty agencies; counterpickets were often driven to the schools during the strike in federally provided vans. Despite all their aspirations to community revolution, these cultural nationalists have no qualms about accepting money from a decidedly nonrevolutionary federal, state or local government. And often no hesitation to do its bidding in the name of the people. These antipoverty leaders, linked with poet-playwright Le Roi Jones (Imamu Amiri Baraka) through a common rhetoric and a common membership in such organizations as the Committee for a Unified New Ark and a common separatist view of urban society, provided the school board with its support and its potential for havoc if the board lost. The school board blessed them by recognizing them as the true community of the city of Newark.

Not that the union was idle in its organization of a "community." The board's flirtation with separatist elements provided enough fear among many whites to make them susceptible to organization in support of the union. Vigilante leader Tony Imperiale, the law-and-order man, again supported what would be an illegal strike.* Ironically, the predominantly white West, North and East wards were hit the hardest by the strike—because parents kept their children home in support of the strike against the black-dominated school board and the perceived influence of Jones (who will never win a popularity contest among whites in the city). In other words, the union was able to exploit racial fear so well that it convinced people to act against the best educational interests of their children. Of course, throughout the three-month ordeal, the average parent, or true "community" member, was en-

---

* The various political combinations in the city really give pause: Le Roi Jones and the city government and the courts, which were to impose heavy fines and jailings on the union leaders, versus the likes of Imperiale and the state's minimal Black Panther Party, which supported the union because of opposition to Jones and, in common with Carole Graves, a mildly Marxist interpretation of society.

tirely ignored. War demands soldiers and discipline, not civilians and diversity.

The strike commenced February 1 and ended April 19. It was a tragic reckoning for Mrs. Graves and for those who believe the union can be changed simply by changing the leadership. The young black woman insisted she had visions of the teachers' union organizing the most oppressed for a joint struggle against the educational oppressor; in the crunch, she reacted as any union leader with less lofty vision might. She ordered a strike, maintained it through some of the ugliest picket-line violence and vandalism since New Orleans, permitted the exploitation of racial fears by organizational ties with white racists—black racists were invariably opposed to the predominantly white union—and ended it without noticeable benefit to anyone. The union had, of course, presented its usual list of demands; but when the strike began, it was forced to protect what it had won the previous year— which it did. Mrs. Graves herself, while in jail—she spent forty-one days there and will likely spend up to a year if the appeals are denied—admitted that the union had won too much too quickly the previous year. But as a union leader, a union concerned about its political ties to the national, she had no choice but to strike against the best interests of the children, the teachers, the city and her own vision of teacher-public participation in the rescuing of a moribund educational system. The union had to act as a belligerent in order to keep aboard the teachers it had frightened into the security and economic-welfare mentality; and it had to keep them in order to remain a large and solvent union, capable of political influence at the national conventions of the A.F.T.

Paradoxically, the Newark union and Mrs. Graves probably gained little in terms of influence on the national. Although she purposely kept the ubiquitous Shanker away from rally microphones and featured Simons and Parrish at the weekly gatherings, the N.T.U. had to turn, ultimately, to the source of money and of power within the A.F.T. for help in paying $250,000 in fines and nearly as much in legal fees. The Newark leadership intends to defy the national by taking the question of whether teachers may strike to the United States Supreme Court—the A.F.T. is against this as a matter of policy for fear the high court will set a national antistrike precedent, but the intention must be backed with funds. After the strike ended, the Newark local, its leadership split into a dozen dagger-wielding conspiracies, its treasury containing $75 and a debt approaching $1 million, was virtually powerless. The A.F.T. would revive it again, no doubt; but on its own terms.

But there will be more strikes like those in Newark and New Orleans. And they will likely be larger and more despicable in their physical and spiritual violence, as the union marches on and the school boards react with little responsibility. Already, staff members have used the Newark experience to persuade teacher-recruits that *this* will happen to you unless you belong to a strong union which can control all aspects of the schools, keeping the "community"—you all know what that means—out of the schools. Control of the schools *is* up for grabs, and the smell of the battle makes good people withdraw and demagogues arise, and drives teachers to the false safety of the union. For now, the battles will tear up only local, self-contained cities and towns. But the trend, tragically for what stabilizing influence a true local community might have on the battle, will be increasingly toward larger units of educational governance—metropolitan-regional, statewide or, perhaps, even national.* It will be a trend to accommodate perfectly well a centralized A.F.T. Many states, finally conscious of what local funding can do to the already overburdened homeowner, are considering education on a statewide level; but they will be taking local con-

---

* The benefits of a regional system are, I believe, obvious in terms of broader financial support and the prospects for ending de facto segregation. But the effects on a national tradition-myth of educational self-governance are likely to be fatal.

trol over hiring, curriculum and personnel away with local spending. That can only improve the prospects for more centralized, more distant, union control. Shanker himself prefers broad national regions, or even national control. The idea of the school as the extension of the people and its hopes, its dreams, its chance for producing a nation of people who do not think alike but who draw from their diverse backgrounds a pluralistic approach to life and learning—this idea, while even now drying up because of the failure of conventional, quasi-representative governance to speak to the people and the thrust for power of private-interest groups (the A.F.T. among them the best organized and least responsive), will certainly wither and die.

With centralized administration of government in education, and with policies determined by a centralized and reform-resistant national union to protect the status quo, the conflicts may just be fought out at a higher level—the A.F.T. against the N.E.A., or A.F.S.C.M.E., with which the N.E.A. has formed an alliance, or with the umbrella administrative groups which have formed in response to the N.E.A.'s parroting of the union line. Whoever emerges from the ashes as antihero of what had been a locally centered, potentially popular school system will have incredible power in determining what children will learn, what kind of children the "experts" will create, what the "final product" will be. There will be reaction, of course, as there is reaction now; but the directionless and angry partisans of local control may very well turn instead from public education to private education, to the establishment of their own schools, pervaded with a racist chauvinism. It is already happening. Whatever the union, if allowed to grow and if fed by the tendency toward more and more centralization, will win may not be worth the price. It may have to destroy public education in order to "save" it, according to its own parochial lights.

This has not been a book of answers, but rather one of unanswered questions and, I hope, of warnings. Public schools which might become extensions of, and responsive to, parents and community life are delicate creatures that must be cared for with patience and with devotion. They will prevail only if everyone who has a stake in the future of our children has a genuine opportunity to act in their behalf through some instrument other than a chronically unresponsive school board, untainted by narrow, private interests related only to job security or economic welfare of the few or, worst of all, related to the political aggrandizement of a national lobby and its leadership. The people must know that the schools are, or should be, the people's schools, maybe the last defense against atomization and alienation in a nation becoming monstrously overpopulated and urbanized. The schools are the people's instruments for the correction of social, economic, political, legal and environmental evils. Or they should be. They may not have been in the past. But there are stirrings and there is confusion; a teachers' union rushing in with promises of security and stability may very well take away the last chance that the people of this nation have for a truly free and public school system.

All in the name of the children—the schools must be saved.

 Index